Recreation Services
LAW AND RISK MANAGEMENT

Nora Rock

2009
Emond Montgomery Publications Limited
Toronto, Canada

Emond Montgomery Publications Limited
1 Eglinton Avenue E, Suite 600
Toronto ON M4P 3A1
http://www.emond.ca/highered

Printed in Canada.
Reprinted November 2019.

We acknowledge the financial support of the Government of Canada. Canadä

The events and characters depicted in this book are fictitious. Any similarity to actual persons, living or dead, is purely coincidental.

Acquisitions and developmental editor: Peggy Buchan
Marketing manager: Christine Davidson
Sales manager, higher education: Dave Stokaluk
Copy editor: Kate Hawkins
Supervising editor: Jim Lyons, WordsWorth Communications
Production editor: Debbie Gervais, WordsWorth Communications
Proofreader: David Handelsman, WordsWorth Communications
Text designer: Tara Wells, WordsWorth Communications
Indexer: Paula Pike, WordsWorth Communications
Cover designer: John Vegter

Library and Archives Canada Cataloguing in Publication

Rock, Nora, 1968-
    Recreation services : law and risk management / Nora Rock.

Includes index.
ISBN 978-1-55239-316-1

    1. Recreation—Law and legislation—Canada.   I. Title.
KE3788.R63 2009   344.71'099   C2008-907590-0
KF3985.R63 2009

Contents

PART III TOURISM AND CASUAL RECREATION

Chapter 6 Management of Parks and Recreation Facilities

Chapter 7 Managing Recreation Programs

Chapter 8 Equipment and Products Law

Chapter 9 Adventure Tourism and Other High-Risk Activities

PART I

Recreation and the Legal Context

CHAPTER 1

Balancing the Benefits and Risks of Recreation

CHAPTER OBJECTIVES

After completing this chapter, you should be able to:

- describe some of the risks associated with recreation;

- list at least six benefits of physical activity;

- explain why even sedentary recreation provides benefits;

- understand the special benefits of recreation that are enjoyed by children and youth;

- describe the role of the recreation provider as a risk–benefits expert;

- understand the basic risk management duties of recreation providers; and

- explain the importance of shared responsibility for risk management.

RISKS IN RECREATION

Thinking back only as far as the 1970s, it is easy to see how radically society has progressed in its attempts to reduce exposure to known risks. For example, since 1976, we have witnessed the following changes:

- the introduction of peanut-free schools and recreation facilities,

- the banning of smoking in the workplace and in public places,

- compulsory seat belt laws and laws relating to child car seats,

- helmet laws for bicycle riders,

- helmet requirements in the NHL and in all youth hockey leagues,

- restrictions on the use of alcohol by boaters, and

- epidemic/pandemic planning not only by health-care facilities but also by businesses of all kinds.

These are only a few of the numerous safety improvements that have occurred in a little over 30 years. The more we know about the risks that we face in our daily lives—and the reasonable interventions available to counteract them—the lower our risk tolerance becomes. This trend leads to an interesting paradox: while our actual life expectancy has never been longer, our perception of the riskiness of our environment is at an all-time high, and we are highly motivated to limit all controllable risks.

There is one area of activity, however, in which risks remain fairly intractable: recreation. Recreation is a broad category that includes, at one end of the spectrum, sedentary activities such as playing bridge, and at the other end, high-risk activities such as heli-skiing and skydiving. Despite many safety innovations, injuries and accidents can occur, from one end of this spectrum to the other. Consider these sobering statistics reported by the Fowler Kennedy Sport Medicine Clinic at the University of Western Ontario:

- Sports injury is the leading cause of disability and death in people aged 9 to 24, recently surpassing motor vehicle accidents.

- Forty-two percent of all injury across all ages is related to sport.

- Canadians suffer more than 1.2 million sports injuries per year.

- Sports injury leads to 8.7 million activity loss days.

- Twenty-five percent of all hospital emergency visits are prompted by sport.

These injury statistics flow from a broad definition of "sport." It includes not only organized team sports played by fit, young players, but also leisure activities, such as cycling and hiking, enjoyed by Canadians of all ages and levels of fitness.

David Ropeik and George Gray are the authors of a US text entitled *Risk: A Practical Guide for Deciding What's Really Safe and What's Really Dangerous in the World Around You.* This book assesses risks of all kinds (including, for example, the risk of catching mad cow disease, absorbing radon from household furnishings, and getting brain cancer from cell phones). Its purpose is to educate people about *relative risks* so that they can make educated judgments about what they should try, what they should avoid, and what they should fear.

One of the reasons that Ropeik and Gray were motivated to write such a text is that studies have shown that human beings do not always make rational judgments about risk. For example, psychological studies show that 63 percent of people are at least somewhat afraid of snakes, while only a very small percentage are afraid of kitchen knives. However, while a person's lifetime risk of cutting herself with a kitchen knife is nearly 100 percent, the likelihood that the average person will ever be injured by a snake is negligible. An objective assessment of the two phobias clearly shows that wasting any mental energy fearing snakes—at least in the case of people who don't work with them—is irrational.

People also tend not to properly take into account the *harm potential* associated with risks. For example, exposure to the risk of kitchen knife cuts is very likely, but death associated with kitchen knife accidents is extremely rare; for this reason, the harm potential of this risk is low. The chance of exposure to rarer risks, such as the risk of being attacked by a tiger, may be very low. However, the harm potential of these rare risks is sometimes very high: human beings have historically fared badly in unarmed combat with tigers. As demonstrated in a *Psychology Today* cartoon in which a person is seen running into the path of a 16-wheeler in an attempt to evade a tiny snake, we humans do not properly assess harm potential when we decide what to fear.

Trevor Butterworth's often-cited example of the effect of irrational risk assessment relates to the September 11, 2001 terrorist attacks on the United States (2008):

> Researchers at Cornell University found that because more people drove instead of taking a plane in the three months after 9/11, there were an additional 725 fatalities from car crashes than during the same period in the previous year. A study by Michigan's Transportation Research Institute took a different tack and came up with a higher figure: 1,018 more traffic fatalities than would have been expected based on earlier trends.

According to Ropeik and Gray (2002, p. 15):

> Ultimately we react to risk with more emotion than reason. We take the information about a risk, combine it with the general information we have about the world, and then filter those facts through the psychological prism of risk perception. What often results are judgements about risk far more informed by fear than by facts.

So, is it rational to be afraid of the risks related to recreation? This is a decision that people must make for themselves, taking into account their own personal circumstances, abilities, and values. However, for those who are responsible for managing recreation facilities, programming, and providing recreation, the question is much more complicated.

Accident statistics certainly compel our attention. In the United States, accidents unrelated to motor vehicles are the eighth leading cause of death for Americans (Ropeik & Gray, 2002, p. 23). Canadian statistics paint a similar picture. They also make it clear that the younger the deceased, the more likely the probability of death by accident. One notable feature of accidental deaths, as a result, is that they rob their victims of more years of life than deaths from natural causes. Two explanations are set out below.

According to Statistics Canada (2003):

> Among various selected causes of death (including colorectal and lung cancers, cerebrovascular diseases, strokes and suicides), unintentional injuries, such as motor vehicle accidents, falls, poisonings and drownings, were responsible for the most potential years of life lost before the age of 75, at 203,799 years; next was suicide at 130,715 years.

According to Ropeik and Gray (2002, p. 23):

> For those who die of so called "natural causes"—the top four killers, ahead of accidents, in the US, the average remaining life expectancy, i.e., the difference between the age at death and the average life expectancy, is between 9.6 and 14.3 years. But for those who die in accidents, the average remaining life expectancy is almost 30 years.

These statistics make it clear that it would be irresponsible for anyone *not* to take into account the real risks of activities that are associated with accidents—and recreational activities fall squarely within this category.

But risk is only half the story.

BENEFITS OF RECREATION

Benefits of Physical Activity

In addition to simply being fun, recreational activities can have other positive influences on the lives of participants. For example, the Women's Sports Foundation, established by US tennis legend Billie Jean King, credits young women's participation in sports with lower rates of teen pregnancy, addictions, depression, and leaving school, and with higher rates of academic success, better body image, and higher self-esteem. The foundation also notes that: "[i]t is no accident that 80% of the female executives at Fortune 500 companies identified themselves as former 'tomboys'—having played sports."

The Public Health Agency of Canada, in its 2003 guide entitled "The Benefits of Physical Activity," asserts that for older Canadians, "weight-bearing physical activity reduces the rate of bone loss associated with osteoporosis and regular physical activity maintains strength and flexibility, balance and coordination and can help reduce the risk of falls. Regular physical activity prolongs independent living."

Falls—especially by the elderly—were listed among the most common causes of injuries and death identified by Ropeik and Gray (2002). Among the lifetime risks deemed by the authors to be most serious—both in the sense of being likely to occur and in the sense of producing serious consequences—were obesity and being overweight. In their discussion of how to avoid these risks, Ropeik and Gray cite increased physical exercise as an effective preventive measure. Exercise is also cited as preventative against the harm associated with other risks deemed significant by the authors, namely, heart disease, cancer, and accidents that do not involve falls.

Benefits of Sedentary Recreation

For many people, sedentary recreation, such as participation in a book club, provides valuable opportunities to build and maintain social networks. Many highly respected medical studies have proven that strong social connections help protect people from physical ailments such as heart disease and cancer. Dean Ornish, a doctor who is best known for his advocacy of nutritional and fitness approaches to circulatory system disease, has also researched and written about what he describes as "spiritual heart disease." This condition has both physiological and psychological symptoms that are triggered by loneliness, isolation, alienation, and depression. Recreation of any kind can help protect against these social ills.

Special Benefits for Children and Youth

Despite the statistics that suggest that children and youth are more likely than any other participants to be hurt during recreation activities, most recreational facilities dedicate considerable resources toward providing recreation opportunities for this group. Studies have shown that despite the risks, this emphasis is well founded. Children and youth do not reach full emotional, social, intellectual, and moral maturity until the end of high school or later, and recreation provides unique opportunities to assist in their development.

In *The Young Athlete: A Sports Doctor's Complete Guide for Parents*, authors Jordan D. Metzl and Carol Shookhoff (2002, pp. 5-12) list the following as examples of ways in which recreation benefits children:

- physical fitness;

- stress relief;

- learning the relationship between practice and skill mastery;

- prevention or reduction of unhealthy habits, such as drug use;

- learning the value of preparation;

- increased emotional resilience and learning to deal with disappointment and misfortune;

- attitude control;

- leadership skills;

- leadership opportunities;

- positive self-identity;

- time management;

- learning the importance of long-term thinking;

- teamwork experiences and skills;

- acceptance of diversity;

- improved relationships with other children; and

- opportunities for supportive relationships with adults, such as coaches.

More information about the benefits of recreation for people of all ages is available on the Vancouver Park Board's website at http://vancouver.ca/parks/rec/benefits.htm.

The strong correlation between recreation and health assists supporters of recreation activities in calling on local, provincial, and national governments to continue and increase economic and policy support for public recreation facilities and programs. While lean economic times and factors such as high fuel costs sometimes put pressure on recreation budgets, the recreation sector is likely to remain an important part of Canada's economy, especially as the population ages.

STRIVING FOR BALANCE BETWEEN RISKS AND BENEFITS

Participants are attracted by the perceived benefits of their chosen recreation activities. These benefits are often widely advertised by the medical community, celebrity athletes, and participants, and by the Canadian tourism industry, which generates more than $60 billion in revenue annually.

Information about the *risks* of recreation is much less widely promoted. This imbalance between what the public knows about fun and what it knows about risk makes it difficult for potential participants to make informed decisions about their recreation choices.

This is where recreation providers come in. Recreation providers—including recreation planners, facility managers, athletics managers, and tourism business owners—are uniquely placed to understand the risks associated with the forms of recreation in which they specialize. The public looks to these individuals as experts in their areas of service.

As experts, recreation providers are expected to maintain a thorough and current understanding of both the benefits and the risks associated with recreation, to communicate these benefits and risks to participants, and to take all reasonable steps to manage, limit, or eliminate risks wherever possible. They are also under pressure, however, to provide the recreational opportunities that their clients demand. These competing responsibilities force recreation managers to strive, on a daily basis, to determine and to achieve an appropriate balance between benefits and risks.

Understanding the duty to balance benefits and risks is at the heart of what it means to be a recreation provider. Even with the best safeguards in place, people are often hurt in the course of recreation, though with widely varying degrees of seriousness. Sometimes, as a result of these injuries, a recreation provider will be subject to legal **liability**. To avoid or minimize this liability, the provider will have to prove that she managed the facilities at least as well as any reasonable recreation manager would have managed them under the same circumstances.

Being reasonable implies actually applying reasoning—in other words, using your head. The law expects a recreation manager, at a minimum, to:

liability
legal responsibility

- learn about risks;

- learn about ways to manage risks;

- refresh her knowledge about both of these topics when that knowledge becomes dated;

- assess the risks associated with her particular programs or facility;

- take well thought-out steps to eliminate these risks where possible; and

- warn potential participants about all risks that cannot be completely avoided to assist them in making their own risk–benefit decisions.

This book is designed to explain how recreation providers can meet these basic legal obligations. In the next two chapters, you will learn more about the legal and regulatory context in which recreation is offered, and about which laws apply to recreation providers. In Part II, you will be introduced to general risk management and risk-financing strategies that can help to control actual risks, manage the potential for harm to participants, and reduce the business costs associated with accidents.

In Part III, you will learn about risk management in specific contexts, including the management of parks and recreation facilities, the management of recreation programs, the tourism and "extreme sport" sector, and the protection of spectators and visitors in sports and entertainment facilities.

A SHARED RESPONSIBILITY FOR RISK MANAGEMENT

As noted above, recreation participants are generally not fully informed about the specific nature of all of the risks involved in their chosen recreation activity. However, with the important exception of children and intellectually challenged participants, most recreation participants have an innate understanding that many activities that are fun are also dangerous. In fact, for many participants, a big part of the attraction of extreme sport comes from the assumption of unusual risks.

In some activities, such as bungee jumping, the element of fear (which flows from perceived risk) is the very basis of the fun. And while most of the risks associated with bungee jumping are controllable by equipment and the actions of human operators, the same cannot be said of every sport. For example, among the 80-plus causes of Canadian alpine accidents catalogued by the Alpine Club, "bad luck" is

---

CASE STUDY

Sharing Responsibility for Accidents: Rozenhart v. Skier's Sport Shop

The case of *Rozenhart v. Skier's Sport Shop* arose because of an in-line skating accident. Robert Rozenhart, a 48-year-old married father, decided to take up in-line skating with his daughter Leslie. He had never tried the sport before, but was an athletic person—a marathoner, cyclist, and swimmer—and he knew how to ice-skate.

Rozenhart and his daughter went to the defendant sports shop, which offered rental skates and in-line skating lessons. There they were provided with rental skates and protective equipment (wrist guards, knee and elbow pads); they had brought their own helmets. Store personnel told them to walk down to a nearby park to await the skating instructor, who was expected to be 10 or 15 minutes late.

At the park, the father and daughter put on their equipment as instructed. While waiting for the instructor, Rozenhart decided to try out the skates to see how they felt. He had been told that in-line skating was much like ice-skating, but had not been told that the procedure for stopping was completely different. He attempted to stop in the way one would on ice skates, fell, and suffered "major, and in some cases permanent, injuries" (these were not described in the court's decision).

Rozenhart sued the sports shop, alleging that it was negligent in not pointing out how the braking mechanism on the skates worked, in failing to discharge a duty of care owed between student and instructor, and in telling him that in-line skating was very similar to ice-skating.

The court found that the sports shop was not negligent for failing to point out the braking mechanism and for failing to offer instruction (since Rozenhart had been told to wait for the instructor before skating). The court did find the sports shop negligent for telling Rozenhart that in-line skating was very similar to ice-skating, without explaining that the braking mechanism was completely different.

However, even though the court found that the sports shop had misled Rozenhart about the similarity between in-line skating and ice-skating, the shop was found to be only 25 percent responsible for Rozenhart's injuries. Because he tried out the skates without waiting for the instructor, when he knew he was a beginner and ought to wait for the instructor, Rozenhart was found to be 75 percent responsible for his own accident and the injuries it caused him. ◇

listed as a cause. In noting that mountain activities have inherent, sometimes unavoidable risks, the club notes: "People are sometimes just in the wrong place at the wrong time."

Despite the limitations on providers' ability to eliminate risk, there remains a demand for access to inherently risky recreation. Providers who are willing to meet this demand generally require that participants commit to sharing the responsibility for risk management. As you will see later in this book, risk-sharing can be accomplished in many different ways. Consider the following:

- participants may waive their right to sue providers,

- participants may purchase their own insurance at their own expense,

- participants may be required to demonstrate an appropriate level of proficiency before engaging in dangerous activities, or

- participants may wear or use safety equipment appropriate to the activity.

In order to require participants to share the risk management responsibilities, providers must effectively communicate the existence and nature of all controllable and uncontrollable risks to participants. Without this communication, participants cannot be expected to carry out their own personal risk–benefit assessments. Proper communication of risk will assist in deterring individuals who don't ascribe a high enough benefit to the activity; it will also assist in forcing those individuals who do ascribe benefits to the activity to assume some of the burden of legal liability should they be hurt.

MANAGING RISKS

Dire Warnings

In fulfilling their responsibilities to participants, recreation providers cannot escape the need to be honest in communicating the serious risks that may be involved in the activities they offer. Might this honest communication turn a few potential customers away? Yes, but that's the point. A responsible recreation provider must force potential participants to make educated, individual decisions about the risk–benefit balance that is right for them.

Consider the following excerpts from the "ride at your own risk" policy of Sea Horse Ranch, south of San Francisco:

> If you get bucked off, thrown off, stepped on, bit, kicked, or licked, join the club.
> SUING IS FROWNED UPON.
> We are extremely sorry when someone is hurt.
> Horseback riding is considered a rugged adventure sport.

A few paragraphs later in this quaint policy, the ranch states clearly that some trail-riding participants "can, and do, suffer serious injury and even death" while enjoying their chosen pastime.

The message is sobering, but it's essential, especially because the activity offered is so enticing: Sea Horse Ranch allows participants to ride its horses down a 45-degree grade, from the top of a 30-foot sea cliff to the rugged Pacific beach, and then to gallop the animals across the sand and walk them in the surf. This author, like many customers before her, read the warnings and tried it anyway, agreeing to share in the risks of a recreation opportunity of a lifetime. ◈

KEY TERM

liability

REVIEW EXERCISES

Review Questions

1. Do people make rational judgments about risk? Do they properly take into account the harm potential associated with risks?

2. Is participation in recreation risky?

3. What are some of the benefits of physical activity?

4. Are there any benefits of sedentary forms of recreation?

5. Do the benefits of recreation justify the risks?

6. Are recreation providers solely responsible for managing the risks of recreation?

Discussion Question

Is our world safer or more dangerous today than it was 30 years ago?

CHAPTER 2

Legal Liability in Tort and Contract

CHAPTER OBJECTIVES

After completing this chapter, you should be able to:

- explain what the common law is and how it differs from statute law;

- list at least three subcategories of tort law;

- explain the concepts of duty of care and standard of care;

- understand how liability is apportioned between the defendants in a tort lawsuit;

- understand how a court may acknowledge a plaintiff's share in responsibility for an accident; and

- describe the basic principles of contract law.

INTRODUCTION

In Chapter 1, you learned about the importance of balancing the benefits of recreation with the risks to participants. The most important meaning of "risk," in the context of recreation, is the risk that a recreation participant will be injured or even killed while participating in a recreation activity. No matter how inherently dangerous an activity may be, everyone—including the provider of the activity—is shocked when an accident happens, and is saddened when someone is hurt. A risk management program is not worthy of the name unless the primary goal of the program is to reduce the likelihood of accidents and injuries to the lowest possible rate.

There is, however, another kind of risk that recreation planners and providers are required to keep in mind: the risk of being found legally liable—and financially responsible—for accidents, or for the financial consequences of broken contracts.

Accidents can leave victims with permanent disabilities that change the course of their lives, making it difficult for them to earn a living, care for themselves, or enjoy the activities that once brought them pleasure. For this reason, courts often order the defendants who have been found responsible for these accidents to pay significant compensation (called "damages") to the victims. Canadian damage awards in personal injury cases can be measured in hundreds of thousands—or even millions—of dollars, especially when the victims are youth or children. While recreation providers almost always purchase liability insurance, it is possible for accidents to exceed the limits of coverage. A provider who makes too many claims may either be denied insurance or be charged so much for insurance that the recreation organization is no longer viable. Problems with contracts, while generally more predictable from an exposure perspective, also have the potential to create financial havoc.

This chapter introduces the common-law disciplines of tort (which includes personal injury law) and contracts. It covers the basic legal principles and concepts necessary for a general understanding of how recreation providers can become legally liable for compensating recreation participants and business partners.

Other areas of the law—including statute law, human rights law, administrative law, and the bylaws and policies of governments and organizations—are introduced in Chapter 3, Legislation, Policy, Procedure, and Administration. The legal concepts introduced in this chapter and the next are referred to throughout the remainder of the book.

HOT TOPICS
Mellow Canadians Show Their Teeth Against Municipalities

Americans are widely considered, by Canadians and others, to be a particularly litigious breed: people who are quick to launch lawsuits in the wake of accidents. The popular wisdom has typically been that Canadians are much less likely to turn to the courts for compensation when they're hurt. ... [however] ... The Ontario Recreation Facilities Association (ORFA) pointed out, in a 2003 press release about increasing recreation user fees, that municipalities tend increasingly to be viewed as an attractive target for litigants. ORFA referred to a 1993 award of $8 million in damages won by an injured teenaged hockey player in litigation against the Township of Lasalle in southern Ontario—which had only $5 million in insurance coverage. ORFA quoted St. Catharines insurance broker Sheldon Rodgers as saying that an emerging trend toward increased litigation by recreation plaintiffs against municipal recreation providers has led to increasing insurance costs and the withdrawal, between 1975 and 2003, of all domestic insurance providers from the market for insurance for municipal recreation activities. Said Rodgers: "if the foreign companies pull out, we will have no-one to insure any recreation activity in Ontario. This puts more than 67,000 Canadian non-profit organizations at risk."

Discussion Questions

1. Why do you think people are more willing to sue municipalities than other plaintiffs?

2. How do you think recreation providers are likely to respond to the growing cost of insurance?

3. Do you think that a campaign designed to discourage people from suing municipal recreation providers would be effective? Do you think it would be ethical? Why or why not?

Sources: For ORFA's comments, see: www.orfa.com/pressrelease/User%20Fees.pdf

The personal injury case referred to by Rodgers is the Ontario Court of Appeal decision *Stein v. Sandwich West (Township)*, 1995 CanLII 1239 (ON C.A.) ◈

THE COMMON LAW

The common law is a body of legal principles, established through court decisions (cases), that govern legal issues or subject areas that are not fully covered by statutes.

It has no single source or code. It can be understood only by reviewing the written words of judges that are published online or in case reporters (books). The common law has its own internal divisions—for example, **tort** law (the law of harms done by people to others) and **contract** law (the law of agreements made between people).

Common-law rules created in legal decisions bind future decision-makers through the principle of **precedent**. In simplest terms, precedent is a method of achieving consistency. It ensures that courts are not free to decide the same issue differently the next time it comes up.

Common-law rules are sometimes the precursors of legislative provisions. In other words, a statute (an Act of Parliament or a legislature) may be created to incorporate the content of what used to be a common-law rule. Statutes are written codes of law that typically deal with a particular subject matter. For example, the Ontario *Horse Riding Safety Act* deals, predictably, with riding safety. Statute law is discussed in greater detail in Chapter 3.

An example of how common-law rules can be converted into statutory form is provided in section 4(1) of the Ontario *Occupiers' Liability Act*. This legislation codifies the common-law concept of *volenti non fit injuria* (which means, in a nutshell, "consent negates liability"), a concept that is discussed later in this chapter under the heading "Voluntary Assumption of Risk."

Statutory provisions, in turn, can be interpreted and informed by judicial rulings. For example, the regulations made under the Saskatchewan *Parks Act* provide that nobody is permitted to construct a dwelling house on the property of Saskatchewan parks without government permission. However, in the 1999 case of *R. v. Sundown*, the Supreme Court of Canada upheld the right of a First Nations hunter to construct a log cabin on Saskatchewan parks property to use as a hunting base. A treaty permitted the hunter to hunt in the park, which was located in his traditional territory. The Supreme Court ruled that building the cabin, which was consistent with native hunting tradition, was incidental to that right. The *Sundown* case, therefore, *interpreted* statute law (the Saskatchewan *Parks Act*) but *created* case law in the form of a precedent. Even though the *Parks Act* does not discuss whether or not First Nations hunters can build cabins on parks property, it is now law in Saskatchewan—and probably anywhere else in Canada where treaties provide for traditional native hunting on Crown land—that such hunters can build hunting cabins.

tort
harm done by people to others for which compensation can be sought

contract
agreement enforceable in law

precedent
court decision that affects future court decisions to ensure consistent application of the law

TORTS

Introduction

"Tort" is French for "wrong." It refers to the wrongs—or harms—that people do to each other, whether intentionally or through lack of care and caution. The kinds of harm covered by tort law are nearly limitless, and can include personal injury, harm to reputation, and damage to possessions or property (including damage to land

and resources). Environmental law, libel and slander law, conversion (theft), child abuse, sexual and physical assault, harm to business prospects, and the law relating to copyright and trademark violations are all distinct legal doctrines rooted in the law of torts. Many of these areas of law are now governed by statutes, such as the *Criminal Code*, the *Environmental Protection Act*, and the *Copyright Act*. However, the area most relevant to recreation providers—personal injury law—is still very much grounded in the common law.

A person who believes that she has suffered injury (either personally or to her possessions) at the hands of another can bring a lawsuit asking the court to make a finding of fault and an order for compensation. The party who starts a lawsuit is called the **plaintiff**, and the party or parties who are required to defend the lawsuit are called the **defendant** or the defendants. The monetary compensation that the plaintiff generally seeks is called **damages**.

A plaintiff can bring a tort lawsuit against any party who (allegedly) harmed her. There is no need for any pre-existing formal relationship between the plaintiff and the defendant. As you will see later, this is one of the biggest differences between tort law and contract law. (Contract law turns on the interpretation of an agreement that the parties made before they came into conflict.)

There is more than one basis on which a court can find a party at fault—and legally liable—in tort. The tort cases in which it is simplest to attribute fault are those that are based on intentional acts.

Intentional Torts

An intentional tort is just that: a harm that one person intends to cause, and does cause, to another. Courts consider a tort to be intentional as long as the person who causes the harm foresees that the consequences of his behaviour are substantially certain. For example, a person who punches another person in the nose, causing a broken nose, is likely to have committed an intentional tort.

Many of the actions that can form the basis of an intentional tort lawsuit are also crimes that can be prosecuted by the police. In fact, most serious intentional assaults form the basis of criminal charges, and are handled in the criminal court system. In these cases, the victims rarely bring lawsuits in civil court.

It *is* possible, however, to sue a criminal (or accused criminal) for monetary compensation under the civil law of tort. A well-known American example is the lawsuit filed against retired football star O.J. Simpson in the wake of two murders of which he was accused, and then acquitted, by a criminal court. Many people wonder how these inconsistent results could have occurred. While rules about the admissibility of certain kinds of evidence played a role, the main reason for the apparently inconsistent criminal and civil results in the Simpson cases relates to the standard of proof. The **standard of proof** is the amount, level, or persuasiveness of the proof that is required to be successful at trial. In a criminal case, the prosecution must prove the defendant's guilt *beyond a reasonable doubt*. In a civil trial, the plaintiff must prove the defendant's fault merely *on a balance of probabilities*—that is, the plaintiff need only prove that it is more likely than not that the defendant was at fault. From a plaintiff's point of view, there are two major advantages in launching a civil action: the standard of proof is easier to meet, and compensatory damages may

plaintiff
party who starts a lawsuit

defendant
party who is required to defend a lawsuit

damages
monetary compensation awarded to a plaintiff for harm suffered

standard of proof
amount, level, or persuasiveness of proof that is required at trial

be awarded. (In Ontario, compensation may also be awarded to victims of crime by the Criminal Injuries Compensation Board; however, the amounts are modest.)

Other examples of lawsuits for intentional torts have arisen in the context of sexual assault, especially in cases in which the assaults occurred in childhood and were ongoing over a period of several years. There have also been some cases of dual criminal-plus-civil prosecutions following incidences of violence in sport.

In 2004, Vancouver Canucks hockey player Todd Bertuzzi punched Colorado Avalanche player Steve Moore from behind, knocking him unconscious and forcing him headfirst to the ice. The assault caused severe injuries to Moore, who was in hospital for nearly six months and never returned to professional hockey. Bertuzzi was suspended by the National Hockey League, and a criminal charge of assault causing bodily harm was laid against him by the police. Bertuzzi pleaded guilty to the charge and was sentenced. He was also sued, in the civil court system, by Steve Moore.

The potential for intentional tort lawsuits in recreation is very real. Todd Bertuzzi was not the only plaintiff named in Steve Moore's lawsuit: the Vancouver Canucks were also named as a defendant. Especially in the context of rough or violent sports (including, for example, hockey, lacrosse, martial arts, boxing, and rugby), recreation providers and managers must do their utmost to ensure that rough play does not cross the line into assault. Violence in sport is discussed in more detail in Chapter 12.

Negligence

Most lawsuits that arise from recreation-related personal injury are founded not in intentional tort, but in **negligence**, which is another class of torts. A plaintiff who is seeking to prove negligence is not required to prove any intentional wrongful action in order to be successful. The traditional law of negligence is based on rights that flow from relationships between people.

negligence
failure of a person to act reasonably that results in harm to another

Instead of intention, the plaintiff must establish the following elements of negligence:

- the defendant owed the plaintiff a duty of care;

- the defendant failed to carry out this duty to the appropriate standard of care;

- the defendant's failure to meet the appropriate standard of care was the cause of the harm or injury to the plaintiff; and

- the harm or injury was foreseeable to the defendant (in other words, the harm or injury was not too remotely connected to the defendant's negligence).

Each of these common-law elements of negligence—the duty of care, the standard of care, causation, and forseeability of harm (remoteness)—has been discussed at length by courts.

DUTY OF CARE

Unless a court finds that a defendant owed a **duty of care** to a plaintiff, it cannot find the defendant liable for any harm that has come to the plaintiff. One person's duty of care to another person is the foundation on which fault is established in a

duty of care
duty owed by one person to act reasonably that is the foundation of a negligence action

negligence action. Generally, a person owes a duty of care to other people who may be affected by his acts or omissions (failures to act).

Duties of care often accompany relationships—for example, neighbour to neighbour, host to guest, parent to child, coach to athlete—but they can also arise between strangers. Anyone who is thoughtless about the potential victims of his actions is usually held accountable when foresight was reasonable in the context. A defendant need not have a relationship with a specific plaintiff, as long as the plaintiff is one of a class of people that the defendant's actions can be expected to affect. For example, a driver who runs a red light and collides with a pedestrian because he is fiddling with his car's CD player had a duty of care to the pedestrian, even if she was a complete stranger, because the driver is expected to look out for all pedestrians.

Recreation providers almost always have a duty of care toward participants because, in providing recreation, they are inviting and expecting people to take part. It is very difficult to argue that you did not foresee an impact of your carelessness on people whom you invited onto your property or into your program. The case law also makes it clear that recreation participants owe a duty of care to co-participants. For example, the case of *King v. Redlich* confirms that hockey players playing together on the ice have a duty of care to each other.

STANDARD OF CARE

standard of care
degree of care that a person must take to prevent harm to others

Once a court has determined that a defendant owed a duty of care to a plaintiff, the next step is to determine whether the defendant lived up to that duty of care. To do this, a court measures the defendant's actions according to an appropriate **standard of care**.

The usual starting point, in determining the standard against which the defendant's actions are to be measured, is the standard of the "reasonable and prudent person in the same circumstances." For example, in the car accident described above, the actions of the driver who hit the pedestrian are compared to the actions of a reasonable and prudent driver who is heading toward an intersection. Since a reasonable and prudent driver would not choose that particular moment to look away from the road to operate a CD player, the court would likely find that the driver failed to meet the standard of care that was expected of him.

However, a court does not always use so general a standard to measure behaviour. The case law makes it clear that certain relationships that involve a duty of care merit the taking of extra care. For example, parents are held to a higher standard of care when dealing with their children than when dealing with the general public. Consider, for example, a man who is using a corrosive chemical paint stripper to refinish the floors in his home. If the doorbell rings and the man lets a tradesperson in, it is likely reasonable for him to leave a painting tray containing paint stripper unattended on the floor while the tradesperson is walking around in the home. However, the man would probably be found to be unreasonable in leaving the chemical unattended while his two-year-old child was walking around the home, because while the tradesperson can be expected to take precautions for her own safety, the toddler's safety is the responsibility of the parent.

Enhanced standards of care have also been applied to people who hold themselves out as experts. For example, in the recreation context, the decisions made by an experienced sports coach may be held to a higher standard of appropriateness than the decisions of a reasonable and prudent person who is *not* an experienced coach. The notion of a special standard for experts received court approval in the decision of *Hamstra v. BC Rugby Union*. This case involved a rugby tryout in which players, under the direction of an experienced rugby coach, were trying out different positions in a game situation. A 17-year-old player was badly injured when a rugby scrum (a group of players holding onto each other in a formation) collapsed. The player sued, alleging that the coach should not have permitted players of different ages, sizes, and abilities to try out together.

While the court found that the coach in *Hamstra* acted reasonably by 1986 standards, it noted that a coach in similar circumstances might be found negligent had the accident occurred in 1989 (the year the case was decided). By 1989, much more was known about the risks of spinal injuries, and coaches would be expected to apply that knowledge in deciding who could and couldn't participate in a tryout.

CAUSATION

Even if the plaintiff in a tort lawsuit can prove that the defendant owed her a duty of care and did not meet the applicable standard of care in carrying out this duty, the plaintiff cannot recover any compensation unless she can prove **causation**. To establish a claim for damages, the plaintiff must prove that the defendant's conduct caused the harm or injury.

causation
the logical connection between harm and the negligent actions of the party accused of causing it

The generally used test for causation is the **but for test**: but for the defendant's conduct, would the harm have resulted? For example, consider the case of a student who falls from gymnastics equipment, breaking his arm. It is later discovered that the equipment was not properly assembled, and could have collapsed at any moment. However, was this error the cause of the fall? If the equipment had been properly assembled, the student would still have fallen. In other words, "but for" the problem with the equipment, the injury would nevertheless have occurred. Therefore, the equipment was not the cause of the injury.

but for test
test to establish causation in negligence action: but for the defendant's conduct, would the harm have resulted?

Alcohol consumption often has a role in causing or contributing to accidents. Some studies suggest that alcohol use is a factor in 25 to 50 percent of adult drownings (Ropeik & Gray, 2002, p. 25). Consider a situation in which a recreation provider rents kayaks to visitors in a provincial park. A couple, who do not appear to be impaired by alcohol, come to the rental office and rent a kayak. They sign a waiver document that contains a warning about operating the kayak while intoxicated. They put on appropriate flotation vests, immediately launch the kayak in full view of the rental clerk, and paddle out of sight. They go to an island, take a 40-ounce bottle of vodka out of a pack, drink the whole thing, forget to put their flotation vests back on, and overturn the kayak on their way back. They drown.

Clearly, in renting the kayak to the guests, the recreation provider has contributed to the circumstances—kayaking—that led to the accident. But did the recreation provider *cause* the accident? Cases like this one, in which it is difficult to attribute a single clear cause of an accident to a single defendant, come before the courts all the time. It is very common, in these cases, for the courts to find that more than one defendant contributed to the harm suffered by a plaintiff, and to attribute liability between the various defendants.

Liability may also be attributed in part to the plaintiff under the doctrine of contributory negligence. This doctrine is discussed below under the heading "Contributory Negligence."

FORESEEABILITY (REMOTENESS)

In general, the law does not hold a person legally responsible for consequences that the person could not have foreseen when he took action. The cause of the harm must be **foreseeable**. For example, in our car accident example, imagine that the pedestrian who was struck by the car was a veterinarian rushing to her office to operate on a dog who was also struck by a car, half an hour before and several blocks away. Because of her own accident, the pedestrian vet doesn't make it to the office, and the dog dies. Because the dog was the sole companion of an emotionally fragile old man, the old man falls into a depression, and is prescribed an anti-depressant. One morning, there is a minor earthquake, and the man's glasses fall from a shelf and shatter. Without his glasses, the old man mistakes his anti-depressants for a different prescription, takes six times the appropriate dose, and dies of an overdose.

In this situation, not only is the car crash linked to the veterinarian's injuries, but a dog and an old man are also dead. While the negligent driver's actions contributed to the chain of events that culminated in these two deaths, the deaths of the dog and the old man were not reasonably foreseeable to the driver. While there was some degree of *causation* between the driver's actions and the old man's death, the consequence was not foreseeable. In a case like this, the law provides that the driver's action was too remote from the harm to attract damages.

The principle of remoteness does not prevent a court from awarding damages that are suffered by a plaintiff with unusual (and arguably unforeseeable) personal circumstances. In other words, the precise consequences of the defendant's actions need not be foreseeable. Consider the example of a plaintiff who suffers an injured knee. If the plaintiff had a sedentary job—for example, writing college textbooks—the impact of a permanent knee injury on future income would likely be modest, and modest damages would be awarded. However, if the plaintiff were a star forward in the NHL, the claim for future economic loss would be very high. The law makes it clear that the defendant cannot complain to the court that she could not have foreseen that the victim of her negligence would be an elite athlete.

Similar to this idea, and of particular relevance to recreation providers, is the **thin skull rule**. The thin skull rule provides that people who commit torts take their victims as they find them, even when the victims have hidden vulnerabilities that make them more susceptible to injury than the average person. If a plaintiff suffers extreme damages as a result of his particularly thin skull, the defendant may be fully liable for all the plaintiff's losses if the cause was foreseeable, even though the *extent of the damages* was not foreseeable.

For example, there are reports every year of young, apparently healthy people who die suddenly while participating in sports. In many cases, investigation of the causes of these deaths reveals that the victims suffered from heart defects or other asymptomatic, long-standing health problems that had escaped prior detection. These cases rarely lead to lawsuits because in most instances the deceased participants were exposed only to the usual risks of reasonably safe activities. In other words, the recreation providers were meeting the standard of care owed to the victim at the time of the death. However, it is entirely possible for an unexpected death to occur in circumstances where a recreation provider is *not* meeting the appropriate standard of care.

Consider, for example, a youth training class at a boxing club. It is widely known in the boxing world that wearing a mouthguard while boxing or sparring greatly decreases the risk of suffering a serious injury from a blow to the head. However, first-time youth participants cannot be expected to know this. Imagine a situation in which a group of 10-year-olds show up for their first boxing training class. The young people try on the sparring gloves that they find on a bench and begin fooling around, punching each other, while the instructor has stepped out of the room to make a telephone call. The instructor has not yet had a chance to explain the importance of mouthguards to the children. One child punches another, who is not wearing a mouthguard, in the side of the head. Even though the punch is not particularly hard, the punched child collapses to the ground and never regains consciousness; eventually she dies of a head injury.

With the help of medical witnesses, assume that the court makes the following findings:

- the instructor owed a duty of care to the boxers, and it was an enhanced duty because of their youth;

- in failing to put away the boxing gloves, and in leaving the room without advising against roughhousing and without explaining the importance of mouthguards, the instructor has failed to meet the standard of care of a reasonable boxing instructor;

- the mouthguard would have made the injury less likely; and

- the main reason the child died was that she suffered from an undiagnosed anatomic abnormality of the skull.

In a case like this, it was unforeseeable to the instructor that a child would die in the three minutes he spent outside the room; however, the instructor (and the boxing club that employed him) would likely be found at least partly legally responsible for the child's death because a cause of the harm (failure to wear a mouthguard) was foreseeable.

SHARED LIABILITY

Many injuries occur when a number of factors converge to create a risk. Different defendants may be responsible for introducing different risk factors, and the result is shared responsibility for the harm caused to the plaintiff.

Consider, for example, injuries caused to a child from the tipping over of a portable soccer goal. (A 1999 US government study reported 23 deaths and 38 serious injuries from this cause between 1979 and 1999.) Imagine a situation in which, after having analyzed the evidence, a judge has determined that three factors contributed to the child's accident:

1. the goal manufacturer was at fault because the design of the goal was faulty and made it prone to tipping forward when weight was suspended from the front bar;

2. the school at which the goal was installed was at fault for not having anchored the goal to the ground as recommended by the manufacturer; and

3. the soccer day camp instructor (who was using the facilities pursuant to an agreement with the school) was at fault for allowing children to play with the goal inappropriately by hanging from the front bar.

Having identified the defendants who significantly contributed to the harm, the court must allocate liability among them. If the individual causes are found to be divisible (as they are in this situation), each defendant is responsible for a proportional part of the damages. For example, the court may find the manufacturer in this case to be 40 percent liable, the school to be 40 percent liable, and the day camp that employed the instructor to be 20 percent liable.

However, the common law concerning shared liability has been modified by statutes in many jurisdictions. In Ontario, the *Negligence Act* provides that where more than one defendant contributed to the harm to a plaintiff, the defendants are jointly and severally liable. Under the doctrine of **joint and several liability**, each defendant can be required to pay the full amount of the damages award. Under the statute, liability is not limited by the proportion of fault allocated to each defendant.

A defendant who is forced, under joint and several liability, to pay more than her fair share has a right (after paying the plaintiff) to seek reimbursement from the other defendants. It is at this stage that it becomes important to determine which party was responsible for what percentage of the harm.

In practical terms, joint and several liability means that if one defendant cannot afford to pay, the other defendants must make up the shortfall. In the recreation context, this tends to lead to situations in which the party with the most money pays, even if this party was only partly at fault.

In some cases, the multiple causes of an injury do not all occur at the same time. A minor injury may predispose a victim to a future, much more serious injury, or a later injury may compound an earlier one. Going back to the soccer goal example, imagine that the injury to the child consisted of a severely broken leg requiring surgery and that while in hospital recovering from the surgery, the child contracted necrotizing fasciitis (flesh-eating disease) as a result of poor sanitary procedures at the hospital, and died.

A case like this is much more complicated, because the risk of the child's death from necrotizing fasciitis is probably not reasonably foreseeable to any of the three defendants (manufacturer, school, and day camp), though a *general* risk of death from an overturned soccer goal is likely foreseeable to these parties. However, in this case, were it not for the negligence of the hospital, the harm to the child would have been much less serious. A complicated case such as this one requires detailed analysis on the part of the court, and the result for the defendants is not easy to predict.

VICARIOUS LIABILITY

In general, people and organizations are legally responsible only for their own actions, and not for the actions of others. An exception to this rule is created by the doctrine of vicarious liability. **Vicarious liability** is imposed when a party is held legally responsible for harm that it did not cause directly. Vicarious liability has important implications for recreation providers, and one of the most important circumstances giving rise to it is the employment relationship.

joint and several liability
a legal principle that makes the parties who contributed to harm jointly responsible for the full extent of damages, so that if one or more parties lack the means to pay, the remaining party or parties are liable for the full amount

vicarious liability
liability imposed on one party (often an employer) for the harmful actions or omissions of another (often an employee)

MANAGING RISKS

Calculating Damages in Personal Injury Cases

One of the reasons that recreation providers dread personal injury lawsuits is that it is very difficult to predict the scope and extent of damages for which they may be liable. Judges in Canadian personal injury cases have awarded damages of many different kinds to personal injury plaintiffs. Categories of damages are sometimes described as "heads" of damages. The following is a list of some of the most common heads of damages (there are others):

- Compensation for medical costs that are not covered by health insurance, and for the costs of rehabilitation.

- Compensation to health insurers for costs spent on a plaintiff (subrogated claims).

- Compensation for pain and suffering at and immediately after the time of injury.

- Compensation for residual loss of enjoyment of life (temporary or permanent) as a result of the injury.

- Compensation to reflect the loss of a limb, or a reduction in life expectancy.

- Compensation to replace income lost by the plaintiff while recovering from injury, up to the point of full expected recovery.

- Compensation for the costs of retraining, if the plaintiff is forced to change careers.

- Compensation for special equipment and services needed during the recovery time.

- Compensation for future economic loss. This is often the most significant head of damages, and is calculated by finding the difference between (1) the projected future income stream that the plaintiff would have had were it not for the injury and any associated disability and (2) the future income stream that the plaintiff is likely to have after the injury. The number is adjusted to reflect reasonable life expectancy. In cases where the plaintiff is too young to have a pre-injury occupation, the court makes an educated guess about a likely future career or class of careers for the plaintiff, taking into account the plaintiff's aptitudes.

- Compensation for other plaintiffs—typically family members of the injured person—to reflect the loss of the plaintiff's future companionship and/or help if the plaintiff is hurt. In some cases, compensation is awarded to other plaintiffs to reflect the loss of an inheritance if the plaintiff dies young.

- Punitive damages to denounce the defendant's behaviour in cases where the defendant has acted with extraordinary callousness or cruelty.

- Prejudgment and postjudgment interest.

A defendant who is found liable is also usually required to pay a significant proportion of the plaintiff's legal costs. ◇

Where an organization employs individuals to provide services, it is widely accepted that the organization can be held legally responsible for harm caused by its employees in the course of providing those services. There are a number of reasons for this; an important one, from a practical perspective, is that the organization makes money from the activities of its employees, and it is fitting that the party that enjoys the profits of an enterprise should also bear the risks.

Vicarious liability is not without limits. In general, employers are responsible only for harm caused by employees while carrying out their proper job duties. When an employee steps clearly outside of his standard job duties—for example, by secretly selling illegal drugs in the workplace—the employer is not usually vicariously liable.

However, if the employer could reasonably have foreseen the harm caused by an employee acting outside the scope of his job duties—and especially if the employer created a circumstance in which the employee was likely to do harm—the lines become blurred. In these cases, courts have sometimes imposed liability on the employer. The most widely reported examples are cases involving sexual assault on vulnerable clients, where the employment brought an employee (who may not have been properly screened) into contact with the clients. Vicarious liability is discussed in greater detail in Chapter 7, Managing Recreation Programs.

CONTRIBUTORY NEGLIGENCE

Often, as in the drunken kayaking example introduced earlier in this chapter, the actions of the plaintiff are partially responsible for his injury. A plaintiff participating in a recreational activity may attempt a feat (a backflip on a trampoline, say) that is beyond her ability, may neglect to put on recommended safety gear, or may simply take insufficient care (a player late for his euchre game at the community centre may rush across an icy parking lot and fall). Where the accident is partly the fault of the defendant and partly the fault of the plaintiff, the plaintiff is said to be contributorily negligent. In determining damages in such a case under the doctrine of **contributory negligence**, the court assigns percentages of responsibility to each party. Thus, where a plaintiff sues for $100,000 but is found to be 75 percent at fault in an accident, she will recover only $25,000 from the defendant. The common-law concept of contributory negligence has been codified into statutes in many jurisdictions. In Ontario, contributory negligence is found under section 3 of the *Negligence Act*.

contributory negligence role that a plaintiff may play in negligently contributing to the cause of or the aggravation of his own injury

Recreation providers who are trying to limit liability for accidents in the context of a dangerous activity should be certain to warn participants about risks (for example, on forms, signs, or—always best—verbally). They should also clearly recommend and, where possible, require the use of safety gear. If a defendant can prove that she clearly warned a plaintiff about risks, and the plaintiff was careless anyway, the defendant has a strong case for establishing contributory negligence on the plaintiff's part. The defendant may even be able to rely on the defence of voluntary assumption of risk.

VOLUNTARY ASSUMPTION OF RISK

As you learned in Chapter 1, Balancing the Benefits and Risks of Recreation, nearly all recreational activities come with inherent risks, and many come with very significant risks. An important part of a recreation provider's job is to clearly communicate these risks to participants.

Before the second half of the 20th century, individuals were much more likely to be found by the courts to be personally responsible for the injuries they suffered when participating voluntarily in dangerous activities under the long-standing rule *volenti non fit injuria*. This rule reflected the courts' view that willing participants should not be able to hold others responsible for the risks they assumed.

Volenti used to offer recreation providers a very powerful defence against liability; however, the current legal trend is to interpret consent much more narrowly, and to require recreation providers to share in the responsibility for avoiding risk. In order to rely on participant consent as a defence against liability—or even as a reason to find that the plaintiff was contributorily negligent—a recreation provider must prove the following:

1. the participant was well informed about all of the reasonably foreseeable risks associated with the activity;

2. the participant voluntarily consented to assume these risks (either simply by participating or, more formally, by signing a consent form or waiver); and

3. the participant's injury was caused by risks that fell within the scope of the communication and consent described in the first two requirements.

The third requirement poses as much difficulty for defendants as the first two. Although courts are unlikely to hold recreation providers liable for injuries that fall squarely within the scope of foreseeable risks, accidents that are found to be caused by an unusual factor are said to be outside the scope of foreseeable risks and may attract liability.

For example, consider a trout farm that rents fishing gear and permits families to fish in one of the ponds used to raise trout. The farm will very likely post signs about the dangers of casting fishing lines near other people, running on the docks, and fish hooks. If a participant is cut by a flying fish hook, she is unlikely to be able to recover damages from the trout farm. However, if the same participant breaks an ankle in a fall when the floating dock she is standing on is unlatched by the child of another participant, she may well recover damages, because this kind of injury would have been controllable by the trout farm, and unforeseeable to her.

From a practical standpoint, it is very difficult to warn participants of all of the foreseeable risks of an activity, to ensure that they understand these risks, and to confirm that they have made an informed and voluntary consent. Most recreation providers simply do the very best they can, using the tools at their disposal—for example, signs, codes of conduct, written waivers, and verbal instructions—to create an environment in which participants are aware of the risks that they face, and are free to decide for themselves whether or not to participate.

Occupiers' Liability

All providers and managers of recreation facilities need to understand the basics of occupiers' liability law, a branch of tort law that blends aspects of both negligence (discussed above) and nuisance (discussed below). Many aspects of occupiers' liability law continue to be developed in the common law through court decisions. However, the basic principles of occupiers' liability have been codified—put into statute

CASE STUDY

Basic Negligence Concepts Illustrated: Hutchison v. Daredevil Park

The 2003 decision in *Hutchison v. Daredevil Park* illustrates many of the basic negligence concepts discussed above.

In August 1997, 49-year-old Norman Hutchison suffered a severely broken ankle in an accident while launching himself down a waterslide at Daredevil Park in Wasaga Beach, Ontario.

After reviewing the facts of the case, the court found that the injury was caused when Hutchison slipped as he entered the slide improperly.

Hutchison alleged that the park owed him a duty of care under the doctrine of occupiers' liability. He alleged that the park failed to discharge this duty in three ways:

1. through the failure of the slide attendant to instruct him about how to enter the slide,

2. by failing to use proper signage and other warnings to alert him to the hazards of the slide at the entry tub, and

3. in not having handrails at the slide entry tub.

The court agreed with the first two allegations but disagreed about the need for handrails.

The defendant alleged that Hutchison voluntarily assumed the risk of injury in opting to ride the waterslide. The court reviewed previous cases about voluntary assumption of risk and concluded that it is very rare, in modern times, for a person to truly consent to all the risks of an activity. The court found that Hutchison did not explicitly consent to all the risks of the activity he undertook in riding the slide. The court did, however, find that Hutchison was contributorily negligent because he did not ask for instructions about how to get into the slide.

The court attributed 80 percent of the fault to the park under the doctrine of occupiers' liability, and 20 percent of the fault to Hutchison under the doctrine of contributory negligence.

In calculating damages, the court made the following findings:

- Hutchison was in severe pain for the three days following the accident, and in considerable pain for several weeks afterward;

- Hutchison made a full return to most activities (including golf) within several months, and he was not permanently disabled by the injury to a significant degree; and

- there were some minor, though permanent, after-effects of the injury, including numbness in Hutchison's toes and an increased propensity for arthritis in the joint.

The court assessed Hutchison's total damages at $45,000. Since Hutchison was contributorily negligent for 20 percent of that amount ($9,000), the damages owed to him by Daredevil Park were $36,000. The court also allowed a subrogated claim for medical costs from OHIP, and claims as permitted under the *Family Law Act* for Hutchison's wife and children. ◇

form—in most Canadian jurisdictions, including Ontario. The Ontario *Occupiers' Liability Act* is discussed in Chapter 3. Specific applications of the law are touched on in other chapters of this book (especially Chapter 6, Management of Parks and Recreation Facilities), but the basic principles of occupiers' liability are introduced here.

Occupiers—people who have control over property, whether or not they own it—have long been charged with a duty of care regarding others who are invited onto or who trespass on the property. The degree of control over property required to form the basis of occupiers' liability does not have to be permanent or exclusive. There may be many occupiers on one parcel of property, and an occupier's control need last only as long as the incident that attracted the lawsuit.

When the common law of occupiers' liability was first developed, occupiers owed different standards of care to people who came onto their property, depending on the reasons for which the people were there. Specifically, occupiers were said to owe a higher standard of care to "invitees" (people who were invited, such as registered program participants) and a lower standard of care to trespassers (people who were unlawfully on the property).

However, Ontario's *Occupiers' Liability Act* has eliminated the different standards of care owed at common law. Now, an occupier of premises has an obligation to take reasonable care that all people coming onto the premises are reasonably safe while there. Instead of creating a different standard of care to deal with trespassers, the law now deems trespassers to have willingly assumed any and all risks involved in being on the premises. However, the legislation makes it clear that an occupier cannot create a danger for trespassers.

For example, consider the situation of someone who snowmobiles across municipal parkland where snowmobiling is prohibited. The *Occupiers' Liability Act* says that the park managers cannot create any dangers (such as concealed pit-style traps) for the snowmobilers (which management may be tempted to do, to discourage snowmobiling). The Act also says that the snowmobiler has willingly assumed all risks involved in taking the snowmobile through the park without permission.

Another application of the duty of care under the *Occupiers' Liability Act* is "host liability" for alcohol-related injuries. Under this branch of liability, courts have found hosts who serve alcohol to be liable, in some cases, for injuries to intoxicated guests. Liability can attach to a host regardless of whether the injury occurs at an event or party, or immediately afterward—for example, during the time in which a guest drives home while impaired. There have also been cases in which a host is sued not by his guest, but by the *victim* of his guest—for example, by another driver who was injured in a collision with the guest. Injured people (plaintiffs) have argued that the *Occupiers' Liability Act* imposes a duty on hosts to make sure that guests do not injure themselves or others as a result of being intoxicated while at a party or event. Alcohol management is discussed in greater detail in Chapter 11, Recreation Spectators.

Nuisance

The law of nuisance deals with one property occupier's interference with another party's use and enjoyment of her own property. To constitute nuisance, an invasion of property need not be intentional or even negligent. As long as the possibility of an impact on the plaintiff's use is foreseeable to the defendant before an action is taken, the action can constitute nuisance.

Nuisance need not and often does not involve an entry by a defendant onto a plaintiff's land. It may instead be the result of the defendant's use of his own private property, which may have harmful effects on the plaintiff's use—for example, loud noises, bad odours, or shade from a new building cast over a neighbour's garden. These kinds of intrusions can attract tort liability under the doctrine of nuisance. A common example, in the recreation context, is the tendency for balls from a golf course to land on adjoining land.

In assessing damages, the courts can award a remedy for almost any kind of interference, temporary or permanent, with an owner's "use and enjoyment" of her property. Any interference beyond that which would not be tolerated by an "ordinary occupier" in the plaintiff's position can be compensated with damages.

Property uses that create potential nuisance claims in the recreation world include:

- noisy activities (for example, municipal fireworks displays);

- activities that attract crowds, especially crowds of unpredictable numbers that may be noisy, drop garbage outside the perimeters of the event, park illegally, or depart noisily at a late hour;

- activities that require bright lighting at night (for example, evening baseball games); and

- activities that pollute (for example, the operation of watercraft that may pollute waters with fuel or motor oil).

In planning new activities, recreation providers should be mindful of their potential impacts on neighbours, and should plan for ways in which potential nuisances can be contained. In some cases, it may be wise to offer benefits to neighbours (for example, free tickets to an event) to discourage complaints, and to reward neighbours for their tolerance.

Other Kinds of Torts

STRICT LIABILITY

strict liability
liability that requires no proof of intention or negligence

due diligence
defence requiring the defendant to prove that she did everything reasonable to prevent a tort from occurring

Strict liability requires no proof of intention or negligence. Once a plaintiff proves that a tortious act was committed by a defendant, the burden shifts to the defendant to prove **due diligence**. Due diligence is a concept similar to standard of care; however, it is a defence that must be proved by the defendant. Rather than requiring the plaintiff to prove that the defendant acted unreasonably, the law places the burden on the defendant to prove that he acted diligently to prevent the tort from occurring. This reverse onus of proof, compounded with the fact that due diligence requires a higher standard of conduct than reasonableness, is often enough to tip the scales in favour of the plaintiff.

Strict liability does not occur in tort law frequently, but is more common within regulatory statutes, such as the *Environmental Protection Act*, which requires polluters and potential polluters to exercise due diligence. The most well-known case of strict liability in tort is *Rylands v. Fletcher*. In this case, the doctrine of strict liability was said to apply in situations involving the escape of water, chemicals, or other dangerous forces from one property onto another. In cases that involve strict liability, the damage to a victim's property does not have to be negligent or intentional. The mere fact of the damage constitutes a sufficient reason to impose liability in all cases except for those involving an "act of God" such as an earthquake. The principle behind imposing strict liability is that there is a social benefit in requiring those who make risky or dangerous use of their own land to account for even the non-negligent consequences of that use, because they are presumably the parties most able to control the danger.

In *Soccer Quest Coaching Inc. v. The Ice Box Arena Co.*, the builder of a soccer arena sued a neighbouring ice arena for contributing to the creation of a marshy area, which interfered with plans to build the soccer arena. In finding that the ice arena was liable in tort to the builder of the soccer arena, the court relied not only on the law of negligence but also on the rule in *Rylands v. Fletcher* (common-law strict liability). The court found that the ice arena met the test for liability because:

1. it engaged in a "non-natural use" of its land (by regularly melting ice and creating water that needed to be disposed of); and

2. this use led, *whether negligently or not*, to the escape of something (water) that damaged neighbouring property.

In general, any time a defendant creates these two conditions, there is potential for a lawsuit (or a prosecution under an environmental statute) based on strict liability.

NEGLIGENCE AND CONTRACT OR BUSINESS RELATIONS

It is generally easier to prove a violation of the terms of an explicit contract than a violation of an unwritten duty of care. The availability of remedies for breach of contract is a key reason why people choose to enter contracts in the first place and to favour contractual solutions over tort litigation in the event of a dispute. (Contract law is discussed below.)

The law of product liability is a good example. Product liability is the name given to an area of negligence that once depended on the existence of a contractual relationship between the parties. This presented a problem because consumers do not always have a direct contractual relationship with manufacturers; more often than not, consumers purchase goods through retailers. The law evolved to allow consumers to assert tort claims against manufacturers in the absence of a contract and to recover damages incurred through losses or injuries from defective or dangerous consumer goods.

For example, the manufacturer of a sports drink now owes a duty of care to the consumer who buys it. Even without a contractual relationship, the manufacturer is strictly liable to the consumer—that is, liable without being negligent. If a drink that reaches the consumer in sealed packaging is contaminated and the consumer becomes ill, the manufacturer is responsible.

INTENTIONAL BUSINESS TORTS

The common law also recognizes a number of business torts, such as deceit (fraud), conspiracy, interference with contractual relations (inducing breach of contract), and interference with business relations. A discussion of the elements that must be proven for each of these offences is beyond the scope of this chapter; however, consider the following business situations in sport that have the potential for business torts:

- teams compete with each other to draft, trade, or otherwise obtain the services of coveted players;

- sponsors compete for the right to sponsor players or events, or attempt to obtain exclusive sponsorship rights; and

- players who have advertising contracts with manufacturers (and whose contracts prohibit them from endorsing other products) can be induced to break their contracts and enter into different agreements with other manufacturers.

CONTRACT LAW

Introduction

Contract law is a very broad legal discipline that encompasses a great number of situations, including commercial transactions, tenancies, domestic contracts, employment relationships, personal service arrangements, and many other issues. All situations that fall within contract law, however, have at their heart one common feature: an agreement (or alleged agreement) between two or more parties.

For example, many recreation program providers do not own their own program facilities, but rather lease space from other providers in which to offer their programs. Consider, for example, a quilting club that wants to use a room at a community centre for a weekly meeting. The club must negotiate the following matters with the community centre:

- the time slot in which it will use the room and the number of weeks or months that the contract will last;

- whether the club will need extra chairs or other furniture for its meetings;

- whether the club or the community centre will be responsible for setting up the tables and chairs and for cleaning up the space after the club's use;

- whether the club or the community centre will be liable for any personal injuries incurred during the meetings (for example, an accident with a knitting needle), and whether either party is required to purchase insurance to mitigate this risk;

- the amount of the rental fee, and how and when it will be paid; and

- the procedure to follow if one party wants to terminate the contract early (if the centre finds a better tenant or the club members lose interest in their project).

A contract may be oral or written, unless a statute says otherwise. For example, agreements for the purchase and sale of real estate must be in writing to be enforceable. Even when a contract is not required to be in writing, written contracts are much easier to prove than oral ones. There are obvious difficulties with proving oral agreements, such as imperfect recollection and the credibility of the parties.

Rules of Contract Formation

Contract law involves determining when contracts are breached (broken), determining who is responsible for the breach, and providing a remedy (usually in the form of monetary damages) to the other party. A party breaches a contract as soon as she fails to do what she promised. The availability of a remedy for breach of a contract naturally depends on there being a legally enforceable contract to begin with. The plaintiff is therefore required to prove that a contract exists.

OFFER, ACCEPTANCE, AND CONSIDERATION

The formation of a contract requires an offer, an acceptance of the offer, and consideration. A contract is said to exist when one party makes an offer (or a counteroffer, if negotiations have gone back and forth a few times) and the other party accepts it, and communicates her acceptance to the offeror. The contract is completed at the time the offeror hears or implicitly knows of the offeree's acceptance. This process is sometimes called the "meeting of the minds."

Contracting parties must have the intention to be legally bound by the terms of the contract and they show this intention by providing consideration. **Consideration** differentiates a legally binding contract from a simple promise, which is usually not legally binding. For example, if a person promises to allow a friend to use his cottage for a week, this promise is not legally binding. It is one-sided—that is, there is a benefit to only one party. Consideration is the benefit that must flow to each party to make a contract binding. An entirely one-sided promise is generally not enforceable under contract law, and courts do not accept moral obligations as proper contract consideration. If the parties want to make an agreement that might appear to be one-sided, sometimes one party pays the other party a token consideration (for example, the sum of one dollar) to satisfy this legal requirement. If, for example, a friend pays one dollar in return for the promise of the use of the cottage, an enforceable contract may exist.

consideration
benefit that must flow to each party to make a contract binding

LEGAL CAPACITY

Another essential element is the capacity to contract. A contract may be unenforceable if it is entered into by an individual who is subsequently found to be lacking the required **legal capacity** to enter into binding contracts. Subject to certain exceptions, a party may lack the capacity to contract as a result of mental incapacity, drunkenness, or being underage. The age at which people can make enforceable contracts varies from jurisdiction to jurisdiction. Problems related to capacity to contract may arise when recreation participants are children or adults with cognitive deficits or mental illnesses. In these cases, parents or legal guardians may need to contract on behalf of the participant.

legal capacity
ability to contract that flows from being of sufficient age and mental ability

Contract Interpretation

In general, all issues regarding the terms of a contract are decided by reference to the contract, and legal rights in a contractual dispute are said to flow from the contract itself. Therefore, it is important that contract terms be precise and clear to enable the courts to understand the agreement and to ensure that the contract represents the contracting parties' intention.

The interpretation of a contract is subject to established legal rules of construction, such as plain meaning. The plain meaning rule simply states that the words in a contract should be interpreted (construed) according to their simplest and most widely accepted meaning, as opposed to unusual or euphemistic meanings. In general, the meaning of the contract is determined without reference to external sources of evidence, such as other documents or oral testimony: this rule is known as the **parol evidence rule**. It is applied less rigidly to standard form contracts, which may be interpreted by the court with reference to an industry standard, and is applied more rigidly in circumstances involving parties who have individually negotiated the specific terms of their contract.

A court generally does not imply "missing" terms into a contract; however, in the interests of business efficiency, a necessary term may be "read in." Factors such as past business dealings between the parties may be considered in determining the appropriateness of reading in a particular term.

Sometimes a statute dictates mandatory contractual terms that the parties may not circumvent. This usually occurs where there is an imbalance of bargaining power, such as a contract between an employer and employee, landlord and tenant, or insurer and insured. Mandatory terms may be legislated to protect the weaker party.

EXCLUSION CLAUSES

An **exclusion clause** is a contractual device that limits the contractual or statutory liability of a party in the event of a breach of the contract. It is a contract term like any other, negotiated between the parties. The standard rules of construction apply to these clauses no differently from any other term of a contract. However, misrepresentation of the purpose of the exclusion clause, or serious unfairness (unconscionability) in its operation, may render the clause inoperative.

Problems with Contracts

MISREPRESENTATIONS

Representations are statements or claims made by parties to a contract in the course of their negotiations. For example, a person who sells an all-terrain vehicle (ATV) may tell the buyer that the vehicle has never been in an accident. As a result of this representation, the buyer may be induced to purchase the vehicle. Representations are not necessarily incorporated into the document as a contractual term or obligation, and as a result, false representations, or **misrepresentations**, do not automatically give rise to an award of damages under contract law. There is no breach of contract. However, there may be tort liability for negligent or willful misrepresentation.

parol evidence rule
common-law rule stating that if the language of a written contract is clear and complete, courts do not look at evidence beyond the contract to interpret it

exclusion clause
contract term that limits the contractual or statutory liability of a party in the event of a breach of the contract

representations
statements or claims made by contracting parties in the course of negotiations

misrepresentations
false statements of fact

MISTAKE

In some circumstances, a court may find a contract unenforceable on the basis that one of the parties was mistaken about the details or the nature of the contract. Two kinds of mistake that might invalidate a contract are unilateral mistake and *non est factum*.

Unilateral mistake exists when one party, with the full knowledge of the other, is mistaken. This mistake arises both in situations of fraudulent misrepresentation and in situations involving one party's acceptance of an offer that the offeror knows is a result of a mistake. In these cases, only the innocent party is entitled to cancel the contract.

Non est factum is a Latin phrase loosely translatable as "I didn't sign that." Modern law has changed the meaning of the phrase to something closer to "I didn't *intend* to sign that" or "this is not my deed or doing." A party may argue *non est factum* in a situation where he has signed the wrong contract or has signed a contract under a complete misunderstanding about its nature. This is an exception to the general rule that, once signed, a document is binding. For a party to successfully plead *non est factum*, the mistaken document must be different in quality or nature, not merely in content, from the intended document. For example, a person who is handed a document to sign when renting ice skates or bowling shoes, and who assumes that the document is a waiver, may later allege *non est factum* if he is told that he actually signed a pledge agreement to sponsor the rental clerk's participation in a 10 km charity race. Also, the party claiming *non est factum* must not have been careless in signing the document.

Occasionally, an injured recreation participant pleads *non est factum* in an attempt to challenge the validity of a waiver of liability that she signed before undertaking the activity. Waivers are discussed in other chapters of this book, especially Chapter 4, Risk Management I: Identifying and Reducing Risk; Chapter 7, Managing Recreation Programs; and Chapter 9, Adventure Tourism and Other High-Risk Activities.

ILLEGALITY

Contracts must be legal to be enforceable. A term of a contract that causes one party to violate a law or regulation is not enforceable. For example, contracts to commit a crime, or contracts that require non-compliance with statutory regulations are illegal and unenforceable. Recreation providers can encounter illegality in many different ways, but should be especially wary when providing recreation that involves heavily regulated subject matter, such as alcohol, gambling, or weapons.

FAIRNESS PROBLEMS

Another class of problems that may interfere with the enforceability of contracts relates to fairness. A court may find a contract unenforceable if the evidence establishes that one of the parties was subjected to any of the following:

- **duress**: direct pressure or threats;

- **undue influence**: indirect pressure, usually in circumstances where one party is in a position of power over the other; or

- **unconscionability**: circumstances so grossly unfair as to be unconscionable.

unilateral mistake
error made by one party with full knowledge of the other

non est factum
claim that a party signed the wrong contract or signed a contract under a complete misunderstanding about its nature

duress
pressure to enter into a contract by way of threat of physical or economic harm

undue influence
pressure exerted on a weaker party that deprives him of the ability to exercise his judgment or free will

unconscionability
serious unfairness

In general, a court does not scrutinize the relative fairness of a bargain between consenting individuals. However, if a contract appears to be extremely one-sided—to the point that an honest and just person would not accept it because it is so unfair to the other person—the court may take a closer look.

Breach of Contract and Remedies for Breach

remedy
judge's order to compensate a plaintiff

In the event of a breach of contract, the wronged party, the plaintiff, may sue the breaching party, the defendant, and seek a remedy from a court. A **remedy** is the order a judge makes to compensate the plaintiff for the breach of contract. Contractual remedies offered by the courts are designed to put the plaintiff back into the position he or she would have been in had the contract either:

- been fulfilled, or

- not been formed.

specific performance
requirement that a breaching party complete his obligations under a contract

An order to force a breaching party to fulfill his obligations under a contract is called an order for **specific performance**. Because the breach of a contract generally leads to a breakdown of the business relationship between the parties, courts rarely order specific performance. This remedy is limited to situations in which a monetary payment of damages does not address the harm caused by the breach.

More commonly, courts compensate an innocent party by requiring the breaching party to pay monetary damages. The plaintiff has the burden of establishing, through evidence, the extent of the damages suffered. Receipts, bank statements, and income tax statements are examples of the kind of evidence that the plaintiff must provide in order to support her claim for damages. In situations where damages are impossible to quantify accurately, an estimate based on evidence is sufficient.

In the event of a breach of contract, the innocent party has a duty to mitigate losses. This means that the plaintiff must take steps to limit or reduce the harm caused by the breach. For example, if the host of a beach volleyball tournament learns, the day before the tournament, that a contracted shipment of sand will not arrive, the host cannot simply cancel all the participant registrations and expect the breaching delivery company to pay for the lost revenue. Instead, the host must attempt to obtain the sand from a different supplier in time for the tournament.

If a plaintiff fails to mitigate, a court may reduce the damages award by the amount that could have been reasonably mitigated. The plaintiff must do that which is expected of a reasonable person to minimize the losses resulting from a breach of contract. If the host is successful in making this arrangement but the sand from the other supplier costs an extra $10 per ton, it is likely that the court will award damages against the original supplier that include the additional cost (for example, $100 if ten tons were purchased) plus any other administrative or convenience costs related to the host's need to replace the supplier.

KEY TERMS

but for test

causation

consideration

contract

contributory negligence

damages

defendant

due diligence

duress

duty of care

exclusion clause

foreseeable

joint and several liability

legal capacity

misrepresentations

negligence

non est factum

parol evidence rule

plaintiff

precedent

remedy

representations

specific performance

standard of care

standard of proof

strict liability

thin skull rule

tort

unconscionability

undue influence

unilateral mistake

vicarious liability

REVIEW EXERCISES

Review Questions

1. How is the common law created, and where is it found?

2. Why must recreation providers understand tort law?

3. When an accident occurs and the victim wants the party who caused the accident to compensate him for his losses, what must he do?

4. What is a duty of care, and why can there be no tort liability without it?

5. What is a standard of care?

6. How do courts decide who is legally responsible for accidents or injuries that have multiple or complex causes?

7. What is the practical impact of joint and several liability on recreation providers?

8. What is vicarious liability, and how can it apply to recreation providers?

9. How does a court's assessment that a recreation participant took inappropriate risks or contributed to his injuries in some way affect the court's finding of liability?

10. What is occupiers' liability?

11. What is nuisance in the context of tort law, and why is it relevant to recreation providers?

12. Why should recreation providers know about contract law?

13. List at least three reasons why a court may find a contract to be invalid.

14. Once a court has decided that one party has breached a contract, how does it remedy the situation?

Discussion Question

While the principle of *volenti non fit injuria* used to offer considerable protection to the providers of dangerous recreation, voluntary assumption of risk is now interpreted very narrowly by the courts. A person will generally not be found to have assumed all the risks involved in a recreation activity, even when she knows that it's risky. Is this a step backward or forward in your view?

CHAPTER 3

Legislation, Policy, Procedure, and Administration

CHAPTER OBJECTIVES

After completing this chapter, you should be able to:

- explain, with reference to the Constitution, how legislative powers are allocated within the Canadian federation;

- identify which statutes apply to a particular recreation business or program, and know where to find copies of these statutes;

- describe the general structure of a subject-specific statute;

- understand the role of general statutes, such as the *Provincial Offences Act* and the *Criminal Code*;

- explain how human rights legislation and the *Canadian Charter of Rights and Freedoms* apply to recreation;

- know how to determine which civil, criminal, or administrative procedures apply to legal issues and disputes that a recreation provider may face; and

- list alternatives to litigation for the resolution of disputes.

INTRODUCTION

This chapter introduces statute law in the recreation context, describing the role of specific statutes, such as the *Motorized Snow Vehicles Act*, and more general legislation, such as the *Canadian Charter of Rights and Freedoms*. It also discusses federal and provincial human rights statutes, and international law. It is intended to give you a very basic introduction to the legal process, touching on civil procedure, administrative law, and alternative dispute resolution. Finally, it introduces the role of policy, both public and private.

LEGISLATIVE JURISDICTION

jurisdiction
law-making authority

Constitution
document that establishes the framework under which all other laws are created and the basic principles to which all laws must conform

Canada has a federal system of government, which means that there is a central government (called the federal government) and numerous provincial governments. **Jurisdiction** to legislate is divided between these two levels of government, as described in the **Constitution**, a piece of legislation that supersedes all other legislation in the country.

In Canada, a comparatively large degree of legislative responsibility is delegated to the provinces. This means that there are many more provincial statutes, and accompanying regulations, than federal ones. Whether a statute is to be provincial or federal depends on its subject matter. Sections 91 and 92 of the Constitution set out a division of powers: a framework that assigns certain subjects to either the federal or the provincial level of government. See Table 3.1.

For example, section 91(27) assigns jurisdiction over the creation of the criminal law to the federal Parliament. For this reason, the *Criminal Code* is a federal law. Section 92(5) assigns the management of "Public Lands belonging to the Province" to the provincial legislatures. Using this power, Ontario passed the *Provincial Parks and Conservation Reserves Act*, as well as a number of more specific statutes, such as the *Kawartha Highlands Signature Site Park Act*.

Municipalities are a third level of government. Their power does not come directly from the Constitution, but rather from statutes passed by provincial governments, such as Ontario's *Municipal Act, 2001*. Municipalities may be cities, towns, and regions. They have the authority, delegated to them by the province's municipal statute, to regulate local issues by passing bylaws.

Although local issues, such as parking, waste collection, and community services, may seem minor in comparison with national concerns, the smooth management of a large municipality is an incredibly complicated task and can give rise to an enormous number of bylaws. Since municipalities often provide recreation services, these bylaws are relevant to many recreation providers.

Sport and recreation are not explicitly referred to in Canada's Constitution. Generally, recreation falls within the definition of "Matters of a merely local or private Nature in the Province," which puts it within the ambit of provincial regulation. However, there are some aspects of recreation that have federal, and even international, dimensions. Consider the following examples:

- *National parks.* Recreation in a national park is governed by the federal laws that apply to these parks.

- *Gambling.* First Nations peoples are within federal jurisdiction, and federal law provides for the establishment of casinos on First Nations reserves.

- *Fishing.* Oceans are governed by the federal government, and federal laws may affect recreational fishing in oceans.

- *Hunting.* Firearms are governed by the federal government, and this may affect hunting.

- *Sporting competitions.* Competition at the interprovincial and national levels engage federal jurisdiction, as well as international law and custom.

Table 3.1 Summary of Canada's Law-Making Powers

Federal Government Law-Making Powers by Subject Matter (Section 91)	Provincial Government Law-Making Powers by Subject Matter (Section 92)
Interprovincial/international trade	Property laws
National defence	Civil rights
Shipping	Contract law
Currency	Tort law
Criminal law	Hospitals
Postal service	Incorporation of companies operating only within a province
Residual powers	Matters of provincial concern
	Municipalities

There are federal statutes that cover issues such as the sponsorship of international sport.

- *Drug testing.* The illegal use of drugs also falls under federal jurisdiction, having an impact on drug-testing in sport.

ACTIVITY- AND ORGANIZATION-SPECIFIC STATUTES

Introduction

There are dozens of statutes and regulations, particularly at the provincial level, that regulate specific recreation activities, facilities, and organizations. Recreation providers who are charged with risk management need to identify all of the statutes, regulations, bylaws, and policies that have an impact on the activities in which they are involved. While some of these are identified in later chapters, it is impractical to cover them all in detail. Also, to do so would have limited usefulness because legislation, and especially regulations, are subject to frequent change.

Instead of attempting to catalogue and discuss the full range of recreation-related statutes, this chapter examines one such statute, the *Motorized Snow Vehicles Act*, by way of example. The following discussion should provide a general understanding of how an activity-based statute is applied and enforced.

Motorized Snow Vehicles Act

The Ontario *Motorized Snow Vehicles Act* is an example of a subject-specific statute: it deals with a single item—motorized snow vehicles—and provides detailed regulation about their use. There are a large number of subject- or organization-specific statutes that apply to the context of recreation. We mention many others in the later chapters of this book without reviewing their content in detail. This detailed review of the *Motorized Snow Vehicles Act* is intended to help you understand how statutes are structured, so that you can better understand the statutes that apply in various recreation sectors.

WEB LINK

Access statutes, regulations, and cases at www.canlii.org (statutes and regulations from most Canadian jurisdictions, court decisions, and some tribunal decisions); www.laws.justice.gc.ca (federal legislation and regulations); and www.e-laws.gov.on.ca (Ontario statutes and regulations).

DEFINITIONS SECTION

Most statutes contain a definitions section (sometimes called "Interpretation"). Usually, it is either the first or the second section of the statute. The definitions section is very important because it establishes the meaning of certain terms that are repeated throughout the statute. The definitions section also excludes certain possible interpretations of the terms it defines, thereby narrowing the application of the statute. For example, the ordinary meaning of "tourism establishment" may bring places like museums and amusement parks to mind; however, the definitions section of the Ontario *Tourism Act* makes it clear that for the purpose of the Act, "tourism establishment" means a place that offers sleeping accommodations.

The definitions section of the *Motorized Snow Vehicles Act* provides definitions for 15 different terms, including:

- motorized snow vehicle,
- highway,
- conservation officer,
- Minister, and
- trail permit.

"Motorized snow vehicle" is defined as "a self-propelled vehicle designed to be driven primarily on snow."

One of the most common and most important definitions in a definitions section is the definition of "Minister" and "Ministry." The government of Ontario is organized into a number of different ministries, and each ministry is in charge of regulating particular activities. Many different Ontario ministries are involved in the administration of recreation law. In the case of motorized snow vehicles, the regulating ministry is the Ministry of Transportation. By checking the definition of "Minister" or "Ministry" in the definitions section, you can quickly determine which part of the Ontario government is responsible for regulating the relevant activity. This can help direct your research or inquiries when you have questions. For example, if you want more information about snowmobiling laws, you can contact the Ministry of Transportation, whether by telephone or online.

REGULATORY PROVISIONS

After the definitions section, it is usual to find provisions that establish regulatory policies relating to the activity that is governed by the Act. The most important aspects of regulatory policy usually are listed first. In the *Motorized Snow Vehicles Act*, the first provision after the definitions section is entitled "Permit needed for driving." This provision makes it clear that no one may drive a motorized snow vehicle in Ontario without first obtaining a permit.

Section 2, "Permit needed for driving," has 11 subsections that describe the legal requirements for permits. The details include the following:

- the dealer who sells the vehicle to the owner must register it with the Ministry;
- after payment of a fee, the owner can obtain a permit from the Ministry for the duly registered vehicle and must display it on the vehicle;

- the permit can be validated by the Ministry as required by the regulations made under the legislation (more on these later in this chapter under the heading "Regulations");

- the Ministry must keep records of permits and their holders;

- not having a permit is an offence, which, on conviction, can lead to a $200 fine (offences are discussed below in greater detail under the headings "General Offence Provisions" and "Provincial Offences"); and

- there are some exceptions to the need for a permit—for example, manufacturers of these vehicles need not have permits to possess the vehicles, and dealers need not have permits to display them for sale.

After section 2, there are a number of other provisions dealing with obligations, such as the following:

- Section 2.1: Trail permit required.

- Section 3: Administrative requirements. For example, a registered vehicle owner must inform the Ministry of a change of address.

- Section 4: Registration number to be kept clean, unobstructed.

- Section 5: Driving on King's Highway or secondary highway. The "King's Highway" is an archaic expression that means public highway; this provision prohibits driving on public highways except in certain circumstances, such as crossing them.

- Section 6: Duty of driver when school bus stopped on highway.

- Section 7: Municipal bylaws. The statute provides that municipalities can pass bylaws that affect (generally by restricting) the use of motorized snow vehicles within municipalities; most municipalities do pass such bylaws, and do not permit the use of motorized snow vehicles in built-up areas.

- Section 8: Crossing roadway. Drivers must cross the roadway only at an angle of approximately 90 degrees.

- Section 9: Driving requirements. For example, drivers must be age 16 or over and have either a valid automobile driver's licence or a locally valid snow vehicle operator's licence.

- Section 10: Operators' licences. These are licences distinct from vehicle permits, and are issued to certify that the operator is aged 12 or over and has passed any tests that may be prescribed by the regulations.

- Section 11: Application of certain Acts. This section makes it clear that the *Highway Traffic Act* and the *Motor Vehicle Accident Claims Act* do not apply to motorized snow vehicles.

- Section 12: Insurance. This section makes insurance compulsory for snowmobile operators.

- Section 13: Duty to report accident. Reporting is required if anyone is hurt, or if there is damage in excess of $400 in value.

- Section 14: Speed limit. The speed limit varies depending on location, and is not the same as the posted highway speed limit.

- Section 15: Careless driving. This section establishes the offence of careless driving of a motorized snow vehicle; it was necessary for the Act to include this, since the *Highway Traffic Act*, which creates the offence of careless driving for cars, does not apply to motorized snow vehicles.

- Section 16: Driver's obligations. These include the obligation to carry licence documents while riding, and to stop at the request of a police or conservation officer.

- Section 17: Stopping for vehicles with red lights. This provision, and provision 17.1 after it, contain 16 subsections that explain the responsibilities of motorized snow vehicle operators when they are being pursued by police vehicles, including the consequences of failing to stop, or of attempting an "escape by flight."

- Section 18: Equipment requirements. This section requires that the vehicle's muffler be in working order.

- Section 19: Towing.

- Section 20: Driver shall wear helmet. This section makes the wearing of a helmet a compulsory requirement.

- Section 21: Vehicle shall bear National Safety Mark. Safety standards for products and equipment are discussed in Chapter 8, Equipment and Products Law.

- Section 22: Risks willingly assumed. This section refers to the *Occupiers' Liability Act*, and provides that motorized snow vehicle operators assume the risks of their activities when they operate the vehicles on premises without paying a fee to do so—including, by implication, while trespassing.

GENERAL OFFENCE PROVISIONS

A review of the list of regulatory provisions highlighted above reveals certain offences created by the statute—for example, the offences of operating a motorized snow vehicle without a permit and evading a police vehicle. As you can see, offences created by a statute can be scattered throughout the statute. Even if there is a provision or section entitled "Offences," it may not provide an exhaustive list of the offences that can be charged under the statute. Only a full reading of the statute will reveal all of the offence provisions.

Like most statutes, the *Motorized Snow Vehicles Act* discusses the general subject of offences and liability near the end of the statute. The provisions that relate to offences include not only section 25, which is entitled "Offences and Fines," but also sections 23 and 24, which are entitled "Liability of Owner" and "Owner may be convicted."

Section 25, the general offence provision, reads as follows:

25. Every person who contravenes any of the provisions of this Act or the regulations is guilty of an offence and on conviction where a fine for the contravention is not otherwise provided for herein is liable to a fine not exceeding $1,000.

Note that while the maximum fine mentioned in this section is $1,000, different maximum fines are described for particular offences, for example:

- failing to stop for a police officer (maximum fine of $10,000);

- attempted escape by flight (maximum fine of $25,000); and

- driving while licence suspended (maximum fine of $5,000).

PROVINCIAL OFFENCES

The procedures for charging and prosecuting offences are sometimes prescribed in part by the statutes that create the offences, but these statutes are not the only source of law. The charging and prosecution of **provincial offences**—offences that are created under provincial statutes—are governed by the *Provincial Offences Act*.

The *Provincial Offences Act* is a general statute that establishes procedures relevant to provincial offences. These general procedures apply any time a provincial statute is silent about any detail of charging or prosecution. Provincial offences are prosecuted separately from criminal offences (which are federal offences), in separate courts, using simplified procedures. A description of the structure of Canada's court system appears in the Extra Credit feature later in this chapter.

provincial offences
offences created under provincial statutes

REGULATIONS

In the *Motorized Snow Vehicles Act*, the provision that appears after the general offence provision is a provision entitled "Regulations." It provides a list of areas that may form the subject matter of regulations passed under the statute. Regulations can exist only under an authorizing statute. If the statute is repealed (rendered no longer in force), all regulations made under the statute are repealed as well.

Regulations differ from statutes because they do not require the formal legislative procedures of first, second, and third readings, royal assent, and often proclamation in order to come into force. Instead, they are created by ministry staff, and can be changed fairly efficiently through a process of notice to the public. Regulations tend to deal with specific administrative or technical details that are not specifically addressed by the legislature, and that may change frequently over time. A common example of a regulation is one that sets administrative fees, such as the fee required to register a motorized snow vehicle. Setting these fees by means of regulation allows the government to easily raise the fee periodically.

There are currently five regulations under the *Motorized Snow Vehicles Act*:

- Designations, which designates certain roads as being "the King's Highway";

- General;

- Motorized Snow Vehicles Operators' Licences;

- Trail Grooming; and

- Trail Permits.

Regulations entitled "General" are usually the longest and most important regulations made under a statute. They often contain a catch-all collection of administrative directives.

OTHER PROVISIONS

Some statutes, though not the *Motorized Snow Vehicles Act*, may contain other kinds of provisions, such as a "purposes" or "principles" provision, and "coming-into-force" provisions.

Purposes or principles provisions appear very early in the statutes that include them, usually in either section 1 or section 2. These provisions are designed to communicate the philosophy or values intended to be promoted or reflected by the legislation. These provisions tend to be more common in statutes that are designed to promote general social benefits or values. An example of such a provision can be found in the *Ontarians with Disabilities Act, 2001*, which states:

> Purpose
>
> 1. The purpose of this Act is to improve opportunities for persons with disabilities and to provide for their involvement in the identification, removal and prevention of barriers to their full participation in the life of the province.

It's important to review purposes or principles provisions because they give you useful clues about the values and policies that guide the administration of the statute.

Coming-into-force provisions appear at the end of statutes, and provide information about the status of the legislation. For example, if the legislation has passed third reading in the legislature but has not yet been proclaimed, this situation will be explained in the "coming-into-force" provision. Sometimes, a statute is proclaimed with certain provisions excluded, with a view to having these provisions take effect at a later date.

STATUTES OF GENERAL APPLICATION

As you learned at the beginning of this chapter, not all statutes focus on a narrow subject matter or activity. Some very important statutes have general application to a wide range of activities, organizations, and circumstances. These general statutes are designed to communicate the government's broad social or administrative policies.

Criminal and Quasi-Criminal Statutes

The Constitution's division of powers allocates criminal law to federal jurisdiction. For this reason, the *Criminal Code* of Canada is a federal statute. (Adding confusion, after criminal law is legislated by the federal government, it is administered by the provinces through the provincial court system.)

There are also certain quasi-criminal statutes. These govern activities that, like traditional crime, pose a risk to the public and can lead to significant consequences such as imprisonment or large fines. Because of their similarities to criminal law, these statutes also fall under federal jurisdiction. They include the *Controlled Drugs and Substances Act*, the *Crimes Against Humanity and War Crimes Act*, the *Anti-terrorism Act*, and the *Firearms Act*. The *Criminal Code* and most quasi-criminal statutes contain both substantive law (offences) and procedural provisions that explain how these offences are to be prosecuted and how penalties are to be imposed.

Possible Criminal and Quasi-Criminal Federal Offences in Recreation

Under the *Criminal Code*:

- *assault* (many forms, including aggravated assault and assault with a weapon) —for example, violence in sport that exceeds the participants' expectations and consent

- *sexual assault, sexual interference* (many categories)—for example, sexual abuse of students by a music teacher

- *threatening, coercion, and harassment* (various criminal forms that apply to serious cases)—for example, one potential player stalking, harassing, or threatening another to discourage that player from trying out for a team; a coach pushing a player beyond his limits to the point of injury

- *unlawful confinement*—for example, refusing to allow a tour participant to return home or to her hotel, or to leave a plane, ship, or other vehicle

- *criminal negligence* (includes a long list of offences, such as criminal negligence causing bodily harm, manslaughter, and failure to provide the necessaries of life to someone to whom they are owed)—for example, a mountain guide allowing inexperienced or young hikers to proceed unattended onto a dangerous trail where a hiker is hurt or killed

- *fraud* (many offences)—for example, failure to deliver promised services and/or to provide a refund

- *gambling and gaming offences, and offences related to prostitution*—for example, having an illegal slot machine on a recreation premises, or allowing recreation staff (for example, exotic dancers) to engage in prostitution

- *failure to protect the safety of workers*—under new employer criminal negligence provisions brought in by the Westray Bill (Bill C-45)

- *many other possible crimes* (including those related to interference with crime scenes or investigations, aiding or abetting violence by recreation participants, violation of wildlife or environmental protection rules, and crimes related to running an illegal business or engaging in illegal business practices)—for example, hosting a cockfight, contrary to the prohibition against this sport

Under the *Controlled Drugs and Substances Act*:

- *doping* (selling or administering an illegal substance) and/or being an accessory to the crime of doping—for example, concealing evidence or impeding an investigation into alleged doping

Under the *Firearms Act*:

- *possessing prohibited firearms*—for example, by a museum that displays firearms not legal for display in Canada

- *registration offences*—for example, where a gun club or firing range allows participants to use or possess unregistered weapons on its premises

- *storage and/or transportation offences*—for example, where a hunting lodge allows participants to leave loaded firearms in open racks while breaking for lunch

- *offences involving licences, permits or unqualified participants*—for example, operating a firing range or a gun club without appropriate licences or permits, or allowing unqualified participants to handle firearms ◈

Since most recreation providers will never run into trouble with the criminal law, a detailed discussion of criminal law is not warranted here. However, the box entitled "Possible Criminal and Quasi-Criminal Federal Offences in Recreation" highlights a few of the offences that can potentially flow from recreation-related activity. You may notice that a number of the listed offences are actually criminalized forms of the tort of negligence, which was discussed at length in Chapter 2, Legal Liability in Tort and Contract.

Criminal law and the potential for criminal charges against recreation providers will be revisited in appropriate contexts in later chapters—for example, in the context of the discussion of abuse of vulnerable participants in Chapter 7, and in the discussion of violence in sport in Chapter 12.

Rights-Focused Statutes

Canada has a number of important statutes that protect human rights. These include the *Constitution Act, 1982*, the *Canadian Charter of Rights and Freedoms*, the *Canadian Human Rights Act*, and the Ontario *Human Rights Code* (and comparable legislation in the other provinces).

The *Canadian Charter of Rights and Freedoms* (the Charter) was passed in 1982, as a schedule to the Constitution. Like the other components of the Constitution, it is paramount to all other legislation in Canada. The Charter enshrines a number of very important human rights and freedoms, and prevents legislatures from passing laws that trample on them. Any law that is found to be in conflict with the Charter may be struck down by a court.

While the Charter guarantees certain rights by prohibiting governments from making laws or authorizing actions that infringe these rights, human rights legislation, such as the Ontario *Human Rights Code*, provides protection to individuals against the infringement of their rights by non-government entities. Human rights statutes provide remedies against the actions of individuals and corporations, as well as government decision-makers, when these parties discriminate against or harass people in relation to:

- access to goods and services,

- employment, and

- housing.

Understanding human rights legislation is very important for recreation providers, who provide services and also employ workers. For example, refusing to allow a child to attend a summer day camp program because the child has a disability may be a violation of human rights law. Policies that segregate participants based on characteristics such as age and sex or that seek to deny participation to people with disabilities may also conflict with human rights law. While such discrimination may sometimes be necessary to protect the safety of participants, any segregation policy that cannot be justified for real and substantial safety reasons may be successfully challenged under human rights law.

Human rights legislation, both at the federal and provincial levels, prohibits discrimination based on a number of specific grounds. The precise list of grounds of discrimination varies from statute to statute, but most human rights statutes include the following prohibited grounds of discrimination:

- race, ethnic, and/or national origin;

- colour;

- religion;

- age;

- sex;

- sexual orientation;

- marital status and family status (often including pregnancy and child-bearing);

- physical or mental disability; and

- pardoned criminal convictions.

The *Canadian Human Rights Act* prohibits the infringement of human rights in federally regulated spheres, such as immigration, federal public service employment, and telecommunications. The Ontario *Human Rights Code* and other provincial human rights codes prohibit discrimination in areas of provincial legislative jurisdiction, such as: housing, real estate, and residential tenancies; contracts and commerce; tort law; family law; employment (except in the federal public service); health care; and education.

Other General Statutes

Other statutes of general application relevant to recreation touch on matters of public health and safety. Some examples follow.

- *Employment law.* There are many statutes that prescribe conditions of employment and rights of employees. These include, in Ontario, the *Employment Standards Act*, the *Labour Relations Act*, and the *Occupational Health and Safety Act*; and at the federal level, the *Canada Labour Code*.

- *Health law.* The operators of public facilities—particularly facilities that contain pools, serve food, or bring large groups of people together—need to be aware of relevant public health laws, such as the Ontario *Health Protection and Promotion Act*. This Act is the parent legislation for important regulations, such as those that govern food premises, public pools, public spas, and recreational camps. Where facilities offer services and programs that affect participant health and well-being, operators also need to be familiar with general health-related legislation, such as the Ontario *Regulated Health Professions Act* and/or subject-specific health-related legislation, such as the Ontario *Massage Therapy Act*.

- *Privacy law.* Recreation programmers who collect personal information must understand their obligations under laws that govern personal privacy, such as the federal *Personal Information Protection and Electronic Documents Act*, the federal *Privacy Act*, the Ontario *Personal Health Information Protection Act*, and the Ontario *Consumer Reporting Act*.

- *Building and fire codes, and related statutes.* Operators of public facilities are required to maintain their facilities in compliance with all applicable local building and fire codes, as well as with such legislation as the Ontario *Technical Standards and Safety Act*, which provides standards for equipment such as elevators and boilers.

- *Environmental law.* Operators of public facilities—particularly those that generate waste, such as arena ice melt-off—need to understand their compliance requirements under environmental laws, such as the Ontario *Environmental Protection Act*, the Ontario *Waste Management Act*, and the Ontario *Safe Drinking Water Act*. Parks operators need to be familiar with legislation that applies specifically to parks—such as the *Canada National Parks Act*—and touches on aspects of environmental protection, as well as with subject-specific legislation, such as the *Ontario Water Resources Act*, the Ontario *Clean Water Act*, and the Ontario *Fish and Wildlife Conservation Act*.

- *Consumer protection law.* Operators must also be aware of laws designed to protect the health, safety, and economic interests of consumers, such as the Ontario *Consumer Protection Act* and the *Tourism Act*.

Some of these statutes are discussed in other chapters of this book. For example, the role of building codes and fire codes is discussed in Chapter 4, which explains the role of facility characteristics in reducing risks, and the *Occupational Health and Safety Act* is discussed in Chapter 7, which deals with managing recreation programs and the employees who run them.

THE CHARTER AND RECREATION

Paramountcy

paramount legislation
legislation that takes
precedence over all other
laws

As part of Canada's Constitution, the Charter is **paramount legislation**—that is, legislation that takes precedence over all other laws in Canada. All laws and government actions in Canada, regardless of the level or branch of government involved, are subject to the rights and freedoms guaranteed to individuals as set out in the Charter. If any law violates the Charter, a court may declare the law to be unconstitutional and strike it down. The Charter also prohibits government actions that infringe on Charter rights, and any action of an agent or representative of any level of government that contravenes a Charter right or freedom may also be challenged.

The Charter can be used to overturn a law or a government action only if a person formally complains by launching a Charter challenge. However, the Charter also influences legislatures when they are drafting new laws because they generally wish to avoid having their legislation challenged. Government officials also make efforts to behave in accordance with Charter principles to avoid litigation.

Scope of the Charter

The rights and freedoms expressed in the Charter do not apply to every interaction between people. The Charter is intended to inform and direct government policy, both the kind that is explicitly communicated by means of legislation, and the kind that is implied through the government's actions.

Since recreation providers do not legislate, the only way in which they can risk falling afoul of the Charter is through actions that can be said to be *government* action. When is a recreation provider a government actor? Decisions made under the Charter have made it clear that the activities of organizations that are created by or under statutes can fall within the scope of government action. Some of the organizations that are subject to the application of the Charter include public schools, national and provincial parks, and municipalities and their facilities (for example, community centres and libraries).

Organizations that have been ruled *not* to be subject to the Charter include universities, colleges, and national and provincial sports organizations that are not created by the government. In some cases, however, heavy involvement by the government in funding sports activities or in selecting funding recipients may trigger the application of the Charter, as explained below:

> It may be that certain programs within a private organization could attract Charter application. For example, Canada's Athlete Assistance Program (AAP) is administered by each national sport governing body that "recommends" potential recipients to the government of Canada, which retains the ultimate decision-making status in the allocation of AAP funds. (Corbett, Findlay, & Lech, 2008, p. 93)

For organizations with close ties to the government, the provisions of the Charter are a necessary consideration in all decisions relating to public access to programs.

Charter Rights and Freedoms

The rights and freedoms protected under the Charter can be subdivided into five groups:

1. fundamental freedoms, such as freedom of conscience and religion;

2. democratic rights, such as the right to vote;

3. mobility rights and other rights that are relevant to life in a federal country;

4. rights within the criminal justice process, such as the right to be free from unreasonable searches or seizures; and

5. equality rights.

The Charter right that is most likely to arise in the context of recreation is the right to equality. The Charter provides:

> 15(1) Every individual is equal before and under the law and has the right to the equal protection and equal benefit of the law without discrimination and, in particular, without discrimination based on race, national or ethnic origin, colour, religion, sex, age or mental or physical disability.
>
> (2) Subsection (1) does not preclude any law, program or activity that has as its object the amelioration of conditions of disadvantaged individuals or groups including those that are disadvantaged because of race, national or ethnic origin, colour, religion, sex, age or mental or physical disability.

As noted earlier, safe participation in some sports and other recreation activities may require the segregation of participants by age, ability, and sometimes gender. In certain cases, activities may not be at all safe for people of advanced age or who suffer from physical disabilities. Providers of activities such as these must be very careful in developing limitations on participation that protect the safety and enjoyment of participants without violating their rights to equality under the Charter. As can be seen from reading section 15(2), however, programs targeted specifically at participants with disabilities do not violate the Charter when they exclude fully abled participants.

injunction
court order that is designed to prohibit an action or require an action

CASE STUDY

Gay Student Permitted to Attend Prom with Partner

More than a year before the spring of 2002, Marc Hall, a 17-year-old Oshawa teenager, expressed his intention to attend his Catholic secondary school prom with his boyfriend. (His school had a policy that required students to submit the names of their prom dates.) In March, about three months before the prom, the school informed Marc that he would not be permitted to bring his boyfriend to the prom, and the school board refused to overturn the school's decision. Marc applied to the Ontario Supreme Court for an **injunction** (a court order designed to prohibit an action) to prevent the school board from excluding him from the prom if he attended with his boyfriend.

The school board argued that allowing Marc to attend the prom with his male date would constitute an endorsement of homosexuality; such an action would run counter to the teachings of the Catholic Church, which the school board has a statutory responsibility to uphold. The school board also argued that its decision to exclude Marc's date from the prom was a valid exercise of freedom of religion under section 2(a) of the Charter.

Marc argued that the board's decision to exclude him from the prom on the ground of sexual orientation was a violation of his section 15 equality rights.

The court granted Marc's application, issuing an injunction to prevent the school from excluding Marc and his date from the prom, or from cancelling the prom altogether. In making its decision, the court held that:

- school is a "fundamental institution" in the lives of young people;

- the recreation opportunities associated with school attendance—including participation in school sports and attendance at social occasions, such as the prom—are important to students' development;

- restricting a student's full participation in school life because of his sexual orientation may represent a failure to value the student's human dignity in a free society in which difference is respected and equality is valued;

- excluding Marc and his date from the prom might well be found, by a trial court, to be an unacceptable violation of his section 15 rights;

- section 93 of the *Constitution Act, 1867*, which gives rights to Catholic school boards to determine matters such as curriculum, is not broad enough to supersede individuals' equality rights; and

- if the injunction were declined, Marc would be excluded from the prom and, since the prom was a one-time opportunity, he would not have another opportunity to attend.

Source: *Hall (Litigation Guardian of) v. Powers*, 2002 CanLII 49475 (ON S.C.) ◇

POLICY

Government Policy

Legislation often sets basic rules for interactions between individuals and their government (consider, for example, legislation governing the licensing of vehicles and drivers); however, sometimes statutes and the regulations made under them cannot include all of the details about how an activity is managed by government. Especially if legislation leaves room for **discretion** in administrative decision-making, the manner in which a law is actually applied often evolves as a matter of government **policy**.

Policies can be formal or informal, written or unwritten. They can also have a wide range of objectives—for example, promoting fairness to users of the system, or prioritizing the government's use of its resources.

Government policy must not, however, have an objective or operate in a way that runs counter to the spirit of any applicable legislation. If policies are found to operate in a way not contemplated by legislation, courts may choose not to support their enforcement.

When an Ontario municipality makes a valid policy—one that violates neither the Charter nor any other applicable law and is made in good faith—this policy cannot be challenged under negligence law because it is an appropriate exercise of municipal discretion. This rule prevents people from attempting to dictate how municipalities spend their tax dollars. The rule can be relevant in the recreation context because it can make it difficult for people to challenge a municipality's decision—for example, to close a public outdoor pool or library, or to convert parkland into commercial space.

As a recreation provider, it is your responsibility to be familiar not only with the legislation that applies to your work but also with the government policies, practices, and guidelines that support this legislation. Often, written accounts of these policies are available from the office of the department, ministry, or local municipality that regulates the programs and services that you provide. For example, if you operate a resort that caters to hunters, your activities may be subject to the policies of the Ontario Ministry of Tourism, and either the Ontario Ministry of Natural Resources or the federal Department of Natural Resources (depending on where your clients hunt). If you manage a network of city parks, your activities are subject to the policies of your municipality, which are usually dictated in part by the provincial ministry that delegates policy-making authority to your municipality.

discretion
freedom to make decisions within limits set by legislation or common law

policy
governmental course or principle of action

Policies, Rules, and Bylaws in the Private Sector

Governments aren't the only organizations that create policies. Most private corporations, associations, and organizations, including those in the recreation sector, have policies of their own. These policies are sometimes called bylaws, not to be confused with municipal bylaws.

Employees are required to comply with the policies of their employer, and may also be required to comply with the policies of organizations with which they do business. For example, if you operate a tour company for active seniors that includes a day's outing to a small golf course, you may decide to arrange for the exclusive use of the course for your group for that day (perhaps even bringing along your own golf pros to offer instruction). It is possible that the golf course has a policy that requires you to sign a "hold harmless" agreement; such an agreement states that your organization, and not the golf course, is responsible for any accidents or injuries that occur during the golf day. You may even be required to purchase and show proof of insurance to back up your agreement.

LEGAL PROCESS AND PROCEDURE

substantive law
law that creates rights and obligations by requiring or prohibiting certain activities

procedural law
law that describes the manner in which substantive law is enforced

The distinction between substantive law and legal procedure was mentioned earlier in this chapter under the heading "Criminal and Quasi-Criminal Statutes." **Substantive law** refers to the "dos and don'ts" expressed in statutes—in other words, the "what" of the law. **Procedural law**, by contrast, refers to the "how" of the law: the rules that describe the steps by which the government and the court system *enforce* the substantive rules.

For example, a statute may provide that no organization can hold a fundraising barbecue in a municipal park without obtaining a permit from the municipality. This prohibition is an example of substantive law. The same statute may provide that in order to obtain a permit, an organization must apply in writing to the municipality, at least ten business days in advance of the proposed event. This rule is an example of a procedural law.

Substantive and procedural law often appear side-by-side in the same statute. However, in order to avoid duplication in the law, and to streamline the administration of government, some aspects of law enforcement procedure—particularly those that relate to litigation and to the prosecution of offences—are gathered into separate statutes, regulations, or codes. The *Provincial Offences Act* is an example of a procedural statute: it focuses on legal procedure, rather than substantive law. Instead of creating obligations by requiring or prohibiting certain activities, it creates procedures to govern the enforcement of substantive laws found in other provincial statutes, such as the *Highway Traffic Act*.

Law enforcement procedure falls into two broad categories: (1) criminal and quasi-criminal procedure and (2) civil procedure. Both are introduced, in very brief and simplified terms, in the sections that follow.

Criminal and Quasi-Criminal Procedure

The procedures for enforcing the criminal law that is contained in the *Criminal Code* are described in the Code itself. Certain basic elements are common to all Canadian criminal prosecutions:

- the laying of charges by law enforcement officers;

- after the laying of charges but before trial, the prosecution's obligation to share information about its evidence (called making disclosure) with the defence (the accused and her lawyer);

EXTRA CREDIT

Levels of Courts in Canada

The Canadian legal system has several checks and balances in place to ensure that parties and issues are dealt with as fairly as possible. One way in which the system promotes fairness is by incorporating multiple levels of decision-making in a tiered court system.

When parties to a civil or criminal case first come into formal legal conflict, their cases are heard at the trial court level. Some **trial courts**, such as the Small Claims Court and the Unified Family Court, are specialized; however, generally the lower courts in Ontario hear a broad range of matters.

trial courts
courts empowered to host full hearing of a case

A trial court typically hosts a full hearing of a case, complete with witness testimony and the entering of exhibits (documents and other objects entered as evidence). At the end of the trial, the judge or jury makes a decision. In a criminal trial, the decision relates to whether the accused person is guilty or not guilty. In a civil trial, the court decides whether the plaintiff has proved her case against the defendant and whether the defendant must compensate the plaintiff.

If either of the parties believes that the trial court has come to the wrong decision, he may be entitled to appeal the case to a different court, usually the **court of appeal** for the province. The court of appeal does not hear evidence first-hand, and witnesses are not commonly called in this court. An appeal court only reviews cases in which the appealing party (called the appellant) suggests that the trial court made an error in law—that is, a mistake in applying the law to the evidence presented at trial. The court of appeal generally does not agree to review any of the interpretations that the trial judge or jury made of the facts presented by witnesses.

court of appeal
a court that reviews the actions and findings of trial courts

If an appeal is allowed, the lower court's decision is reversed. If an appeal is denied, the lower court's decision is upheld.

In very limited circumstances, a decision of a provincial court of appeal may be appealed to the **Supreme Court of Canada**, the highest court in the country. However, this Court decides only a limited number of cases every year, and there is no automatic right to appeal a case to this Court, except in certain serious criminal matters. Otherwise, only parties with cases of national importance and general public interest are granted leave to appeal to the Supreme Court. ◇

Supreme Court of Canada
highest court of appeal in Canada

- the filing of a plea (usually "guilty" or "not guilty" but there are other possible pleas) by the defence;

- unless the charges are dropped by the law enforcement body or thrown out by the court, a verdict of guilty or not guilty (if the accused pleads guilty, this verdict is reached without the need for a trial); and

- in the event of a guilty verdict, the imposition by the court of a sentence (punishment).

There are also a number of rights that apply to all people who are accused of a crime, such as the following:

- the right to be presumed innocent until proven guilty,

- the right to counsel,

- the right not to incriminate oneself,

- the right to be told of the charges, and

- the right not to be held in custody without reason.

The finer points of criminal procedure, however, can vary, depending on the seriousness of the offence and the choices made by the prosecutors and the accused. There are three kinds of offences in Canadian criminal law:

1. summary conviction offences (the least serious offences),

2. hybrid offences (offences of moderate severity that offer choices for prosecutors in the selection of procedures), and

3. indictable offences (the most serious offences).

> ### MANAGING RISKS
>
> ## Offence Examples
>
> An example of a summary conviction offence is section 201(2) of the *Criminal Code*: being found, without lawful excuse, in a "common gaming house" or "common betting house"—a place in which illegal betting or gaming is going on.
>
> An example of a hybrid offence is section 266: simple assault—that is, an assault that is not aggravated by injury to another person, intent to injure or kill, use of a weapon, robbery, or sexual touching.
>
> An example of an indictable offence is section 221: causing bodily harm by criminal negligence. This offence carries a maximum prison sentence of ten years. ◈

summary conviction offence
relatively minor offence that is prosecuted without a preliminary hearing or jury

indictable offence
serious offence that is prosecuted with full and formal criminal procedure

hybrid offence
offence that may be prosecuted using either summary conviction or indictable procedures at the discretion of the prosecution

The procedure for prosecuting a **summary conviction offence** is relatively simple. There is no requirement that a preliminary inquiry be held, and proceedings are conducted by a judge without a jury. The sentences that may be imposed for summary conviction offences are generally less severe than those available for indictable offences.

When an accused is charged with an **indictable offence**, the offence is tried in accordance with a full and formal procedure. The additional steps incorporated into this procedure are designed to maximize the accused's opportunity to make full answer and defence to the charges, and to ensure both actual and apparent fairness in the process. A well-known feature of indictable procedure is the option, available to an accused, of having evidence of his alleged crime heard and ruled on by a jury.

When an accused is charged with a **hybrid offence**, the prosecution is entitled to choose whether to use the simpler summary conviction procedures (which save time and money, but which may limit the sentences available), or the formal indictable procedures (which take more time and resources, but which allow for stiffer sentences on conviction). Often, the prosecution makes a decision to proceed by way of indictment either where the accused is a repeat offender or where there are aggravating factors—for example, where the crime involved an unusually high degree of violence or cruelty.

For the specific details of criminal procedure, you will need to review the *Criminal Code* itself. It is also important to remember that not all criminal charges result in a trial. In many cases, negotiation between the defence and the prosecution results in the exchange of a guilty plea for a lesser sentence, a reduction in the seriousness of the charges, or the dropping of some charges. In some cases, an accused who would otherwise be charged can avoid charges through diversion. Diversion is a process in which an informal warning is given and the accused voluntarily undertakes rehabilitation-focused penalties such as community service or the payment of reparations.

When a person is charged with a quasi-criminal offence—for example, an offence created by a provincial statute or a federal statute other than the *Criminal Code* (such as the *Controlled Drugs and Substances Act*), the procedure is similar but not identical to criminal procedure. Understanding what to expect in such a prosecution requires that you review the statute that creates the offence, and any other statute or code that may govern procedure (for example, the *Provincial Offences Act* or the Rules of Court).

Civil Procedure

Civil procedure is the procedure that governs lawsuits brought by private individuals, corporations, or organizations, such as actions in tort or contract law. Procedure in the civil court system is codified in part by the Ontario Rules of Civil Procedure, a regulation made under the *Courts of Justice Act*. Many courts and tribunals have their own rules of practice; for example, practice in the Supreme Court of Canada is described in the *Supreme Court Act*, and practice before the Ontario Labour Relations Board is governed by the Board's Rules of Procedure.

Because of the amount of detail contained in procedural statutes and codes, it's not practical for recreation providers to attempt to develop a general familiarity with these documents. Instead, recreation providers need only know that enforcement and court procedures are often incorporated into statutes and codes, and that these documents become an important resource when—and if—circumstances require involvement in legal proceedings or appearances before administrative tribunals.

PLEADINGS, DISCOVERY, AND OTHER STEPS

A plaintiff commences a lawsuit by serving a statement of claim on a defendant and filing a copy with a court. The defendant is required to respond, within a specified time, by serving and filing a notice of defence. These two documents—the statement of claim and the statement of defence—are called **pleadings**, and serve to frame the issues in the case.

After the filing of pleadings, the parties must follow a long series of steps to prepare for trial. These steps and the eventual trial itself are governed, in Ontario, by the Rules of Civil Procedure, a long and detailed code of procedure that forms regulation 194 under the *Courts of Justice Act*.

A detailed review of the Rules of Civil Procedure is beyond the scope of this book; however, it is useful to point out that one of the most prominent steps in the pre-trial phase is known as discovery. Discovery is a process by which the parties are required to share their evidence with each other. One of the key purposes of discovery is to allow the parties to better understand their own chances of success in the lawsuit because this can pave the way for an out-of-court settlement. Settling out of court and avoiding a trial is the most common way in which personal injury claims are resolved in modern-day Canada.

pleadings
documents exchanged between the plaintiff and the defendant in a civil action that set out their respective cases

LIMITATION PERIODS

limitation periods
time periods that limit when plaintiffs can launch lawsuits

Limitation periods are an important consideration for parties who want to bring a tort lawsuit. A limitation period is just that: a finite period of time within which a court is able to consider a claim based on a particular set of facts. In Ontario, the *Limitations Act, 2002* establishes a general limitation period for tort lawsuits. According to this Act, a party must commence her legal proceeding no later than "the second anniversary of the day on which the claim was discovered."

Determining when a claim is "discovered" can be complicated. For example, the consequences of an accident, exposure, or other event may not be apparent immediately after the event occurs, but may come to light months or even years later. A person who is alleging a delay in the discovery of a claim needs to provide evidence of that delay.

There are exceptions to the general limitation period. For example, if the plaintiff was a minor (below a particular age, usually 18) at the time that the claim arose, the limitation period does not begin to run until the plaintiff reaches adulthood. There is also an exception that suspends the running of the limitation period while the victim of an assault is incapable (physically, mentally, or psychologically) of pursuing the claim. These exceptions have allowed adults to assert tort claims based on abuse that they suffered as children.

Section 16 of the *Limitations Act, 2002* lists many more specific exceptions; for example, it provides that there is no two-year limitation on a person's right to pursue overdue child support from an ex-spouse or a tax refund from the government, or to seek enforcement of a court order. Because of the large number of exceptions, it is essential that all potential plaintiffs check the relevant limitations statute before pursuing (or abandoning) a claim.

To complicate matters further, the *Limitations Act, 2002* is not the only source of limitation periods. Limitation periods can also be found in a wide variety of other statutes, regulations, and bylaws. Particularly noteworthy are municipal laws, which often specify very short limitation periods that require very prompt action on the part of plaintiffs seeking to recover damages against a municipality. For example, the Ontario *Municipal Act, 2001* provides that a person who is injured on a highway or bridge in an Ontario municipality must file notice of his claim with the city clerk within ten days of the accident.

INTERNATIONAL LAW AND CUSTOM

International law is a very broad area that is subject to a great degree of uncertainty and change. As you might expect, wide philosophical differences between nations have made it impossible to create a comprehensive system or code for resolving the innumerable disputes that arise across borders. However, there are some court-like bodies and tribunals that exert a limited international jurisdiction. Examples are the United Nations–affiliated International Court of Justice, which is a non-criminal tribunal, and the International Criminal Court, which is based in Rome.

A wide variety of arbitral boards, usually chosen by the parties, arbitrate international commercial disputes using the guidelines developed by the United Nations Commission on International Trade Law (UNCITRAL).

An area of international law that is of particular interest to some recreation providers is international sports competition law. Events such as world cups in various sports, the Olympics, and the Special Olympics give rise to a very large number of disputes on various subjects, both within nations and between them. All major international competitions have their own dispute resolution organizations and procedures. If issues that are new to these organizations arise, the tribunals consider principles of international law and custom, which have developed from previous rulings and from past accepted practice.

The Europe-based International Court of Arbitration for Sport (CAS) provides a well-respected independent, third-party process for the resolution of sports disputes within or between national sports federations, where there is no competition-based tribunal that has jurisdiction over the dispute, or where such a tribunal is unable to resolve it.

TRIBUNALS AND ADMINISTRATIVE LAW

Courts are not the only decision-making bodies that resolve legal disputes. Many regulatory schemes allow for the resolution of disputes by an administrative **tribunal**, created specifically to deal with the subject matter of a statute or group of statutes.

A well-known example of an administrative tribunal is the Human Rights Tribunal of Ontario, which hears Ontario human rights matters. Other administrative tribunals with which recreation providers may be familiar include:

tribunal
person or group of persons charged with making formal administrative decisions

- the Ontario Labour Relations Board,

- the Workplace Safety and Insurance Appeals Tribunal,

- the Ontario Municipal Board,

- the Ontario Conservation Review Board, and

- the Dispute Resolution Secretariat of the Sport Dispute Resolution Centre of Canada.

In addition, most Canadian sports organizations, such as Skate Canada and Athletics Canada (track and field sports), function as private tribunals, providing formal mechanisms for the resolution of member disputes on issues such as eligibility to compete.

The processes used by administrative tribunals vary widely. Some tribunals, such as the Canadian Human Rights Tribunal, have fairly formal, complex procedures that are similar in many ways to the procedures seen in traditional courts. Small private tribunals—for example, the dispute resolution bodies of small associations, such as individual golf clubs—are considerably less formal; these tribunals may not hold hearings, and instead resolve disputes by means of written correspondence.

When a recreation provider needs to take part in a dispute before a tribunal, her first step will be to learn about the procedures in use at the tribunal. In some cases, this information can be obtained from the tribunal in printed form or downloaded from a website. In other cases, such as those involving small private tribunals, the procedures are explained in the letter that initiates the dispute resolution process. If

MANAGING RISKS

When to Hire a Lawyer

Many courts and tribunals allow parties to appear before them without legal representation. While avoiding the need to hire legal help may appear to be a money-saving option, it doesn't always produce a savings in the long run, especially if the absence of a lawyer leads a party into making costly mistakes.

Situations in which hiring a lawyer may be useful include:

- criminal proceedings of any kind;

- other formal court or tribunal proceedings;

- informal proceedings in which the risks to the party, should she not succeed, are high—for example, where there is the chance that the party will receive a large fine, lose a licence to practise her profession, lose a licence to offer a particular kind of program, or suffer damage to her professional reputation;

- proceedings that constitute an appeal from an earlier proceeding in which the party was not successful, especially where the current proceeding is "the end of the road"; and

- proceedings in which there is a high level of animosity or ill will between the parties, or a serious imbalance of power between the parties.

Hiring a lawyer is not, however, essential in every case. In some very informal settings, where parties are hoping to negotiate a solution to a simple problem during informal meetings or phone conversations, injecting a lawyer into the process too early may create a perception that a party is eager to become confrontational, or expects the dispute to escalate. ◈

the procedures are not clear, the recreation provider may wish to call the tribunal office or the administrator in charge of the tribunal to clarify points of procedure.

As a general rule, the more formal the tribunal procedures, the more appropriate it may be for a party to hire a lawyer to represent her in the process. A lawyer can help avoid inadvertent mistakes—such as missing a key deadline—and may bring a different perspective to the issue, alerting the client to resolution possibilities that she had not previously considered. Finally, a lawyer can assist in informal negotiations with other parties, because he brings a level of neutrality to these discussions, which is especially helpful if relations have broken down between the parties.

In most cases, tribunals are very effective in resolving disputes because the decision-makers on these boards are often experts in the subject area of the dispute (which is not always the case with judges in traditional courts). In a few cases, however, there is the option of appealing a decision made by an administrative tribunal to the traditional court system. The legislation that creates the tribunal explains whether or not this is an option.

Alternative Dispute Resolution

While this chapter has provided an overview of the civil and criminal justice systems, it's important to recognize that the majority of disputes between parties—whether they be individuals, corporations, or government bodies—are not resolved in a courtroom. According to the Ontario Ministry of the Attorney General, over 90 percent of civil cases settle before trial.

Litigation is a highly formalized, adversarial process. It is notoriously expensive, and in most cases, is capable only of producing a win–lose result: one party's victory is the other party's loss. Litigation has the potential to alienate litigants from each other. It can turn relatives or friends into enemies, and can permanently sever business or commercial relationships.

In some cases—especially if there has been malice, fraud, or other counterproductive roots to a conflict—litigation may be the appropriate avenue to resolution. Most conflicts, however, are not so sharply drawn; and parties can usually benefit from a creative, collaborative approach, and perhaps even from a solution that benefits both sides.

Alternatives to litigation begin at the very informal, interpersonal level. When conflicts arise, there is almost always an opportunity for the parties to negotiate a solution. Where parties have not been able to solve their problems on their own, sometimes a more structured process for negotiation works. **Alternative dispute resolution (ADR)** is a term used to describe a range of recognized strategies—for example, structured negotiation, mediation, and arbitration—that are designed to help settle disputes without recourse to the traditional courts.

alternative dispute resolution (ADR)
strategies, such as structured negotiation, mediation, and arbitration, that are designed to settle disputes without recourse to traditional courts

Many of the administrative bodies described in the previous section use ADR strategies to resolve the problems that come before them. If a recreation provider has a conflict to resolve and there is no tribunal that has jurisdiction over the issue, the recreation provider can take steps to arrange a mediation session by suggesting to the other party that a private mediator be hired to assist. The recreation provider can also hire a lawyer to negotiate a settlement, either with the other party directly or through the other party's lawyer.

KEY TERMS

alternative dispute resolution (ADR)

Constitution

court of appeal

discretion

hybrid offence

indictable offence

injunction

jurisdiction

limitation periods

paramount legislation

pleadings

policy

procedural law

provincial offences

substantive law

summary conviction offence

Supreme Court of Canada

trial courts

tribunal

REVIEW EXERCISES

Review Questions

1. What is a statute?

2. Why are some statutes created and administered by the federal government, and others by the provincial governments?

3. Are sports federally or provincially regulated?

4. Why do different cities and towns have different laws about matters such as parking, for example?

5. How can a recreation provider determine which statutes apply to his business or services?

6. Why read the definitions section of a statute?

7. Is the *Criminal Code* the only statute that creates offences in Canada?

8. If a provision creates an offence but is silent about what the penalty is or what procedures apply, where would you look for this information?

9. What are regulations, and do they apply to recreation providers?

10. Can a recreation provider be charged with a crime? What about a recreation *company*?

11. Do recreation providers have to comply with human rights legislation? What about the *Charter of Rights and Freedoms*?

12. What is the difference between law and policy?

13. How do you find out what will happen after a lawsuit, complaint, or other proceeding is filed or commenced, or after you are charged with an offence?

14. What is an administrative tribunal?

15. What alternatives exist to the traditional court system?

Discussion Question

Were you surprised by the range of laws and types of legal regulation that affect the recreation sector? What steps might you take, as the director of a recreation provider, to ensure that you are adequately managing the legal aspects of your business?

PART II

Risk Management: General Principles

CHAPTER 4

Risk Management I: Identifying and Reducing Risk

CHAPTER OBJECTIVES

After completing this chapter, you should be able to:

- explain why and how new recreation businesses must identify all of the risks reasonably associated with their programs;

- list at least three programming changes that can alter an organization's risk profile;

- identify the roles of management and staff, and the impact of the physical environment in reducing risk;

- list at least three pieces of legislation that regulate safety in a building used by the public;

- understand the importance of developing safety policies; and

- explain the role of insurance in protecting the economic health of recreation businesses.

INTRODUCTION

As you learned in Chapter 1, Balancing the Benefits and Risks of Recreation, many kinds of recreation expose participants to risk. Despite recent advances in several areas of personal safety, such as the mandated use of seat belts and bicycle helmets, many of the risks associated with recreation have proven to be difficult or impossible to eliminate.

The fact that there may be limits to risk reduction in recreation, however, does not lessen the responsibility of recreation providers to do everything possible to promote the highest attainable level of safety for client participants. Consider, for example, the safety efforts you would expect of a swimming teacher to whom you had entrusted your own child. Would you demand anything less than the highest possible level of safety? Our laws and the courts that enforce them set standards no less exacting.

Simply having good intentions, doing your job, and hoping for the best is an insufficient safety effort. Protecting your clients—and, in turn, the viability of your business or organization—requires planning, execution, ongoing analysis of successes and failures, and a commitment to the continual improvement of your procedures, equipment, and the expertise of your staff.

Reacting to accidents when they occur is not risk management, regardless of the appropriateness of your reactions. Risk management is proactive: it requires taking planned action, every single day, to reduce the likelihood of accidents. Active risk management can be summarized in the following steps:

1. identifying risks that may affect participants' safety or the viability of your business;

2. taking action to reduce these risks;

3. communicating the existence of any risks that cannot be eliminated to participants and potential participants so that they can make an informed decision about whether to engage in the activity;

4. requiring that all recreation participants and business partners accept an appropriate share of the risk burden;

5. controlling and limiting the impact of accidents and other incidents on victims and on the business and its reputation; and

6. documenting and analyzing accidents and incidents so that adjustments can be made to prevent their recurrence.

All recreation providers—regardless of their size or the nature of the services they offer—must incorporate these steps into their risk management program. Failure to address any one of these tasks can leave the recreation organization vulnerable to civil liability, regulatory sanctions, or even criminal charges.

RISK IDENTIFICATION

Introduction

Before any steps can be taken to manage the risks inherent in a particular type of recreation service, the recreation provider must identify all of the reasonably foreseeable risks associated with the planned activities. To borrow from the negligence terminology used in Chapter 2, Legal Liability in Tort and Contract, "reasonably foreseeable" risks are risks that are not too remote from any actions or omissions of the recreation provider and that can cause harm to potential plaintiffs. What constitutes a foreseeable risk varies depending on the nature of the recreation business. Consider the example of lightning, which often accompanies storms.

A library that holds an outdoor poetry-reading program in a courtyard is unlikely to be found negligent for failing to post "beware of lightning" signs. Should rain start falling, the participants will quickly move inside. In contrast, a golf course would be prudent to post signs urging players to return to the clubhouse immediately at the first sign of ominous weather. Playing golf ranks high on the list of activities in which participants have been struck by lightning because it takes place in a wide-open flat area with nowhere to escape to quickly. Therefore, lightning belongs on a list of "risks to be managed" when setting up a golf course, but not when developing a library reading series.

Once all the reasonably foreseeable risks associated with a business have been identified, the recreation provider should consider whether each risk is a **controllable risk**—a risk that can be eliminated or reduced—or an **intractable risk**—a risk that cannot be eliminated or reduced.

These types of risks should be examined separately since they need to be managed in two different ways. While a variety of steps may be taken to reduce or eliminate controllable risks, intractable risks may be addressed by informing potential plaintiffs of the risks, and shifting liability onto them as much as possible. The classification of each risk as controllable or intractable provides a framework for planning the next steps: risk reduction and risk communication.

It is also important to review risks, both periodically and with any change in the business. Consider the following changes in circumstance that would require a re-appraisal of risks:

- the addition of new programs;
- a change in client demographics (for example, the addition of older, younger, heavier, smaller, less experienced, more experienced, disabled, or alcohol-impaired participants);
- a change in program timing (for example, the rescheduling of a daytime activity to the evening);
- a change in weather;
- a change in venue or a move to a new facility;
- a change in the equipment used; or
- the addition of new, less experienced staff.

Because risks change, the business's risk profile should be updated often so that adjustments can be made.

Start-up

Because the potential economic impact of some accidents can be catastrophic, most recreation providers would be unable to protect the viability of their businesses without purchasing insurance against the risk of claims. The cost of insurance varies widely depending on the risks anticipated by the insurer; where risks are high, insurance costs are likewise high. In some cases, the insurance costs associated with a particular business may be prohibitive. The provider may discover that it cannot earn enough revenue to offset these costs. For this reason, risk identification needs to be addressed before the final decision to establish a recreation business or service is made. Risk financing is discussed in greater detail in Chapter 5, Risk Management II: Communicating and Sharing Risk.

Identifying risks before the recreation provider has gained experience in providing the planned services in a chosen facility and community can be a challenge. Research and consultation are essential at this stage.

controllable risk
a risk that can be eliminated or reduced

intractable risk
a risk that cannot be eliminated or reduced

When it comes to managing physical risks, activity-related associations, such as the Alpine Club of Canada (a national mountaineering organization), and general safety-promotion organizations, such as the Canada Safety Council, can be excellent sources of current information. Many of these associations keep accident statistics and gather and share industry **best practices** for promoting safety. They may also hold conferences about emerging issues, legal considerations, and other key topics. Joining the associations that are prominent in your area of service helps you build contacts and partnerships within the industry, and may even help bolster your organization's reputation as a safe place to enjoy recreation.

best practices
industry procedures that are most efficient in promoting and maintaining safety

Another source of start-up safety data is statistics. Safety statistics can help you understand which kinds of accidents are most likely in your area of service, so that you can provide accurate warnings to clients, insure against the right risks, and focus on the right priorities. Knowing the data about accidents in your field may even help tailor your policies.

Sources of injury and accident statistics include:

- activity-specific member associations;

- the Ontario Recreation Facilities Association;

- Statistics Canada;

- US sources of health and safety information, such as the Food and Drug Administration;

- the Canada Safety Council;

- the Canadian Institute for Health Information;

- the Canadian Institute of Child Health; and

- the Canadian Centre for Occupational Health and Safety.

For example, the Alberta Centre for Injury Control and Research has compiled statistics on fatalities related to all-terrain vehicles (ATVs). It studied 20 ATV-related deaths in Alberta between 1999 and 2002, and discovered the following:

- at least 60 percent of the fatalities were the result of head injuries;

- 45 percent of those killed, or nine persons, were children and teens;

- of the children and teens killed, two were passengers and seven were drivers, and the drivers were all from 10 to 15 years old; and

- alcohol was involved in 45 percent of the deaths.

Statistics like these might prompt the new operator of a trail system for ATVs to develop a strict helmet policy, prohibit alcohol (and conduct sobriety spot checks), and limit the minimum age for drivers to 16 years.

If a recreation provider caters to or encourages the participation of people with disabilities, she should consider contacting support and advocacy organizations that are knowledgeable about these participants' particular medical conditions and disabilities. These organizations may be able to provide useful information about the special needs and vulnerabilities of these participants. For example, some horseback-riding schools offer classes specifically targeted toward participants who have cerebral palsy, or other conditions that cause physical limitations; a facility seeking to introduce such a program for the first time may benefit from the specialized information available from the Ontario Federation for Cerebral Palsy.

When deciding where to start in the risk identification process, recreation providers should try contacting member associations. For example, consider a university student who has decided to create a summer "ghost walk" business that involves leading participants on evening walking tours of a historic neighbourhood. After joining a tourism association, he may learn that the rate of trip-and-fall claims against walking tour businesses triples when those businesses operate after dark. This information may prompt him to map out a new tour route that avoids potential tripping hazards, such as uneven curbs.

Legal requirements, such as obtaining licences, permits, or other clearances essential to the legal operation of the business, must also be addressed.

When Programs Change

A new risk review should be conducted any time there is a change in program offerings. Entirely new programs come with entirely new risks; but even minor changes to existing programs can create new risks. For example, moving a daytime outdoor program to the evening results in changes in available lighting, which can heighten tripping risks and make participants less visible to traffic. An evening time slot may also attract more mosquitoes, increasing the risk that participants will be bitten and prompting the recreation provider to recommend that participants use insect repellent.

Lowering the minimum participant age, increasing the participant–instructor ratio, operating in a different season, and offering a course for beginners are all examples of changes that can affect patterns and levels of risk. Recreation providers must be aware of these potential changes so that they can train staff to handle them, and adapt policies, signage, and insurance coverage to suit the new conditions.

An Ongoing Task

Risk identification is never a one-time process. Because the factors that influence risk are continually changing, recreation providers should treat risk identification as a continual process. Conducting regular inspections of recreation premises and equipment is essential for all recreation providers.

In Ontario, regular inspections are mandated for all workplaces by the *Occupational Health and Safety Act*. Some workplaces that offer activities and programs for the public are subject to further inspection requirements under other legislation and regulation as well. For example, establishments that offer amusement rides or operate ski lifts are governed by the *Technical Standards and Safety Act, 2000*, which regulates both of these kinds of devices. Regardless of legislative requirements, all recreation providers have an obligation to their clientele to ensure that their premises are safe and free of hazards, and that all equipment is in excellent working order.

An effective inspection program requires planning and policies to support it, because the keys to identifying safety problems are regularity and consistency. Inspections must be undertaken at appropriate intervals by individuals who are competent to recognize hazards and problems when they occur.

When developing an inspection policy, a recreation provider needs to consider the following:

- *How often inspections of equipment and premises should be conducted.* High-risk equipment may need to be inspected hourly or, as in the case of parachutes, before every use. Low-risk premises may only need to be inspected daily, while premises that are free of known hazards, such as remote parks, may only need to be inspected weekly (though they should be inspected promptly after storms).

- *A specific list of features or hazards to be checked.* A vague "look around" is not an inspection. Inspectors should be required, for example, to test latches and buckles, check the stability of stacked items, and check floors for spills and trip hazards. Sources for inspection checklists are discussed later in this section.

- *Appropriate inspection personnel.* In a small workplace, only one person (for example, the person who opens the facility in the morning) may need to be designated as an inspector. However, in a larger facility, such as a sports stadium, many inspectors may be needed, with each one responsible for a designated area. When choosing inspectors, the recreation provider needs to consider whether the designates have sufficient familiarity with the equipment and premises to be able to identify problems as they develop.

- *Documentation of inspections.* From a liability point of view, an inspection that is not documented is an inspection that did not happen. It is essential to keep a record of inspections so that a recreation provider can establish that she met the standard of care owed to clients. The degree of detail that is required in the records varies with the complexity of the inspection and with the level and types of risks present. For example, a pool inspection form might require the inspector to note that life-saving equipment is available and in good condition, pool decks are dry and unobstructed, locker rooms are secure and tidy, cabinets containing dangerous chemicals are locked, the first-aid kit is in good order, material safety data sheets are available, and the phone and lights are working. It might also require that the results of water quality tests be recorded. Each element of the inspection should have a checkbox or other appropriate place where the inspector can indicate that a check was in fact made. Completed inspection forms should be collected in a book, file, or other system for safekeeping.

- *Appropriate staff response to newly identified hazards.* It is not enough to discover and document hazards. They must be acted on! The inspection policy must specify to whom a hazard should be reported, and within what time frame. Prompt action must be taken to eliminate the hazard. If it is serious and cannot be immediately eliminated, there must be a protocol for deciding whether and how to cancel programs or to close facilities. If it is minor and cannot be immediately eliminated, steps must be taken to warn participants—for example, by cordoning off areas, posting new signs, and giving verbal warnings.

There are many resources available to assist recreation providers in developing inspection policies. Facility and hazard-specific inspection checklists are developed by many member associations. For example, the Ontario Recreation Facilities Association has published a set of suggested guidelines for air quality in arenas; and the Canadian Playground Safety Institute has developed guidelines for the inspection of playgrounds. For more general applications, recreation providers can turn to the Canadian Centre for Occupational Health and Safety, which offers detailed and comprehensive inspection checklists for many different kinds of premises.

Physical inspection of premises and equipment, while important, is not enough. Some recreation risks flow not from the premises, but from the participants and staff and the interactions between them. **Interpersonal risks** can include:

interpersonal risks
risks that arise through interaction between individuals

- emotional abuse or ridicule of participants, or undue pressure from coaches and parents;

- bullying of participants by other participants or by staff;

- sexual abuse or harassment of participants by other participants or by staff;

- discrimination against participants;

- cheating, favouritism, or other unfairness in team or participant selection;

- corrupt judging, evaluation, or ranking;

- illegal gambling or betting;

- violence, whether unrelated to the activity or part of it;

- excessive risk-taking by participants that is not adequately controlled by staff (for example, beginners attempting sports that require expert skills);

- alcohol and drug abuse on premises that are not adequately monitored by staff; and

- outbreaks of contagious illnesses.

Managing these interpersonal risks requires adequate supervision of all programs, appropriate staff screening and training, and a workplace culture in which staff wrongdoing is not tolerated, and worrisome incidents are promptly reported.

To build a safe working environment and to foster integrity and responsibility on the part of staff, management must commit to listening to all staff concerns and complaints. A culture of open communication must be actively fostered.

It is often useful to provide a variety of ways for staff to communicate their concerns and obtain guidance. For example, staff may be encouraged to share their experiences of problematic situations at regular staff meetings, so that all staff can learn from their colleagues' experiences. There should also be procedures in place for staff to share their concerns privately with a trusted manager, or even anonymously. If management listens to staff concerns and takes appropriate steps to solve problems, staff will be more likely to share their concerns openly.

Where a client base includes vulnerable participants, such as children, the elderly, or people with disabilities, it is essential that an anti-abuse screening and surveillance policy and system be adopted and reviewed regularly.

RISK REDUCTION

Introduction

Once the risks associated with a recreation program or business have been identified, the operators must take every reasonable step to reduce these risks. The "risks" relevant to recreation providers include both risks to participants—which the recreation provider is morally and legally obligated to reduce—and risks to the operation, such as the risks of a catastrophic lawsuit or other penalty. The distinction between these two kinds of risks is more theoretical than real because anything that poses a risk to a participant's safety also threatens the viability of a business. The following discussion includes reference both to direct risks and to liability risks.

Like risk identification, risk reduction is an ongoing process. Just as new hazards emerge over time, so do new solutions. Safety technologies improve every year, and with each new accident, operators gain insight into the dangers of their services and how these dangers can be avoided. A responsible recreation provider knows that it is essential to make a commitment to upgrading and enhancing her knowledge over the long term, and to putting new learning into action in the form of safety and service improvements.

The following discussion of general risk reduction strategies is divided into three categories: the role of management (including policy-making), the role of staff, and the role of facility characteristics and equipment in reducing risks.

The Role of Management

Senior managers in a recreation business are in a challenging position: they are ultimately responsible for the safety of their facility, but they are sometimes far removed from day-to-day activities and therefore have little direct experience with the risks that these activities involve.

Management must build a culture of safety, and set the tone for staff interactions with participants. Managers also need to maintain an up-to-date familiarity with the trends both in accidents and in accident prevention in their area of service. Maintaining this familiarity can require attending conferences regularly, pursuing new training, and ensuring that the staff hired to lead activities are as well qualified as possible.

Armed with the latest risk reduction information, managers are well placed to sow the seeds of a safety-first culture in their organizations. When managers dem-

---

EXTRA CREDIT

Newly Hired Staff Inject New Thinking

Because newly hired staff are often younger than senior management and have been trained more recently, their career knowledge is often more up-to-date than that of senior management. As long as there are senior staff in the organization who can compensate for young employees' lack of practical experience, hiring recent graduates is an easy way to bring cutting-edge industry knowledge into your organization. ◊

onstrate, through their own actions, that the safety of participants and staff is the organization's first priority, this value trickles down to staff. Those staff who are eager to succeed in the organization will mirror management's safety-first attitude, and a culture of safety will emerge in the organization. That culture can then be nurtured and maintained by rewarding safe operation—for example, by making good safety performance a prerequisite for obtaining promotions and bonuses.

An added advantage of a strong culture of safety is that the emphasis on safety may be noticed by participants and by the public. Then, if an accident does happen, the participants involved may be more likely to attribute the cause, at least in part, to bad luck—and not just to failures on the part of the organization.

One way to emphasize safety within an organization is to create a risk management committee to gather and analyze risk management information. If a workplace has several different divisions—such as a recreation centre with a pool, a skateboard park, a martial arts studio, a squash court, a summer day camp program, and a small library—a representative from each division, plus representatives from the indoor and outdoor maintenance teams, should be chosen to sit on the committee. Committee members, with the help of the management team, can decide on a mandate (what they expect to accomplish) and can assign specific roles (for example, secretary, committee chair, or management liaison) among themselves.

In general, the role of risk management committees is to help ensure that information about emerging risks and problems is effectively channelled to senior management and the board of directors. Because of their knowledge of their particular work areas, members may also have unique insights into potential solutions; for this reason, many risk management committees are involved in policy development and risk remediation planning.

With or without the help of a risk management committee, senior management is responsible for creating comprehensive and detailed safety and risk management policies for the recreation business. Even for fairly small operations, this can be a daunting and time-consuming task; however, it is essential. Without current and well-considered policies in place, the organization will be unprepared to manage risks, and to react appropriately if accidents or other problems occur. Policies allow for prompt, coordinated action, which is always preferable to the alternative—hasty reaction.

Recreation organizations serve the public, and this means that they must develop two different streams of policies. **Internal policies** are designed to manage tasks and processes that are internal to the operation. **External policies** are designed to manage the relationship between the organization and its clients, including: the terms of client participation in recreation activities; third-party relationships; and public relations.

Internal policies include personnel policies, facility and equipment management, and fire and other emergency management. Examples of each are listed below.

Personnel policies:

- hours of operation and holidays;
- staffing levels and staff qualifications; hiring and screening of staff; staff scheduling and holiday and sick time coverage;
- new staff training and ongoing learning/career development;
- surveillance and supervision of staff who work with vulnerable clients;

internal policies
policies that govern tasks and processes within a recreation organization

external policies
policies that govern the relationship between a recreation organization and its clients, including client participation, third-party relationships, and public relations

- discipline;
- drug or alcohol screening (if appropriate);
- human resources matters, such as pensions, benefits, income tax withholding, employment insurance and workers' compensation withholding, and termination management;
- chain of command, reporting structure, and approvals; and
- confidentiality issues, such as handling client confidential information and the organization's confidential information, creating intellectual property/technology policies, and designing non-competition agreements for departing employees.

Facility and equipment management:

- opening and closing procedures;
- inspections, including inspection schedules, checklists, and reporting;
- periodic testing of equipment;
- specialized inspections (elevators, for example);
- building security, including alarms and security lighting;
- cleaning and daily maintenance;
- snow removal and other grounds management;
- purchasing and replacing equipment;
- physical plant improvements/maintenance budgeting, schedules, and approvals; and
- standards review and compliance.

Fire and other emergency management:

- evacuation and fire drill procedures;
- procedures for coping with other foreseeable emergencies, such as storms and severe winter weather;
- procedures for dealing with staff and client medical emergencies;
- first aid and internal first responder/CPR preparedness; and
- pandemic planning.

External policies concern issues such as customer service, third-party relationships, and public relations. Examples of each are listed below.

Customer service:

- handling client confidential information;
- client screening (for age-restricted activities and alcohol impairment, for example);
- managing client violence, confrontations, and harassment of others;
- refund and related policies;
- emergency contact policies (in case clients are hurt in an accident);

- diversity, non-discrimination, and anti-harassment policies;
- handling client complaints; and
- accident response plans (from a public relations/liability-management perspective).

Third-party relationships:

- policies to govern the organization's relationship with other businesses with which it may have dealings. These businesses may include:
  - a landlord or leasing company;
  - a lawyer, accountant, bank, or insurer;
  - suppliers;
  - contractors (for example, a self-employed martial arts teacher who offers classes on the recreation provider's premises);
  - group/events users (for example, a company that rents a golf course for a company golf day or a club that rents a meeting room); and
  - sponsors and advertisers.

Public relations:

- marketing and communications;
- the making of public statements in the wake of major accidents;
- fundraising; and
- media relations, press releases, and the giving of interviews.

Another important role of management is to undertake strategic planning—that is, long-term planning for the direction of the business. Policies concerning strategic planning may affect both external and internal dynamics. Examples of strategic planning policies are listed below.

Strategic planning:

- planning for policy review;
- managing the ownership and administrative structure and decision-making authority;
- planning for financing;
- general liability management;
- image management;
- planning for business growth, program additions/changes, and major asset acquisition; and
- planning for new business directions, windup of certain activities, and windup of the business.

These lists, as you can see, are very long, yet some organizations have even more areas in which policy development is required. In some cases, each of the items listed above may require multiple policies. For example, in relation to "hours of operation," a business that is highly weather-dependent, such as a sailing school, may require a detailed policy for making weather-cancellation decisions, and for communicating these decisions to clients.

Problems can occur when a business adds new activities before it has a chance to develop policies to manage them. Consider, for example, a botanical garden that develops a reputation as an attractive site for wedding photographs. Suppose someone requests to have the wedding ceremony itself on the premises. If the botanical garden agrees and hosts the wedding before it has a chance to develop policies about the serving and use of alcohol, it may run the risk of liability if someone becomes intoxicated and has an accident.

Management is responsible for having policies in place before problems occur. The best way to tackle this task is to develop policies as soon as the need arises. For example, when the business is first launched, policies that specify who will deal with the lawyer, bank, insurer, and accountant can be drafted. While the facility prepares to hire its first employees, personnel policies can be developed. Also, as the organization grows in size and sophistication, policies will need to be revisited. The task of policy review should be managed according to its own policy, which is designed to bring order, routine, and thoroughness to the review process.

The Role of Staff

Properly selected, screened, and trained staff are a recreation organization's greatest asset in reducing risk. Because staff are on the front line of customer service, it is their job to communicate risk and policies to clients. Front-line staff are also in the best position to identify new hazards as they develop, and to react when accidents happen.

Staff selection and training are important for the successful operation of any business, and are crucial elements of risk management. It is vital to hire staff who understand the services you offer, who understand how to manage risk, and who work well with clients. Competence, integrity, and reliability are essential traits for staff who work with the public. Knowledge of services and safety procedures can be augmented by appropriate training.

Staff who work with vulnerable participants should be very thoroughly screened and subjected to a police check. In some cases, there are limits on other forms of screening (for example, drug and alcohol testing, health screening, mental health inquiries). However, an appropriate probation policy should be put in place to allow the organization to release staff who prove to be incompetent or untrustworthy during the probation period.

The organization is responsible for providing thorough training to staff in all aspects their work, including safety policies and procedures. It is acceptable to administer tests to verify staff understanding of what has been explained in training; however, poor testing results should be viewed as an indication that the training is flawed and needs improvement.

Many organizations provide thorough training to permanent employees, but only rudimentary training to temporary and seasonal workers. This is a serious mistake. Statistics show that this tendency is at least partially responsible for the high frequency of on-the-job injuries suffered by workers aged 16 to 25, which is the age group most likely to work temporary and seasonal jobs. Train your temporary workers as thoroughly as your permanent employees!

Staff training should not be a one-time event. Successful organizations know that investing in the development of staff will benefit the organization. Therefore, when opportunities present themselves, staff should be supported in seeking upgrading for their skills and abilities, certification in new areas, and refresher training to improve the currency of their skills and knowledge.

Finally, staff who work with the public are often required to remain at their posts for safety reasons, and are not at liberty to seek out management when problems arise. To allow staff to respond appropriately to hazards and incidents, a sufficient complement of well-trained supervisors must be available at all times as a resource for program staff. These supervisors serve the additional role of assessing staff competence, and of providing surveillance for staff who work with vulnerable clients.

Once trained and supported with adequate supervision, good staff can be expected to:

- know and apply company policy consistently and fairly;

- notice and report hazards promptly to supervisors;

- communicate any concerns about safety, policies, or co-worker performance to supervisors;

- communicate risks clearly and consistently to participants, and request participant acceptance of those risks before proceeding (this skill includes explaining and enforcing completion of waivers);

- provide a thorough orientation regarding activities for all participants;

- assess participant skill levels accurately and control participation accordingly;

- identify and provide extra help to participants at special risk of injury;

- enforce safety policies, such as the use of protective gear;

- terminate activities promptly if participants fail to follow safety policies;

- cancel activities or exclude participants if hazards (extreme weather, alcohol-impaired participants, or problems with equipment) warrant;

- defuse conflicts and intervene if violence or harassment occurs;

- treat clients with courtesy, fairness, and respect for diversity, human rights, and human dignity;

- respond appropriately in emergencies, providing first aid and compassionate support while managing confidential information; and

- make prompt, honest, detailed, and useful reports in the wake of incidents.

To ensure that staff make a valuable contribution to safety, the employer must create a working environment in which it is easy and comfortable for staff to report concerns as soon as they arise. Management must respond to concerns promptly, and should offer thanks for disclosure. It is appropriate to reinforce the message that staff are being entrusted with the safety of the organization's valued clients, and that safety is the recreation provider's first priority.

The Role of Facility Characteristics and Equipment

Because safety and the purported lack of it are such newsworthy topics, it is easy to lose sight of how much safer today's world is than the world of 50 years ago. Our cars have seat belts, airbags, and safety glass; our water supply is quality-tested hourly; we wear helmets to cycle and ski; our shampoo has been adjusted to our skin sensitivities—the list goes on.

The houses we live in and the buildings in which we shop, study, work, and play are designed and built in compliance with dozens of strict safety standards to protect us from all manner of hazards, from bumping our heads, to tripping over steps, to falling off balconies, to walking into glass panes, to being trapped in fiery blazes. Similar standards apply to consumer products, and when safety failures are reported, few companies hesitate to issue money-back recalls.

However, when thinking about safety innovations, it's useful to remember that behind practically every new safety standard and protective device lies tragedy: the most powerful motivators for safety design are accidents, injuries, and illnesses.

FACILITY SAFETY

Most recreation providers are not experts in the construction business. Nevertheless, they have a responsibility to ensure that the facilities into which they invite the public comply with all applicable safety standards.

Facility safety standards can be found in a number of different statutes, regulations, and bylaws, such as the following:

- building codes,
- fire codes,
- electrical safety codes,
- municipal bylaws, and
- the Ontario *Technical Standards and Safety Act, 2000.*

Government and municipal buildings are also subject to accessibility standards in accordance with legislation such as the *Ontarians with Disabilities Act, 2001.*

Newly built facilities must pass inspection by building, fire code, and other inspectors before they can be opened to the public. In some cases, and particularly with respect to fire code and elevator safety, regularly scheduled inspections are also required. Recreation providers must check with local inspection agencies to determine their compliance responsibilities under local bylaws and codes.

Buildings must remain in compliance with safety codes as long as they are in use. A building is usually required to remain in compliance with the building code that existed at the time of the building's construction. Since codes change frequently, building occupants cannot be expected to renovate every time there is a change. However, new additions are required to comply with the code in effect at the time of construction.

Fire code compliance may require upgrading in some instances, depending on the nature of the facility and the purposes for which it is used. Fire codes place the onus on the building owner to create emergency evacuation plans and to conduct

---

Anti-Smoking-Law Compliance

In the spring of 2006, Ontario's *Smoke-Free Ontario Act* came into force. The legislation bans smoking in all "enclosed workplaces" and "enclosed public places," which include not only buildings but also spaces such as parking garages, worksite trailers, and taxi cabs. Under previous laws and bylaws, some public spaces were permitted to offer designated smoking rooms, but this is no longer the case: smoking is now completely banned indoors. Employers can build covered outdoor shelters to accommodate smoking employees, but these structures cannot be enclosed: they must consist of no more than two walls and a roof.

The owners of workplaces and public places are required to enforce the law by posting signs prohibiting smoking near entrances and exits, in washrooms, and "in other appropriate places"; by requiring that anyone found smoking stop doing so; and by removing from the premises anyone who refuses to comply.

All other provinces have similar anti-smoking legislation in place.

Some buildings are governed by even stricter rules set out in municipal bylaws. For example, a Toronto bylaw prohibits smoking within nine metres of certain kinds of facilities, such as hospitals and long-term care facilities. Some businesses not subject to these bylaws choose to enforce similar distance-based rules as a matter of private policy, and post signs prohibiting smoking within nine metres of their doors.

Failure to comply with anti-smoking laws can result in fines, both for corporations and individuals. ◇

---

fire drills. Recreation providers who offer activities to the public should ensure that staff have a good understanding of these drills. In the event of a fire or other emergency, clients will generally not have had a chance to practise evacuating, and will therefore rely on staff to lead them to safety.

The needs of people with disabilities require special consideration when planning for an evacuation. Especially where the recreation provider serves children or adults with cognitive problems, a "missing person" drill and a mechanism for accounting for all building occupants in the event of an evacuation should also be developed.

Once a building has been inspected and found to be safe, it cannot necessarily be counted on to remain that way. Building materials deteriorate with age, and repairs will be needed over time. An appropriate inspection program helps a recreation provider keep track of the condition of the facility and plan for repairs or renovations.

Other factors, besides wear and tear, can affect the safety of facilities. These include:

- overcrowding,
- spills and flooding,
- air contamination from leaked gases or moulds,
- the spread of bacteria or viruses related to poor sanitation or food service practices,
- temperature extremes,
- improper storage of equipment and goods (such as storage that creates a topple risk), and
- poor organization of interior furniture that creates obstacles that could hinder evacuation or cause tripping.

Regular inspections and common sense alert recreation providers to these hazards. A facility closure plan, or a plan for restricting access to certain areas of the building, should be in place to govern situations in which hazards arise.

EQUIPMENT SAFETY

Many forms of recreation require the use of specialized equipment, and some require safety gear. Like many other consumer products, recreation and personal protective equipment is subject to standards of construction and performance that are updated regularly as innovations emerge. Equipment selection, maintenance, and renewal are discussed in detail in Chapter 8, Equipment and Products Law.

Insurance

Adequate insurance coverage is essential for all recreation businesses. It is important to understand, however, that insurance reduces only one kind of risk—that is, the risk to the economic viability of the business in the event of a large legal claim or many claims. Insurance does nothing to prevent accidents or other harm, or to reduce the severity of damage or injury. At most, the proceeds from an insurance payout can assist victims in paying for medical costs and in replacing lost income.

Because the funds from insurance claims go to the victims, insurance benefits both recreation providers (by protecting their financial stability) and their clients. Appropriate insurance coverage can also protect the reputation of a recreation provider or industry by allowing it to be seen to be "doing the right thing" for victims. This usually involves offering a prompt and fair settlement of claims.

The basic principle of insurance is the transfer of the economic risk of an activity to another party—the insurance company—in exchange for a fee. The insurance company takes on the *uncertain* risk of a *large* loss in exchange for the insured's payment of an insurance premium. By taking on the uncertain risks of many clients, the insurance company is counting on the odds that only a fraction of its clients will experience claims within a particular time. By pooling and investing the premiums, the insurance company creates a fund from which it can pay whatever claims may arise. The cost of insurance—the amount of the premium—is set by the insurer. It is designed to reflect the insurer's estimate of how many claims it will receive, and how much money will be needed to pay these claims.

Compare, for example, the probability that a car will be involved in an accident over a ten-year period with the probability that a house will burn down during the same time. It is more likely than not that a car will be involved in an accident in a ten-year period, but very unlikely that a house will be destroyed by fire. For this reason, even though the house would cost perhaps ten times more to repair or replace than the car, the one-year premium for an average house is generally less than the one-year premium for a car. (Another reason that the car insurance costs more is that a car is more likely than a house to injure a third party, such as a driver or passenger in another car, or a pedestrian.)

In the recreation context, premiums are influenced by similar factors: the likelihood of an accident happening, and the estimated cost of a claim that would flow from a typical accident. For this reason, dangerous activities—those that generate a high rate of accidents or a modest rate of very serious accidents—can be very costly to insure.

In some cases, the high cost of liability insurance for providers of dangerous activities is warranted. The insurer may have at its disposal detailed and current statistics about the kinds and rates of claims that can be expected. In these cases, an insurer's estimate of the premiums required to offset the claims that it is likely to pay may be quite accurate. Supporting data are usually available to an insurer when an activity, though dangerous, is widely offered and has been practised for many years.

If an activity is rare or new, insurance companies may have little statistical information on which to base their claims estimates. They may also have few similar clients across whom they can spread the risk of claims. In these situations, insurers tend either to inflate their premiums to compensate for their uncertainty or to decline to insure an activity provider altogether. For example, the Tourism Industry Association of Canada (TIAC) identified what it called an "insurance crisis" in the tourism industry across Canada at the beginning of the 21st century. The TIAC cited "exponential increases in insurance premiums, significantly higher deductibles, and reduced or unavailable coverage." In response to the crisis, the TIAC formed an outdoor and adventure tourism working group in January 2004, whose mandate was to negotiate a group liability insurance program. Although this initiative did not result in the creation of a program, it did help to raise awareness of the needs of the sector.

Recreation industries can sometimes improve their access to adequate and affordable insurance by forming groups and negotiating insurance programs that meet their needs. By approaching insurers as a group, the businesses provide an insurer with a pool of clients, which can make it easier for the insurer to estimate claims risk and set fair premiums.

Determining the precise insurance needs of a business is a complicated task. Recreation providers can benefit from the expert advice of an insurance broker who is experienced in dealing with recreation business clients. Help may also be available from industry member associations.

Protecting Third Parties

Some recreation activities pose a risk not only to the participants that engage in them but also to neighbouring homes and businesses. Consider the activities that emanate from a popular nightclub that attracts crowds, serves alcohol, and closes late. A business like this attracts considerable foot and car traffic, and it discharges a large number of jolly, often intoxicated, patrons all at once at closing time. These patrons occasionally do damage to neighbouring businesses, drop litter (or worse) on lawns, and wake light sleepers. They may even increase the risk of drug traffic, assaults, and other crimes in the area.

While zoning laws tend to keep nightclubs away from homes, there are steps nightclub owners can take to minimize the impact of their business on the neighbourhood:

- posting employees on the sidewalk to remind patrons to respect the neighbours;

- obeying liquor service laws, particularly with respect to overserving;

┌───┐
│ **MANAGING RISKS** │
└───┘

Fore! (Containing Errant Golf Balls)

A common third-party risk associated with the operation of golf courses is the risk of balls being hit onto neighbouring property. This risk is particularly acute if a golf course is situated in an urban neighbourhood or borders closely on a residential development.

Lawsuits based on golf ball damage to houses, landscaping, and vehicles are fairly common, and sometimes successful. Inevitably, the golf course argues that homeowners who buy houses bordering on golf courses are well aware that the view goes hand in hand with the risk of being pelted by balls. Homeowners argue that there are ways to contain errant golf balls, and that the golf course has a duty to protect them. The courts have held that any unreasonable intrusion on neighbouring property amounts to nuisance, and can form the basis of a lawsuit. In considering what amounts to unreasonable intrusion, courts have held that no use of land that produces substantial discomfort to others or that causes material damage to property is reasonable.

There are ways to protect neighbours from flying golf balls. Golf courses can install natural barriers, such as tall hedges, which provide only partial protection against ball escape. They can also install highly effective ball-retaining nets. These nets, however, are expensive and require regular maintenance, repair, and replacement. The decision about what efforts will be made to keep balls on the course requires a careful analysis of the cost of the options compared with the potential costs of a lawsuit, and the moral obligation to protect one's neighbours. Courts look favourably on golf courses that take preventive steps that are reasonable when the frequency of ball escape is considered. If a golf course makes no effort at all to protect its neighbours, a lawsuit is much more likely to be successful. ◇

- installing fencing around parking lots to limit trespassing on neighbouring property;

- providing outdoor trash containers; and

- requiring that patrons exit from a door that leads away from homes and businesses.

Nightclubs are not the only kinds of recreation businesses that can potentially bother neighbours. Consider the following:

- ice rinks that allow ice scrapings to melt uncontrolled onto neighbouring lands;

- ballparks that pollute the atmosphere with bright night lighting;

- outdoor bandshells and concert halls;

- outdoor food festivals and beer tents, which create litter and noise nuisance; and

- zoos, from which animals escape occasionally.

If a recreation provider identifies a risk of causing a nuisance for a third party, it should consider whether modifications to the physical layout of its facility, or the purchase of special equipment, would help to minimize the risk of a nuisance claim.

KEY TERMS

best practices

controllable risk

external policies

internal policies

interpersonal risks

intractable risk

REVIEW EXERCISES

Review Questions

1. At what stage in the establishment of a recreation organization should risk identification begin?

2. List three examples of controllable risks, and three examples of intractable risks. Why do these different kinds of risks require different management strategies?

3. List five programming, location, demographic, or other changes that can lead to changes in a recreation organization's risk profile.

4. Why might a recreation provider want to review statistics about injuries related to the kinds of activities it offers?

5. List at least four components of an effective inspection program.

6. What are interpersonal risks, and what can recreation providers do to minimize them?

7. Does compliance with building, fire, electrical, accessibility, and other codes guarantee a building's safety? Why or why not?

Discussion Question

Is it ever morally acceptable for an organization to offer a recreation activity that exposes participants to a significant risk of serious injury or death when it is well aware of these risks?

CHAPTER 5

Risk Management II: Communicating and Sharing Risk

CHAPTER OBJECTIVES

After completing this chapter, you should be able to:

- understand the nature and scope of recreation risks that must be communicated to participants;

- describe at least three methods for communicating risks to participants;

- identify communication barriers that can pose challenges;

- explain the role of documentation and record-keeping in risk reduction;

- understand what it means to build a culture of safety in a recreation organization; and

- describe what it means to be an industry safety leader.

COMMUNICATING RISK

Introduction

Once the risks associated with proposed recreation activities have been identified and reduced as much as possible, the recreation provider must consider how to protect the recreation business against the potential consequences of intractable risks, which cannot be controlled.

One aspect of this task is to purchase insurance coverage, as explained in Chapter 4, Risk Management I: Identifying and Reducing Risk. It is also very important to effectively communicate risks to clients, so that they can share in the decision about whether or not to participate in an activity, and in the responsibility for staying safe.

When communicating risks, the recreation provider is responsible for fully disclosing the likelihood and seriousness of risks. Disclosure includes a discussion about how badly a person could be hurt and, if relevant, the possibility that a person could be killed. Understating or being vague about risks to boost business is never acceptable. The recreation provider should also highlight the client's own risk avoidance role—for example, by drawing attention to the kinds of behaviour that can increase risk. A good example of this is a sign at a go-kart track that prohibits intentional collisions and getting out of a vehicle outside the stopping zone.

The need to be comprehensive and specific, however, must be balanced by the need to be clear and effective. Specific and detailed warnings do no good if they are not understood, or if they are so lengthy that the client stops listening or reading. The need to be thorough, clear, and effective has always posed a challenge for recreation providers, but the fact that it is difficult is not an excuse for neglecting this essential responsibility.

There are many ways in which recreation providers can communicate risks to clients, and using more than one method often boosts the likelihood of successful communication. Clients differ in the ways in which they absorb and remember information. Some clients read all about the organization's activities on its website, and a warning placed there may be effective for them. Other clients may be auditory learners: they may dislike reading and need to hear warnings spoken by human beings before they pay attention. Some clients may forget what they hear, and may understand risks best if they take home reading material to consider later. Finally, some clients may not understand the recreation provider's language of communication, and may learn best from pictorial signs. These methods of communication are discussed throughout this book; the remainder of this section provides a basic overview.

Risk Management Training for Staff

Since customer service and program staff have personal contact with clients, staff are the main conduit for verbal and hands-on risk communication. To be able to communicate risks clearly, thoroughly, and effectively, staff need to be very well informed not only about the risks themselves but also about the importance of risk communication, their own role in the process, and the safety and liability consequences of failing to warn clients.

Appropriate risk communication should be positioned as a primary job duty, assessed by means of performance reviews, and made a prerequisite for promotion. An employer might offer good risk communication performers some form of special recognition, such as a gift certificate, identification as a "safety leader" in a company newsletter, or even a simple verbal acknowledgment in front of peers at a staff meeting.

Verbal Warnings

Armed with good training, customer service and program staff are able to speak effectively to clients about risks. Although many situations make it necessary for staff to address participants in groups, one-to-one verbal communication of risks is the most desirable method of risk communication. Communicating risks to a participant one-to-one offers the following advantages: the participant is likely to pay attention to what is said to him directly; a verbal exchange allows the staff person to identify any communication barriers, such as a language barrier; one-to-one communication affords the staff person the opportunity to ask the participant whether he has understood the warning, and to offer clarification; and finally, one-to-one

---

MANAGING RISKS

Barriers to Communication: An Example

The following recreation activity was planned in a way that created a barrier to risk communication.

At a community event in a small town, a rock-climbing facility set up a portable rock-climbing installation consisting of a plastic tower with footholds to which climbing harnesses were attached. The area around the base of the tower was cordoned off with ropes so that spectators could come no closer than three metres to the tower. Participants waiting to climb the tower were required to stand in line in a cordoned-off queue area. Non-participants (including the parents of child participants) were not allowed in the queue or in the area surrounding the climbing tower. The roped-off areas were set up to keep onlookers secure—a safety initiative. However, by excluding parents from the area in which child participants were strapped into climbing harnesses and oriented to the activity (and perhaps warned of the risks) the recreation provider put the people responsible for assessing the reasonableness of risks—the parents—out of earshot of any warnings! ◇

---

communication makes the staff person a witness to the participant's receipt of the warning.

Often, verbal risk communication is best handled during orientation, when staff introduce clients to activities and equipment. For example, when taking a new horseback-riding student on a tour of the riding facility, an instructor can explain the need for the rider to wear a CSA-approved helmet and shoes with a one-inch heel. Instead of simply listing the required equipment, however, the instructor should add that the heels are needed to hold the rider's feet in the stirrups, which minimizes falls; that almost all beginners, and even experienced riders, do experience falls; and that while a helmet can help protect against head injuries, falls can result in broken bones and sometimes more serious harm, such as paralysis or death. The instructor may also wish to add that the facility is highly committed to providing as safe a riding experience as possible, but that horses are by nature unpredictable, and not all risks can be avoided. This detailed, honest, and balanced discussion provides an opportunity for the client to make up his mind about whether or not to proceed. It can also help to bolster the validity of any written waiver that the client may be asked to sign before participating.

When a verbal warning is given to one person, it is fairly easy to confirm the recipient's understanding—for example, by simply asking, "Do you have any questions?" and "Do you understand?" When a warning is given to a group, however, the situation is more complex. Consider, for example, a tour guide leading a cycling tour who calls out to the riders behind her to watch for broken pavement ahead. There is always the risk that someone in the group

- cannot hear the warning;

- doesn't understand the warning, perhaps because of a language barrier; or

- isn't paying attention.

The adequacy of a group warning depends on the circumstances. In the cycle tour example, the risk is minor, and the riders at the back of the pack will see the riders in front of them navigate the obstacle. In this case, it is likely not necessary or practical to stop the ride before every obstacle to allow for individual warnings. However, when the risks are higher—for example, when a group of beginners is being taken whitewater rafting—it may be sensible to make time to highlight key risks to each participant individually—for example, by moving through the group to check the fit of each person's personal flotation device. Taking the time to speak to individual participants allows the instructor to identify special client risk factors—for example, clients who don't speak the instructor's language, who seem especially nervous, or who seem to be under the influence of alcohol or drugs.

If a recreation provider serves child participants or participants with cognitive deficits, it is not enough to warn the participant himself. The parent, assistant, or guardian who accompanied the participant must be warned also, because that person is responsible for the participant's care, and for making the decision about whether participation is worth the risk. Staff need to be trained to warn the right person.

A recreation provider who is committed to safety will require that activity staff both provide a detailed orientation to all new activity participants and allow the participants the opportunity to ask questions. The complexity of an appropriate orientation should be determined by the difficulty of the activity and the seriousness of the potential risks. In some very low-risk contexts (for example, a typical minigolf range), risks may be communicated by signs alone, or by kiosk staff, who can warn participants to stay on the footpath, use clubs only for the purpose intended, and watch for stray balls. For high-risk activities (for example, skydiving) a full-day training session may be necessary.

The verbal communication of risks need not be restricted to the orientation phase. As in the cycling example described above, program staff may find that risks emerge during the course of an activity. In some cases, a decision to stop the activity may be warranted; in others, additional risk-specific warnings may be sufficient.

Where emerging risks relate to client factors, such as a client's refusal to follow the rules, to play safely, or to use protective gear, activity staff must be assertive in correcting the client's conduct. If attempts to restore order fail, staff must bring the activity to an immediate halt. This requires the exercise of authority and, in many cases, backup from other staff and/or a supervisor. Conflict over stoppages can be minimized by providing effective warnings during the orientation phase about the operator's right to exclude non-compliant participants for safety reasons.

Finally, an underused aspect of risk communication is *praise*. When participants are praised for following safety rules, many goals are accomplished: the participant group is reminded of the safety rule in a positive way, other participants are motivated to play safely (because many people are naturally competitive), and the organization's commitment to safety is reinforced in the minds of the participants—something that can help to dissuade lawsuits if anything does go wrong.

Visual Warnings and Signs

Posting signs can be a convenient way for recreation providers to warn participants about risks. Signs can be graphic—containing images and symbols that convey a message—or they can be composed of words. Language-based signs are generally most effective when their message is brief. This is particularly true when the signs are intended for motorists. Motorists may have only a moment to read the signs as they drive by, and small print may be illegible to some readers.

The effectiveness of signs varies widely with the circumstances of their use. A sign is effective only if it's seen before a hazard is encountered, and so placement is key. Signs also lose their impact over time if readers are exposed to them regularly. Using too many different signs in a single area also reduces reader impact. Because readers often make the unconscious decision that they don't have the time to read and retain *all* of the sign messages, they make no attempt to read *any*.

The most effective signs are generally the simplest. Consider the effectiveness of a black-on-yellow graphic depiction of rocks tumbling from a cliff onto a car or a person. Now compare it with the following message in black on white: "Caution. This area is subject to rockslides, especially in spring and during rainstorms. By driving on this roadway, you assume the risk of personal injury and/or damage to your vehicle." The graphic sign is more effective for at least four reasons:

1. It can be understood in a split second.

2. Black-on-yellow is a colour combination that we have been conditioned to associate with hazards.

3. It is accessible to people who cannot read or who do not understand English.

4. The image of rocks falling on a car or a person creates a strong emotional impact.

Signs with more than four or five words of text should be reserved for situations in which the reader is expected to approach on foot, and ideally to pause in front of the sign—for example, at a gate or closed door or in an area where customers line up for service.

If a sign is intended to convey a limitation of liability, it is necessary to ensure that customers see, read, understand, and agree to it. This may involve a staff person asking customers to read the sign. In other words, the sign is not a substitute for an oral exchange, but can be used to reinforce it.

One of the main drawbacks of warning signs is that they do not offer an opportunity for the reader to ask questions, or for the recreation provider to confirm the reader's understanding. Some experts recommend that a sign designed to enforce good safety behaviour in an unstaffed area—for example, a municipal playground—should list a telephone number that readers can call to ask questions, leave comments, lodge complaints, or report hazards or criminal activity. The use of a telephone number on a sign can serve three useful purposes:

1. The receipt of telephone calls can be recorded as proof that the sign is being read, which may be useful in the event of a future claim.

2. A telephone number allows the recreation provider to learn about new hazards, such as a fallen tree branch, as they arise, and not only when inspectors visit.

3. A telephone number also reinforces the message that safety is everyone's responsibility, and not only that of the facility owner.

Visual hazard reminders include more than just signs. Yellow paint or reflectors on curbs, crosswalks, sign bases, and other topographical features help pedestrians and drivers to identify areas that may pose a hazard. Caution tape can keep people away from repair or construction, accident scenes, and other restricted areas. Buoys or paint on treacherous rocks can keep boaters away from marine hazards. If there are features in your recreation facility that pose a potential hazard and there are ways to make them more visible, it is prudent to do so.

The Fine Print: Waivers and Written Material

When participants are asked to sign a waiver of rights to limit a recreation provider's liability for harm, significant detail may be required to properly communicate the risks involved in the activity. Usually this information is provided in written form.

However, written communications have major drawbacks. It can be difficult to prove that a participant has actually read the warning in its entirety, and has understood it. Demanding that clients read long documents on the spot is impractical. Having customer service or program staff go through long documents point by point may be equally unrealistic, depending on the activity offered.

At the very least, where the recreation provider is relying heavily on a waiver, a staff person should make it clear that the client is expected to review any written material provided, and that it contains a limitation of liability and/or a waiver that may affect the client's legal rights.

Written risk communication documents work best in situations that allow clients reading time. For example, a package mailed out to clients who are booking a tour vacation or children's summer camp session is more likely to be read than a brochure handed out to participants who have already arrived at a recreation facility. Even then, recreation providers need to remember that not all clients will receive the package on time, and that some clients will ignore it or not be able to read it because of a language barrier.

Where written risk communication documents and waivers are necessary, recreation providers should make every effort to keep the documents as brief and clear as possible. Plain language should be favoured over legalese, and documents should carry clear and bold titles that communicate their nature and importance—for example, "Warning!," "Limitation of Liability," or "Waiver of Rights."

When a client is asked to sign a waiver, the document should be clear and precise in its description of what exactly the client is giving up. Staff who distribute risk communication documents should take the time to draw clients' attention to them, and to explain their importance. Waivers are discussed in detail in Chapter 9, Adventure Tourism and Other High-Risk Activities.

SHARING RISK

Introduction

Waivers and statements that limit liability are one means by which recreation providers seek to share participation risks with other parties—in this case, with participants.

Requiring that others bear some of the risks of recreation activities is not only fair, it also promotes safety. By demanding that participants consider and consciously accept the risks associated with their choices, a recreation provider can motivate them to help avoid risks by following rules, paying attention to training, and using safety equipment.

Participants are not the only parties that should be asked to share in risk-bearing. Business partners, such as landlords, suppliers, and third-party users of recreation facilities, have a role to play as well.

Property Owners

A recreation provider that does not own the premises on which it operates must depend on the owner to minimize risks by maintaining buildings and grounds in good repair.

The relationship between a recreation operator and the owner of the facility in which it operates is governed by a contract. In some cases, where the recreation provider rents space over the medium or long term from a facility, the governing contract is a lease. Where the recreation provider uses the facility on a temporary or occasional basis, the contract may be a licence. Finally, where the recreation provider is hired by a facility to deliver programs (for example, where a belly-dancing teacher is hired by a fitness club to teach an evening class), the relationship may be governed by a contract for service.

In all three of these cases, it is important that the recreation provider makes sure that there are terms in the contract that set out the property owner's responsibility for maintaining the facility in good repair and free from hazards. Typically, the owner bears the cost of this maintenance. An owner who intends to pass the cost on to the recreation provider must state that this is the case in the contract.

There should also be terms to govern what will happen if the recreation provider discovers a problem with the facility. If something breaks, leaks, or becomes otherwise unsafe, how soon will the facility owner come to fix it? Long delays, or the need to conduct repairs during business hours can mean disruption to the recreation business. The recreation provider should negotiate terms that require prompt repairs with a minimum of disruption to programs.

There should also be a term that allows the recreation provider to get out of the agreement if the property owner defaults on its maintenance and repair responsibilities. Where the contract between the recreation provider and the facility owner is a licence, there should be terms that explain whether or not the recreation provider will be offered additional usage or access privileges to make up for any lost time.

Finally, the contract between the recreation provider and the facility owner should clearly state which party is liable in the event that a recreation participant is hurt and makes a claim for compensation. Most personal injury plaintiffs file their claims against all potential defendants—that is, against both the property owner and the recreation provider, among others—but it is still useful from an insurance-planning standpoint for potential defendants to consider this issue.

Suppliers of Goods

When a recreation provider needs to purchase or rent equipment, vehicles, or other materials from suppliers in order to run its business, it should require these suppliers to bear some of the risk associated with the use of their equipment or materials.

As in the case of lawsuits involving property ownership, injured parties generally sue all potential defendants, including both recreation providers and the suppliers of any equipment being used at the time of the incident. Nevertheless, recreation providers can reduce potential legal time and cost by purchasing only equipment that a supplier is willing to stand behind. A good supplier sells only equipment that meets all industry and legal standards, offers product warranties, and carries insurance to cover the cost of lawsuits.

For recreation providers, sourcing high-quality equipment and materials from honest and fiscally secure suppliers is essential to ensure participant safety, and to protect against unexpected liability related to manufacturers' defects, design problems, and equipment failure. Equipment standards and product liability are discussed again in Chapter 8.

Third-Party Users

Some recreation providers—particularly those who operate facilities such as sports fields, ballparks, golf courses, arenas, swimming pools, ski hills, and program rooms—may find it cost-effective to allow the use of their facilities by third-party groups. Consider, for example, a private members-only ski hill that allows members to host ski days for the companies where they work.

This kind of use generally carries a fee, and can provide a helpful revenue stream to the recreation provider. However, any time participants use a recreation facility, there is a risk that someone will be hurt. If the recreation provider is not directly supervising the facility use—for example, while a third party is running programming at the facility—the recreation provider has diminished control over safety and risk reduction.

hold harmless agreements
agreements that make users of recreation facilities responsible for assuming risk of any claims arising from use

Because of this diminished control, recreation providers should require that all third-party users sign **hold harmless agreements**. These agreements make it clear that the third-party user is responsible for assuming the risk of any claims that may arise through its use of the property.

A lawyer should be retained to draft a hold harmless agreement that suits the recreation provider's business, and that can be adapted to apply to third-party uses as they arise. If there is ever any question about how to adapt the agreement to suit new circumstances, the proposed version should be shown to the lawyer for approval.

In addition to signing third-party agreements, third-party users should be required to provide proof of insurance coverage sufficient to compensate accident claimants. If a participant is hurt and the third-party facility user does not have enough insurance to cover the claim, the facility owner must make up the difference. The facility owner's insurance agent can recommend an appropriate quantum of insurance coverage that should be required of third parties. Where the cost of this insurance makes the cost of renting the facility prohibitive for third parties, the facility owner can consider bearing a share of the risk.

DAMAGE CONTROL AND COMPENSATION

Introduction

Once an accident or other serious incident has occured, there are two kinds of risks that need to be managed: the risk of further harm and the risk of legal liability.

If the recreation provider has devoted sufficient attention to policy development, there should be a policy in place to dictate how the organization will respond in the event of a problem. This policy should provide procedures that cover the following general matters:

- moving uninjured people out of harm's way (for example, by evacuating a building);

- contacting first responders (911);

- providing competent first aid to victims;

- arranging transport of victims to hospital or other medical care facilities;

- contacting family members of victims;

- securing the accident site or any area that has been damaged by an accident, fire, explosion, spill, or other event;

- providing immediate emotional or practical support, as needed, to survivors or onlookers;

- cancelling or resuming programming, depending on the circumstances;

- preparing an incident report for internal use;

- contacting legal counsel and, if appropriate, an internal or external media relations specialist for advice on information management;

- contacting the insurance company;

- debriefing staff;

- arranging counselling, if warranted, for staff and onlookers;

- providing any necessary information to the workplace safety and insurance board, if there were any employee victims;

- making any compulsory reports (for example, to environmental protection agencies or to the Ministry of Labour);

- contacting victims the day after the accident (or after an appropriate interval) to offer sympathy and help; and

- conducting an internal investigation.

Preventing Further Harm

The most important goal after an incident is to avoid further injury or property damage. All recreation providers should have staff members with first-aid credentials; ideally, there should be at least one such staff person on duty at all times. Staff with first-aid training should be encouraged to keep their knowledge up-to-date, so that they don't aggravate an injury in their attempts to help the victim.

If there is uncertainty about whether to call first responders, it is better to err on the side of caution and to call. It can be difficult to judge the severity of injuries immediately after an accident. Injured staff should be given the rest of their shift off and offered transportation to a clinic, doctor's office, or hospital when appropriate, or should be offered a ride home if first aid is all that is needed. If the injured party is a client, the client's contact person should be called immediately, and if that person cannot be reached, a staff person from the recreation organization should accompany the client to hospital if he is being transported.

Any injured person—whether employee or client—should be contacted soon after the incident, usually the next day, by someone in the recreation organization. The objective is to make it clear to the victim that the recreation provider sincerely regrets that the victim was hurt, and to offer reasonable assistance. A followup call is not an admission of liability; it's a matter of compassion and humanity. Studies, such as *Aftermath: The Social and Economic Consequences of Workplace Injury and Illness*, have shown not only that accident victims are less likely to sue if they are treated with compassion, but also that they are more likely to make a full physical recovery. The recreation provider should be prepared, in some cases, to be told that the victim does not want to accept the call.

If an incident has caused damage to equipment, the equipment should not be used before it is repaired, even if that means cancelling the rest of the program for the day. Where there is property damage to an area and clients cannot be effectively excluded from the area, again, programming will often need to be suspended. The recreation provider should counter any complaints about cancellations with a statement that the safety of participants is the organization's first priority.

Managing Liability

The best way to manage legal liability is not to attract any in the first place. From a public relations perspective, steps taken by recreation providers to *prevent accidents* are almost universally praised, and they improve the public image of the organization. By contrast, steps taken by organizations to *avoid legal liability* in the wake of an accident are viewed with distaste, and erode favourable public opinion.

A good business reputation can, in itself, reduce the likelihood of personal injury claims. The public knows that litigation is expensive, and injured parties and their legal counsel take many factors into account when deciding whether or not to sue, especially if the injuries are fairly minor. One of these factors is the reputation of the potential defendant. A recreation provider that earns, values, and protects its reputation as an organization that cares about participant safety is less likely to be successfully sued than one that lacks such a reputation.

Steps that can be taken to cultivate a reputation as an organization committed to safety include:

- communicating risks effectively and praising participants for safety compliance;
- running or sponsoring safety-focused programs—for example, a bicycle safety rally for children;

- offering free classes on aspects of safe recreation;

- speaking about industry best practices at conferences; and

- handling injury claims fairly.

If an accident does happen, it's important to have accurate information about the details. All incidents should be promptly, fully, and honestly documented by eyewitnesses, as soon as these eyewitnesses are no longer needed to help the injured party or other participants. Eyewitnesses should be encouraged to write down not only what they saw but also what they heard people say about the incident, and what was done by recreation staff in response to the incident. Report-writers should be prompted to list the full names of other eyewitnesses (including participants).

Eyewitness incident reports should be promptly reviewed by managers. It is never acceptable for managers to request changes to these reports, but it's fine for managers to point out gaps in the information provided, and to request that the person who made the report add any necessary information. This information should be added in a way that makes it clear that the addition was made after the initial report, perhaps in a different colour of ink and labelled with a date, if the information was added on a different day.

Incident reports should be filed for safekeeping, and their existence should be reported to the organization's lawyer, who may choose to assert a claim of litigation privilege over them. Such a claim maintains the confidentiality of the reports in the event of a lawsuit.

When an accident is serious, the organization should conduct a formal investigation, following the policy in place for investigations. The organization's lawyer should be contacted by the time an investigation has begun, and may have advice about points to consider. An investigation generally involves examining the accident site before it is cleaned up or otherwise disturbed, and interviewing witnesses. Investigation reports, such as incident reports, should be honest, detailed, filed securely, and given to the lawyer for safe handling.

In carrying out an investigation, the organization should avoid placing its focus on laying blame—that is, identifying the party responsible for the accident. Most accidents have many causes, and a blame-focused investigation often suffers from tunnel vision and misses key information. Failure to identify contributing factors means that the organization will have no opportunity to address these factors, and a similar incident might happen again. Investigators must remember that the goal of an incident investigation is not to find a culprit, but to prevent further incidents.

While an initial post-accident followup call to victims is almost always appropriate, further communications should be undertaken only after consultation with a lawyer, who may have advice about what should be said and/or asked.

Another essential task after an incident is to call the insurance company. Like the call to the lawyer, this contact should be made on the same day as the incident because the insurance company may need to perform its own investigation before the site is cleared. It is often a good idea to call the lawyer first and the insurance company second. If the insurance company chooses not to send an investigator, the organization may want to take photographs of damage to property and equipment; doing this may later help to support insurance claims.

At some point after the accident, the recreation organization may be contacted by a victim or his lawyer to inform it that a claim is being filed. In some cases, the first news will come in the form of the service of a statement of claim; however, a phone call will likely follow shortly afterward because most plaintiffs hope to reach a negotiated settlement and thereby save themselves the cost of prolonged litigation. When such a call comes in, the caller should be referred directly to the organization's lawyer.

Ideally, the lawyer will have already discussed the possibility of a claim with the recreation provider, and will have received the recreation provider's instructions about whether and how the claim should be settled.

Negotiating the settlement of personal injury claims is a delicate task that requires the cooperation of the lawyer, the insurer, the recreation provider, and in some cases a public relations specialist. In the great majority of cases, settling a personal injury case is preferable to going to court. Litigation is costly, both in terms of money and in terms of the organization's reputation. Showing a willingness to consider the plaintiff's claim, to assume a reasonable share of liability, and to negotiate a fair settlement is usually the best position for the recreation provider to take. An extremely hard-line approach will alienate not only the plaintiff victim, and possibly the general public, but also the decision-maker (judge and/or jury) who will ultimately decide on compensation, if the case ends up in court.

costs
a portion of the successful party's legal costs that is paid by the unsuccessful party

It is common practice in Canada to charge **costs** (a portion of the plaintiff's legal costs) to losing defendants. The proportion of costs that a defendant is ordered to pay can be higher if the defendant is also ordered to pay damages that exceed an amount that the plaintiff was willing to settle for before trial.

Early informal attempts on the part of the defendant recreation provider to settle claims may be made verbally by a lawyer over the phone. Since these offers are not drafted in writing and saved in a file, the fact that they were made should be documented by the lawyer in his notes.

Recreation providers who treat personal injury victims with compassion, humanity, and fairness earn their reputation as business owners with integrity, a quality that is essential to the long-term survival and profitability of any business.

LEARNING LESSONS

As noted above, the most important post-accident goal, for a recreation provider, should be the prevention of future accidents. To prevent future accidents, the recreation provider and its staff need to understand the factors that led to the accident. Several suggestions to assist in developing this understanding are listed below:

- document safety incidents, however minor;

- investigate serious incidents;

- track minor and major incidents over time to look for trends and patterns;

- pay attention to accidents that happen at other organizations in your field, so that you can learn from the mistakes of others without having to make them yourself;

- encourage staff to report safety concerns, and to use group discussions to solve problems; and

- incorporate new knowledge into future policy-making and training programs.

Where an accident was the result of damaged or defective property or equipment, repairs should be made immediately, and safety features should be added wherever possible. Never assume that an accident was an isolated event or the result of one person's clumsiness; take potential hazards seriously.

Finally, be sure that the training that you provide to staff reflects your organization's specific experiences, including accidents. Using concrete examples of problems that have arisen in the past teaches new staff that you consider safety to be an ongoing commitment, and that your regret over past failings has served to motivate you to improve. A safety-first attitude is contagious, and it is your organization's best insurance against accidents.

BECOMING A RISK MANAGEMENT LEADER

As you learned near the beginning of this chapter, joining member associations is a good way for start-up recreation providers to learn about the business of recreation and risk management. With luck and hard work, however, start-up organizations eventually become industry veterans, and the recreation providers who run them find that newcomers to the industry are turning to *them* for guidance.

If you have the good fortune of becoming successful in your industry, consider taking the time to share your knowledge, experience, and successful practices with newcomers to your field. Safety is not a competition; it's a responsibility that all recreation providers owe to their clients and their clients' families. Recreation organizations with a strong safety record have a wealth of knowledge that they can offer to the industry as a whole, and there are many ways to share the wealth.

Recreation providers can run seminars at member association events; they can participate in standard-setting initiatives; they can publish papers, books, and guides; they can offer training and certification programs for staff new to the industry; or they can simply be receptive to questions and inquiries from other organizations. If your organization embraces the role of a safety leader, your entire industry will benefit, new clients will be attracted, and your tourism or recreation niche will flourish in your region, province, or country.

KEY TERMS

costs

hold harmless agreements

REVIEW EXERCISES

Review Questions

1. Why must activity risks be communicated to participants?

2. Why is one-to-one verbal communication the most desirable means for communicating risks to participants?

3. What factors limit the effectiveness of signs and other visual risk communication tools?

4. What is a culture of safety?

5. Why is it preferable in the great majority of cases to attempt to settle personal injury claims through negotiation, before the cases wind up in court?

6. What are the benefits to a recreation organization of being perceived as a safety leader?

Discussion Question

One of the most common risk reduction problems in the recreation sector is insufficient communication of risk. Recreation providers often make two mistakes: they wrongly assume that participants understand the risks associated with the activities they pursue; and they rely too heavily on detailed written material such as waivers and limitation of liability statements to communicate risk, even though it has been proven that verbal communication is much more effective for most clients.

What challenges and barriers make it difficult for recreation staff to provide verbal communications about risk? Build a list, and then go back and propose at least one solution for each barrier.

PART III

Tourism and Casual Recreation

CHAPTER 6

Management of Parks and Recreation Facilities

CHAPTER OBJECTIVES

After completing this chapter, you should be able to:

- describe what is meant by occupiers' liability, and explain the standard of care that applies to occupiers;
- list some of the risks associated with pools, ice-skating arenas, and other specialized-use spaces;
- explain how managers can minimize physical risks in parks;
- describe how park managers can monitor interpersonal risks;
- understand the special risks associated with playgrounds, off-leash dog parks, and skateboard parks; and
- explain how the managers of beaches and campgrounds can take steps to protect visitors and the environment from harm.

INTRODUCTION

This chapter introduces some of the legal issues that may arise for the owners or operators of buildings and outdoor facilities devoted to recreation. Legal issues that emerge from the operation of participant programs are discussed in Chapter 7, Managing Recreation Programs.

Many of the liability issues discussed here pose a threat to all building owners, not just those who operate recreation facilities. However, the following features of recreation facilities may increase exposure to lawsuits:

- they are situated in public places, where access is uncontrolled;
- they may specifically cater to people with disabilities, who may be less able to avoid hazards; and
- potential plaintiffs tend to view municipalities and other public facility owners as having ample funds to pay compensation for injuries.

As you learned in Chapter 4, general liability insurance is expensive and can some-times be difficult to secure. Controlling insurance costs, protecting the public, and maintaining a facility's image as a safe place to play all require careful attention to potential hazards, and to the surveillance and maintenance required to limit them.

This chapter covers general legal issues that may affect the following types of facilities: general-use buildings; pools; arenas; other specialized-use indoor spaces, such as squash courts and rock-climbing walls; parks; playgrounds; walking and cycling trails; off-leash dog areas; skateboard parks; beaches; and campgrounds.

GENERAL-USE BUILDINGS

occupiers' liability
duty that imposes liability on occupiers of land or buildings for any harm caused to visitors, invitees, or trespassers

Any person who is in control of property—which includes both buildings and land—has a duty to protect from harm any person who comes onto the property. This duty, which is known as **occupiers' liability**, arose under the common law, and has since been codified in provincial statutes in most jurisdictions in Canada. In Ontario, the statute that governs occupiers' liability is the *Occupiers' Liability Act*.

Section 1 of the *Occupiers' Liability Act* defines an occupier as including:

(a) a person who is in physical possession of premises, or
(b) a person who has responsibility for and control over the condition of premises or the activities there carried on, or control over persons allowed to en-ter the premises,
despite the fact that there is more than one occupier of the same premises.

In the event of an accident on recreational or other premises, this definition al-lows courts to determine that more than one party is responsible. A decision that liability should be shared is appropriate in cases where an accident had causes that were related both to the features of a building and to the way in which the building was used. Whereas the building's features are likely to be the responsibility of an owner or landlord, the way in which the building was used could well be the respon-sibility of the recreation-providing tenant.

The usual tort law standard of care—that is, the duty to take the care that a rea-sonable person would take to prevent reasonably foreseeable harm—applies to most occupiers' liability situations. This means that an occupier must maintain her prem-ises in good repair, and must take steps to ensure that unusual risks are brought to the attention of visitors. Where possible, an occupier must also block off access to dangerous areas.

An unusual risk is anything that is unexpected or that cannot be readily identi-fied by someone who is new to the building. An example may include water that has dripped from a leaking roof and accumulated on the floor. Such a puddle may not be immediately obvious to visitors, and so it needs to be either cordoned off or clearly identified with "wet floor" signs.

Perhaps the most common class of unusual hazards flows from Canada's winter weather. Weather-related slip-and-fall hazards lead to dozens of lawsuits in this country every year. For this reason, snow and ice removal, and the use of anti-slip flooring and slip hazard signs inside buildings, in parking lots, and near entrances and exits are essential for facility maintenance. When building a facility or when planning for its use, it is important to consider snow removal, the location of plowed snowbanks (refrozen snow melt-off causes many slips and falls every year), and icicle and roof snowpack risks. In some locations, carrying supplemental insurance to cover heightened slip-and-fall risks is a good idea.

The standard occupiers' liability rules apply to **invitees**—that is, people who are invited onto the premises by an occupier. An invitee need not have received a specific personalized invitation to visit; he may simply be among the class of people who are entitled to come onto the premises. In the case of commercial premises and most recreation facilities (except for private clubs), any member of the general public who attends during business hours is an invitee.

A different set of rules applies to **trespassers**—that is, people who come onto premises uninvited or after business hours. A trespasser is also a person who goes into an area that is clearly marked as off-limits—for example, a room marked "staff only," an area clearly cordoned off while repairs are taking place, or a locked activity room.

Under occupiers' liability law, occupiers are not permitted to leave hazards unguarded in a manner that intentionally threatens the safety of adult trespassers. When trespassers are children, the standard of care that an occupier owes is essentially the same standard that is owed to invitees. There are two reasons for this higher standard. First, if security at a facility is so poor that children can easily gain access, then it's difficult for an occupier to claim that access was truly prohibited in any meaningful way. Second, prohibitions designed to keep adults out and to warn of risks are not as effective against children, who are naturally curious, may not be able to read, and may have less discerning judgment than adults.

Finally, the law recognizes the concept of an **attractive risk**—that is, a risk that by its very nature tends to lure children into situations that endanger them. An ex-

invitees
people who are invited onto premises by an occupier

trespassers
people who come onto premises uninvited, or after business hours

attractive risk
risk that tends to lure children into situations that endanger them

---

MANAGING RISKS

Legislated Limits on Liability for Recreational Use

To help promote the recreational use of both public and private lands, many jurisdictions have passed legislation that limits the liability of property owners for injuries suffered by people who are allowed to enter the land without charge for recreational purposes.

In Ontario, section 4(3) of the *Occupiers' Liability Act* provides that occupiers who allow recreational use of certain kinds of properties free of charge owe only the trespasser standard of care to those recreational users. In other words, occupiers cannot deliberately conceal or create risks.

In Ontario, the kinds of properties that are covered by the recreational user risk provisions are listed in section 4(4) of the *Occupiers' Liability Act*, as follows:

    (a) a rural premises that is,
       (i) used for agricultural purposes, including land under cultivation, orchards, pastures, woodlots and farm ponds,
       (ii) vacant or undeveloped premises,
       (iii) forested or wilderness premises;
    (b) golf courses when not open for playing;
    (c) utility rights-of-way and corridors, excluding structures located thereon;
    (d) unopened road allowances;
    (e) private roads reasonably marked by notice as such; and
    (f) recreational trails reasonably marked by notice as such. ◇

Limiting Liability: A Trend?

In some places outside Canada, the trend toward limiting the liability of recreation providers has been extended to other contexts. For example, in 2003, the Civil Liability Amendment Bill (which amends the Western Australia *Civil Liability Act*) was passed. That legislation made significant changes to negligence law—protecting public-policy makers (for example, a public parks authority that makes decisions about whether or not to provide lifeguards at beaches on government land) in many situations and creating a cap for economic loss claims arising from certain accidents. Many Canadian policy analysts have suggested that similar legislation might help to contain escalating insurance costs here in Canada. ⋄

ample of an attractive risk is a large, unstable dirt pile. Children enticed by the prospect of digging may cross flimsy barriers and could be seriously hurt or killed if the pile shifts and buries them. Occupiers are required to consider whether a risk may qualify as an attractor to children and take extra precautions to keep children away. Adults cannot successfully rely on the attractive risk doctrine because they are expected to use their judgment and obey no-trespassing signs. Covering a dirt pile with a tarp that is secured with cords and heavy weights is most likely a reasonable precaution.

POOLS

The risks related to pools are well documented: unless appropriate supervision and screening of deep-end swimmers are provided, pools present a risk of drowning. According to the Child Death Review Unit of the Office of the Chief Coroner of British Columbia, children are much more likely to drown than adults. In the case of preschoolers, they are more likely to drown in pools than in natural bodies of water, and more likely to drown in private pools than in public pools. For youth, natural bodies of water (lakes, rivers, ponds, and oceans) are the most common locations for drowning, and drowning is often the result of high-risk behaviour. A lack of supervision is almost always a factor in the drowning of both youth and preschoolers.

Public pool operators are generally well informed about the need for supervision. As long as a pool does not become overcrowded, operators typically provide adequate supervision during the usual operating hours. However, some drownings, especially in outdoor pools, occur outside these hours, when trespassers gain unauthorized access to the pool. It is the responsibility of pool operators to ensure that pools are well secured. For outdoor pools, this means high fences and locked gates and doors.

Other design features of pools and pool surroundings can help contribute to safety. Depth markings, both on pool decks and in the water, can help prevent dives into too-shallow water. Sufficient clearance around diving boards prevents swimmers from hitting their heads or other body parts on boards, decks, or other surfaces. Finally, pools must be equipped with appropriate, good-quality, and readily accessible rescue equipment.

There are other pool risks besides drowning. Pool chemicals can cause burns or poisoning, and must be kept in locked storage when not in the physical custody of pool staff. Wet decks, change room floors, slides, and diving boards pose a slipping risk. Pool operators should opt for slip-resistant surfaces in these areas, should discourage running in the pool vicinity, and should ensure that all edges and borders are clearly marked. Finally, the air quality in indoor pools has been associated with some risks to health. These risks may be negligible for occasional pool users, but may warrant protective measures for staff. Staff should be encouraged to wear respiratory protection when handling volatile chemicals. They should also ensure that air filtration, venting, and circulation systems are in good working order and turned on while the pool is staffed.

ICE-SKATING ARENAS

Ice-skating arenas are the scene of a variety of different activities and host many participants. Both figure skating and hockey are sports with a relatively high rate of injuries, but even leisure skating can pose risks. Careful attention to arena safety can help minimize accidents.

Safety measures include the following:

- shatter-resistant glass above the arena boards, if the ice is to be used for hockey or ringette;

- puck containment nets that extend from the top of the glass to the ceiling to protect spectators;

- secure latches for gates, and markings to make the location of exit gates readily visible from the ice surface;

- markings at the base of boards to make it easy to see where the ice surface ends;

- smooth edges on boards, and minimal gaps between panels;

- adequate lighting;

- an effective ventilation system;

- slip-resistant flooring at exits from the ice surface, and between the ice surface and change rooms;

- safe spectator seating, including safe steps in the seating area, with coloured markings to help climbers distinguish steps;

- restricted access barriers for the resurfacing machine passageway; and

- adequate drainage to prevent flooding in the case of ice melt-off.

Like any other recreation facility, an arena requires regular inspection, maintenance, and cleaning. Special attention should be paid to hazards—for example, glass that is not well secured and water on change room floors or in the shower area. The ice surface itself should be checked and (ideally) resurfaced after every hour of use to prevent dangerous pits and cracks from developing.

Maintenance areas must be kept just as safe as public areas. In 1996, a 21-year-old arena employee in London, Ontario was killed when a poorly located pilot light in a maintenance room ignited gasoline fumes from an ice-resurfacing machine. This tragic accident led to some safety innovations. For example, arena construction standards now require that pilot lights be placed in locations where they will not come into contact with combustible vapours, and more attention is now paid to marking ice surface exit gates.

The quality of air in arenas is an issue that has attracted attention recently. Testing of some arenas in Canada has revealed levels of ultrafine particulate pollution that exceeds the level expected in such high-pollution areas as freeways. The use of electric, instead of propane or gasoline-powered, ice-resurfacing machines may help to reduce levels of particulate pollution. A ventilation system that is in good working order and appropriate for the size of the arena is also essential to ensure good air quality.

OTHER SPECIALIZED-USE INDOOR SPACES

Some recreation facilities offer other types of specialized-use spaces, including gymnasiums with gymnastics equipment; tennis, squash, and racquetball courts; indoor rock-climbing walls; curling rinks; and bowling lanes.

Each of these facilities comes with its own particular set of risks and safety challenges. These challenges are often best understood by the member associations that promote and study particular activities. Equipment suppliers, such as suppliers of gymnastics equipment (including pommel horses and ceiling-mounted rings), are also good sources of information about issues such as clearance around equipment and minimum load ratings for flooring.

Before offering a new specialized activity, a recreation provider should be certain that the space chosen for the activity meets all legal and voluntary standards, and that the staff who will run the activity are qualified and experienced.

Inspectors of special-use spaces must have adequate knowledge of the relevant activities to be able to identify potential hazards as they appear. For example, in the case of a large municipal recreation centre that contains a pool, a gymnasium, and squash courts, the person who is inspecting the squash courts should have a specific understanding of the risks common to squash, so that she will be able to notice problems that may emerge in that particular space.

PARKS

Introduction

The following discussion of parks includes both landscaped (mowed and planted) leisure parks and gardens, and "natural" parks and conservation areas in which only the trails, boardwalks, and docks are maintained.

A special safety challenge that arises in parks is lack of supervision. While there may be a few groundskeepers, naturalists, or summer program staff, parks are not staffed in the manner of other recreation facilities. Most of the time, park users and park staff do not encounter or even see each other. This lack of supervision has some potential consequences:

■ Park staff cannot personally point out hazards to users, so hazards must be identified by other means.

- Park staff are not available to enforce conduct rules, so there is a potential for uncontrolled high-risk behaviour by park users.

- Park staff are unavailable to monitor interpersonal risks, so there is a potential for interpersonal violence and/or sexual misconduct in parks.

- Finally, there is usually a delay between the emergence of a hazard—for example, a bear wandering into the human-use section of a park—and the discovery of the hazard by park staff.

Suggestions about how to minimize the harm that may flow from these consequences are set out below.

Communicating Hazards

Because the opportunities for giving verbal risk warnings to users of parks are limited, park managers will need to use other means to communicate risks. The most common risk communication tools used in parks are signs and barriers.

Careful attention must be paid to the placement of risk communication signs. It is generally a good idea to place these signs at the entrance to the park; however, parks often have many possible points of entry. Visitors may enter most frequently near a parking lot associated with the park or near busy pedestrian intersections; however, park managers should not forget that a few visitors will enter by climbing fences, from adjoining private property, or along beaches.

The number of general warning signs posted and their placement will vary depending on the layout of the park, and the seriousness of the risk. Some parks, including small municipal parks and parks without water features or playgrounds, may be quite low-risk. The priority for the managers of these parks may be to limit interpersonal risks—for example, by posting usage rules such as "no entry between dusk and dawn" and/or "dogs must be leashed at all times." Signs containing such warnings as these should be posted at the most heavily travelled entries to the park. When posting signs, park managers should consider lighting: a "no entry between dusk and dawn" sign is useless if it cannot be read after dusk! For legibility, signs should be posted where they can be illuminated by safety lighting—for example, near parking lots.

Where risks relate specifically to a particular location in the park—for example, a playground—warning signs should be posted near that location. A playground sign might read:

> **This equipment is designed for use by children between the ages of 7 and 12 years. Playground equipment is used at the user's own risk. To report damage to equipment or any other concerns about this park, please call 1-800-555-5555.**

Where risks relate to a specific area that is large—for example, a beach or a marsh—reasonably spaced signs should be placed along the perimeter of the high-risk area.

In some cases, risks may be seasonal or intermittent. For example, in a conservation area that contains a creek, the risk of high water or flooding during the spring snow melt or after severe storms may need to be drawn to the attention of visitors. Visitors who have come to a park during safer times of the year may not be aware of the new risk, and so park staff should post eye-catching signs that cannot be ignored by return visitors. To make seasonal or emergency postings easier, park managers may choose to leave room on permanent signposts for the addition of the seasonal signs.

Physical barriers also play a role in communicating risks. Consider, for example, a park in which heavy rains have created a natural sinkhole near a trail. Park staff may choose to mark the sinkhole with caution tape affixed to stakes. This barrier will likely not be strong enough to keep a trail user from falling in, but the caution tape will alert any reasonable person to the fact that there is a hazard beyond the tape, and that it is best to stay clear.

Some unfenced parks have gates across roadways that are closed and locked at night. While these gates effectively keep car traffic out, pedestrians can often walk around them. However, the presence of the locked gate should communicate, to reasonable users, that entry into the park is prohibited or discouraged while the gates are closed. The use of these barriers, especially in conjunction with signs, can help parks limit their liability for after-hours mishaps.

Finally, park websites provide another opportunity for communicating hazards. While few people use a website to plan a visit to a small municipal garden, many people do research conservation areas and provincial and national parks online before visiting. Highlighting salient risks on the park's website (for example, noting that the park contains poison ivy and providing information about how to identify it) can be an effective means of reaching these users.

Controlling Uses: Risk-Taking and Interpersonal Violence

Controlling the behaviour of park users without directly supervising them poses a significant challenge for park staff. Besides including messages about limitation of liability on signs, there are other means by which park staff can encourage appropriate behaviour in parks. One example is the use of security lighting. Consider, for example, a municipal park that acts as a shortcut between a residential area and commercial businesses. Ensuring that walkways and seating areas are brightly lit at night can help to limit crimes such as muggings and sexual assaults. Consensual criminal activity (such as drug-dealing), however, may simply be driven further into the shadows.

Where significant problems with drug-dealing and trash-dumping develop in a particular area, park managers may choose to install security cameras, along with signage that alerts visitors to the existence of the cameras. The signs themselves may act as a significant deterrent.

When installing security cameras, it is important to consider whether the cameras constitute an invasion of privacy. On private property (for example, in an outdoor amusement park, or in a privately owned parking lot), the property owner is entitled to install video surveillance; however, posting signs alerting patrons to the fact that they are under surveillance is a good idea. The law with respect to video surveillance in publicly owned places like city streets and municipal parks is less clear; while public video surveillance is on the rise in Canada, the legality of this practice has not been confirmed. Because a park is a public place, visitors in outdoor areas have no reasonable expectation of privacy. However, it is reasonable for patrons to expect privacy in park washrooms and change rooms. There have been cases in which park managers have installed cameras in these areas in an effort to control public sexual activity. People caught on camera in these areas have successfully challenged the use of cameras in many cases.

However, lighting and security cameras are fixed devices, and savvy users can learn to avoid them. On the other hand, foot patrols by security officers can prove much more difficult to anticipate and avoid. Where park managers have concerns about risk-taking or crime, arranging for patrols by park staff or security officers may be warranted.

The key to effective patrols is the element of surprise. If staff patrol a regular route on a regular schedule, problem visitors will quickly learn to avoid the patrols. The route and schedule should be varied so that the arrival time of patrols in any particular location is unpredictable.

In problem areas, staff should patrol in pairs. Where the risk is lower, single patrollers may be adequate, as long as backup is within range of portable radios. Staff at some large parks use cars to conduct patrols. However, the light and sound from an approaching car can give wrongdoers plenty of time to escape. In daylight, at least, bicycle patrols can be more effective as well as less likely to pollute the park environment.

Hazard Identification in Large Parks

Besides helping to control visitor behaviour, safety patrols can alert park staff to natural hazards, such as fires, fallen tree limbs, flooding, collapsed bridges, or dangerous animals. Safety patrollers should be trained to be on the lookout not only for dangerous visitor behaviour but also for changes in the natural environment.

All parks should have an organized inspection schedule and protocol that is appropriate to the park's usage pattern, size, and features.

PLAYGROUNDS

According to the Canadian Paediatric Society, each year an average of 28,500 children who have been injured on playgrounds are treated in Canadian emergency rooms. The frequency of playground injuries has always been a cause for concern. However, most park managers feel that the benefits of playgrounds and physical activity outweigh some of the risks of injury, and that the best way to balance safety with fun and health is to make playgrounds as safe as possible.

The Canadian Standards Association has created standards for play structures. Only equipment that meets these standards should be selected in the construction of new playgrounds.

Standards for playground equipment continue to evolve, and park managers have a duty to monitor changes to standards, and to replace outdated equipment on a reasonably regular basis.

A key way to minimize playground injuries is to select the appropriate ground surface beneath play structures. A fall on a hard surface is much more likely to cause injury than a fall on a soft surface. Some options for the ground beneath play structures include sand, wood shavings, and synthetic dense-foam surfaces. Minimizing the maximum fall height can also reduce the potential for injury (1.5 metres has been suggested for preschoolers, and 2.3 metres for older children).

In an ideal world, playgrounds would offer supervision by park staff. Adequate supervision has been shown to greatly reduce the likelihood of injury because supervisors tend to correct risk-taking behaviour and the misuse of equipment. However, costs generally make the provision of supervision prohibitive for most municipal playgrounds.

To compensate as much as possible for the lack of supervision, park managers should install signs near playgrounds. These signs should require that children be supervised while playing, and indicate the age range for which the equipment is intended. Where appropriate, specific high-risk behaviours (for example, wearing scarves or other loose clothing while playing, climbing the slide, or standing outside guardrails) should be discouraged. Signs should include a telephone number that users can dial to report hazards and problems.

When budgets permit, it is ideal to fence off playgrounds and to provide a gate. Doing so provides two benefits: when the playground is in use by children, the fence can help exclude dogs; and in winter, when equipment can be icy and surfaces hard, the playground can be locked.

Finally, park managers should inspect all playgrounds at least daily, checking for loose or broken equipment, foreign objects in the surface material, and other possible hazards.

HOT TOPICS
Greener School Grounds

Traditional school and daycare grounds tend to share predictable features: an open expanse of grass and/or concrete, and perhaps a play structure or two. Some parks and schools, however, have adopted a newer approach that incorporates more tree cover, more shade, easy-care (often native) plants, and opportunities to learn about the natural environment. These grounds provide an interesting environment for children while helping to regulate the temperature outside the school and to promote clean air.

In some cases, outside organizations, such as the non-profit organization Evergreen, provide instructions about how to create these greener school grounds. Under certain circumstances, they may also help with funding.

Discussion Question

Can you identify any safety benefits likely to accompany the move to "greener" school grounds? What about new risks? ◇

WALKING AND CYCLING TRAILS

Like the large parks in which they are found, walking and cycling trails are typically designed for unsupervised use. The interpersonal hazard management challenges discussed above in the context of parks apply to walking and cycling trails as well.

In some large parks with trails, illegal overnight camping poses an additional hazard. Campers may light fires in fire-sensitive areas or may fail to extinguish fires properly. In some cases, they may even be unaware that fire bans and limits on burning are in effect because it is generally only in parks that allow camping that fire bans and limits are widely publicized and enforced. For this reason, it is a good idea to communicate the risk of fire to users, even in areas where no camping is permitted.

To ensure the safety of users, walking and cycling trails should be inspected at least daily in light-use areas, and more often in more heavily used areas. Park staff should check for signs of fire, flooding risks, fallen limbs across pathways, and damage to bridges. Where a trail-marking system is in use, staff should remember that although they are familiar with the trails, many users are not. Trail markings need to be clearly visible, and all directional arrows must point in the direction that properly delineates the path. The general condition of trails should be monitored as well so that the park can plan for repairs and improvements.

In some areas, naturalist associations may make regular use of a particular set of trails. It may be possible for park managers to partner with these associations to help maintain trails and keep them safe. Local associations may be willing to provide volunteer trail walkers who can help with inspections, and park managers can help support these partnerships in various ways—for example, by allowing the associations to run gift shops on parks property, or by linking to the associations through the park's website.

Finally, many parks ban the use of motorized vehicles (motorbikes, all-terrain vehicles, and snowmobiles) on walking and cycling trails. Regular patrols help to enforce these bans, as do contact telephone numbers on park signs so that users can report the unauthorized presence of motorized vehicles.

OFF-LEASH DOG AREAS

Some parks have designated areas in which dog owners are allowed to let their dogs play freely. Some, but not all, of these areas are fenced. Instead of designated areas, some parks have off-leash *hours*.

Off-leash dog areas pose potential risks to both people and dogs. Dog bites are a very common injury in Canada, and dog attacks are occasionally sufficiently serious to cause permanent disability, or disfigurement, or even death. Because dog owners generally accompany their dogs into off-leash areas, they are at risk of dog attacks from the dogs of other owners. (On the other hand, the restriction of unleashed dogs to these areas can be expected to decrease the risk of dog attacks for people who use other parts of the park.)

The key to controlling risks in off-leash areas is the careful screening of dogs. Aggressive dogs and female dogs in heat should not be permitted to enter these parks. Determining whether or not a dog is aggressive, however, is very difficult because animals are unpredictable. A policy that provides for banning dogs that have actually demonstrated aggression in the park is a good first step toward making off-leash areas safer.

Dogs that are not well-controlled by voice commands may also need to be excluded, especially from parks without fences. These dogs may move outside the off-leash area, and owners may have trouble containing them. The need to keep dogs safely within the off-leash area must be communicated to owners, and owners who allow dogs to escape should be subject to sanctions.

From a design standpoint, off-leash areas need to be clearly marked as such, and easily identifiable by members of the public who wish to avoid free-ranging dogs. In smaller parks, or where there are playgrounds or walking trails within reasonable proximity to the off-leash area, fencing is a very good idea. Larger, more remote parks can use other means to delineate the off-leash area. It may be possible, for example, to situate an off-leash area on one side of a roadway or river that divides the park. In all off-leash areas—large and small, remote or not—clear signs regularly spaced around the entire perimeter of the park should alert the public to the presence of dogs running freely.

Some municipalities have developed policies to govern the introduction and management of off-leash dog parks. For example, the policy in force in Toronto addresses the following issues:

- a municipal licensing requirement for all dogs that use dog parks (a rabies vaccination is a prerequisite for obtaining a licence);

- a permit requirement for commercial dog-walkers, who are required to carry liability insurance;

- exclusions for uncastrated male dogs and female dogs in heat;

- proximity to playgrounds, horticultural displays, skateboard parks, and other sensitive areas;

- signage for off-leash parks;

- a procedure for applying to create an off-leash dog park;

- the role of dog owners' associations (these associations are not required to carry liability insurance for Toronto park use but are required to do so elsewhere);

- limited exemption provisions for dog parks that existed before the development of the policy; and

- enforcement of rules and fines for non-compliance.

Where an off-leash dog park policy exists in a recreation provider's community, proving compliance with the policy may assist the recreation provider in managing its liability should a claim be filed.

SKATEBOARD PARKS

In an effort to keep skateboards off staircases, benches, and other outdoor structures not designed for the sport, many municipalities have built designated skateboard parks with special equipment. Like other sports, skateboarding is associated with injury risks. Most skateboarders are young, most young people are blessed with the ability to heal quickly from injuries, and most of their injuries are fairly minor. Anecdotal evidence also seems to indicate that injured skateboarders are less likely to sue than other potential plaintiffs. Nevertheless, skateboard parks scare recreation providers because by introducing a skateboard park where there was no skateboard park before, a park manager automatically assumes new risks. There are two possible choices: refuse to build a park and let skateboarders take their chances on the city hall steps, or build a park and make it as safe as possible.

There are many ways to reduce risk in a skateboard park:

- wearing helmets;
- wearing other protective equipment, such as wrist guards, and elbow and knee pads;
- avoiding high-risk behaviour, such as attempting unusual tricks;
- avoiding overcrowding;
- excluding aggressive participants;
- ejecting skateboarders who are under the influence of alcohol or drugs; and
- having adult supervision.

Providing all-day staff supervision is beyond the budgetary reach of many recreation providers. However, it is certainly possible to offer a limited number of supervised time slots during the week. Parents of young children or parents who are particularly concerned about the risk of injuries from horseplay or overcrowding may appreciate the opportunity to bring their children to the skateboard park during these supervised times. As an added bonus, skateboarders who are most likely to engage in high-risk skateboarding, to use profanity or drugs, or to bully other skateboarders are likely to avoid the park during supervised sessions.

Most skateboard park providers develop rules for the use of their parks. Since the parks are not staffed for much of the day, signage is the most popular means for communicating these rules. To maximize the likelihood that skaters will follow the rules, signs should be kept brief and simple, such as the following:

> **Use of this park is a privilege, not a right.**
> **Helmets mandatory.**
> **Maximum 20 skateboarders.**
> **Park closed dusk to dawn.**
> **No alcohol, drugs, or smoking.**
> **No boards on guardrails.**
> **Respect your fellow skateboarders.**
> **This park is regularly patrolled; participants found**
> **breaking the rules will be banned from further attendance.**
> **In case of emergency, the nearest telephone is outside**
> ***Donuts Now* at 400 Westney Rd.**

If the sign indicates that the park is patrolled, the recreation provider must actually conduct patrols, and patrol times should be frequent but unpredictable.

Finally, some skateboard park providers require that users register with the park administration and sign a waiver before being permitted to use the park. This policy can be enforced, to some extent, by issuing permit cards to registered users. Whether a waiver would be effective in limiting the liability of the park for accidents is a matter of conjecture, and complicated by the fact that most skateboard park users are minors. However, even if a waiver is not an effective means of avoiding liability completely, having signed waivers on file does provide some proof that a park made efforts to communicate the risks of skateboarding to participants. (Waivers are discussed in greater detail in Chapter 9, Adventure Tourism and Other High-Risk Activities.)

A more positive way to communicate skateboarding risks is to offer free orientation and training sessions. Staff running these sessions (which can be scheduled at a regular time each week throughout the skateboarding season) can instruct participants about the appropriate use of the park's equipment, and can make recommendations about the use of protective gear. If these sessions are offered, it may be useful to document and keep on file the names of participants.

BEACHES

Introduction

A recreation provider who has control of waterfront that is accessible to the public should always assume that some people will go into the water. This presents a drowning risk. In some locations, there are additional risks, including hypothermia, illness from microbes in the water, injuries related to rocks in the water, and injury arising from collisions with watercraft.

If a risk is obvious—for example, a high cliff at the water's edge with boulders below—there is no obligation to draw attention to the risk with specific signage. However, if a risk is not obvious—for example, an inviting beach with dangerous riptides—the risk should be communicated to the public through the use of well-placed signage in an area where there have been drownings due to riptides.

If a recreation provider has in some way increased or contributed to risks—for example, by constructing a segment of a bike trail that runs along the edge of a cliff—the risk should be reduced or eliminated, for example, by installing a guardrail. If the risk cannot be reduced, it should be communicated with signage.

Water Contamination

Different communities handle water contamination in different ways. One of the most common systems for communicating contamination risks is a flag system: recreation providers use coloured flags to mark a beach as safe or unsafe for swimming. (Usually a green flag means safe, and a red flag means unsafe.) Communities that use a flag system are required to test the water quality at regular intervals and to determine whether certain contaminants, such as E. coli bacteria, exceed the limits of safe exposure.

One of the pitfalls of the flag system is that the contamination status of beaches can change quickly in response to certain environmental changes, some of which are not well understood, and testing may not occur often enough to catch these shifts. Also, different stretches of the same lakefront can have markedly different levels of contamination. Where a beach has been shown through testing to have significant shifts in contamination status, it is useful to post signs stating that swimming should be avoided for 48 hours after any heavy rainfall.

Drowning

It is generally accepted that undeveloped natural waterfront is a signal to visitors to swim at their own risk. However, where a recreation provider creates an inviting beach by removing rocks, pouring and grooming sand, and building parking lots nearby, there is an enhanced duty to protect visitors. At minimum, visitors should be warned of some of the risks. For example, signs should be posted that state that the beach is unsupervised and that swimming is "at your own risk." If the water is intrinsically dangerous—for example, subject to riptides or killer sharks—creating an inviting beach may add to the risk.

Many recreation providers who create unsupervised beaches take the additional steps of providing life-saving equipment near the water and/or roping off the beach where the depth drops off sharply. If lifeguards are hired, recreation providers should ensure that the number of lifeguards is sufficient to supervise the expected number of swimmers, and that the lifeguards are fully trained in both rescue and resuscitation techniques. Many drowning-based legal claims in the United States, where litigation is more prevalent than in Canada, are based on incompetent rescue.

When lifeguards leave their posts for breaks, either they should be relieved by other lifeguards, or their absence should be indicated. In this way, swimmers (or their parents on their behalf) can make an informed choice about when to go into the water.

The presence of lifeguards should not be used as a rationale for failing to warn swimmers about risk. Even when lifeguards are present, signs should prohibit swimming by unaccompanied children, swimming after supervised hours, swimming while under the influence of alcohol, swimming alone, and high-risk play.

Collisions with Watercraft

Every year in Canada, watercraft collide with swimmers, usually with tragic results. Swimmers are difficult for boaters to spot, especially when a swimmer is alone. The easiest way to prevent swimmer–watercraft collisions is to keep boating and swimming separate.

Recreation providers who provide beaches along bodies of water used by boaters should use highly visible, closely spaced buoys to delineate the swimming area. Where possible, signs should be used to warn boaters away from swimming areas, and swimming within the marked area should be enforced by lifeguards. Where it is absolutely necessary for boats to approach the shore in areas used by swimmers, a "dead slow" speed limit between the shoreline and the buoys should be enforced. Finally, signs should also warn swimmers never to swim alone.

CAMPGROUNDS

Many of the safety issues identified above for parks and walking trails also apply to campgrounds; however, campgrounds come with additional risks. Many campgrounds permit the use of open firepits for cooking and entertainment. In hot and dry weather, the risk that fires will spread beyond firepits increases considerably. Campground managers should monitor the conditions of the natural environment, and when the risk of fire is high, a partial or complete fire ban should be considered.

Even if no fire ban is in effect, campground staff should conduct regular park patrols, and should approach campsites where fires appear to be excessively large, or to be burning unattended.

Even when it is not burning, firewood can pose a risk—to the natural environment. Some parts of Canada are infested with insects that can be transported to unaffected areas on firewood. For example, firewood from Toronto may not be transported to areas farther north that have not been affected by the emerald ash borer. Using the campground website to advise travellers about firewood transport restrictions can help prevent the spread of infestation.

Many campers consume alcohol on campsites. Alcohol is permitted in provincial parks unless the park has an alcohol ban in effect, which sometimes happens on long weekends in summer. The consumption of alcohol by campers can lead to an increased risk of drowning, burn accidents, motor vehicle accidents, and tripping injuries. The public consumption of alcohol by other campers can also dissuade families with young children from visiting campgrounds. To ensure that the park's alcohol policy is being followed, campground staff should conduct regular walkabout patrols.

Because of low lighting, winding roadways, and other factors, motor vehicles pose a serious risk in some campgrounds. Cars, pedestrians, and bicycles are required to share the road in an environment with low visibility. For this reason, speed limits must be set very low and strictly enforced by campground staff.

Finally, in some parts of Canada, bears or other wild animals can be attracted to campers' food stores, or to garbage disposal sites. Parks frequented by bears must develop comprehensive bear-management policies, and should post signs and hand out written material explaining to campers how to react if they encounter a bear.

KEY TERMS

attractive risk

invitees

occupiers' liability

trespassers

REVIEW EXERCISES

Review Questions

1. List at least two factors that may contribute to an elevated risk of personal injury claims against recreation facilities as compared with, for example, private office facilities.

2. What is occupiers' liability?

3. Must occupiers protect the safety of trespassers?

4. List at least two risks, other than drowning, that can exist at pool facilities.

5. Where can recreation providers gain information about standards for specialized-use spaces, such as rock-climbing installations and gymnasiums?

6. What is the biggest safety-related challenge for managers of parks and what are its consequences?

7. List three steps that recreation providers can take to help improve safety in playgrounds.

8. List three steps that recreation providers can take to improve the safety of off-leash dog parks.

Discussion Question

Reducing and communicating risks in large, undeveloped outdoor spaces poses unique challenges to recreation providers. Most individuals understand, instinctively, that if they hope to be safe in the outdoors, they must assume a share of active responsibility for their own safety. What can an outdoor recreation provider do to promote a culture of responsibility for parks users?

CHAPTER 7

Managing Recreation Programs

CHAPTER OBJECTIVES

After completing this chapter, you should be able to:

- list the kinds of interpersonal risks that can threaten recreation participants;

- explain direct employer liability for harm caused by employees;

- describe whether, and under what circumstances, employers are liable for the actions of volunteers or contractors;

- explain the doctrine of vicarious liability, and describe the factors that support a finding that an organization is vicariously liable for harm;

- list strategies that a recreation provider can employ to minimize the risk that participants will be physically, sexually, or emotionally abused by staff; and

- understand the importance of adequate screening, training, and supervision of recreation program staff.

INTRODUCTION

Chapter 6, Management of Parks and Recreation Facilities, discussed strategies for minimizing risks that flow from the physical environment in which recreation takes place. In this chapter, we examine the risks that arise from participation, and from the interactions between participants and program staff, and among participants.

This chapter deals mainly with recreation programs that do not have serious competition as their central feature, but that focus instead on recreation, education, health promotion, and fun. These programs sometimes have elements of competition (consider, for example, children's soccer), but when the programs are well designed, winning is not their central focus.

An issue that is reserved for a later chapter (Chapter 12) is violence in sport. Understanding the fine line between "playing hard" and committing assault is a challenge for regulators in a wide range of sports. In the context of recreational programs, however, the issue is clearcut: there is no place for violence in recreation.

interpersonal harm
harm that results from interactions between participants and program staff or among the participants themselves

The kinds of **interpersonal harm** that are covered in this chapter are often more difficult to identify—but no less serious—than physical violence. It is an unfortunate reality that harassment, emotional abuse, and sexual abuse occasionally arise in the context of recreation. Creating mechanisms and strategies that help prevent these harms, allow identification of problems in their earliest stages, and correct and sanction wrongdoing is an essential responsibility of every recreation provider.

This chapter introduces interpersonal risks in two different contexts: between the participants and the program staff; and among the participants themselves. It also touches on problems between children and parents (or other spectators) that arise in the context of recreation.

LIABILITY FOR THE ACTIONS OF STAFF

Introduction

Recreation participants can suffer various kinds of harm at the hands of staff. After explaining the general basis of employer's liability, this chapter focuses on physical and sexual abuse, and then on harassment and emotional abuse.

When a participant suffers harm as a result of his interactions with a staff person, the employer is almost always responsible for the conduct of the staff person. Therefore, the organization is liable for the harm to the participant.

ordinary course of business
on an employer's premises, during usual working hours, and while an employee is performing her regular job duties

How the law extends responsibility to the organization can vary depending on the circumstances. In many cases, a staff person causes harm to a participant in the **ordinary course of business**—in other words, on the recreation provider's premises, during usual working hours, and while the staff person is performing her regular job duties. Consider, for example, a case in which a staff person bullies, insults, or teases a participant in front of other participants. In these cases, the law views the staff person as a representative of the organization: her actions are those of the organization, and the organization must take responsibility for the harm done. The technical name of the legal doctrine under which this responsibility is imposed is ***respondeat superior***. Throughout this book, we refer to it as "employer's liability."

respondeat superior
legal doctrine under which liability is imposed on an employer for harm caused by an employee in the ordinary course of business while carrying out a usual job duty

In other situations, a staff person may cause harm to a person who has been a recreation participant *outside* the ordinary course of business. The harm may occur away from the business premises or after hours; or the staff person may cause harm to the participant while doing something that is *not* part of the staff person's job.

Such a situation might arise if a teacher drives a student home after a class, and sexually assaults the student while parked in front of his home. Cases like this one are complex because: offering rides home is likely not part of a staff person's job; the organization would certainly have advised the staff person not to assault or harass participants; and the organization has little means of controlling what its staff do when they are off duty.

Holding an organization responsible for the off-premises, after-hours, or unauthorized wrongdoings of its staff may seem unfair. However, it's important to realize that in many of these cases, staff gain access to their victims, and build relationships of trust with them, through their work with the recreation organization. The recreation organization brought the staff person and his victim together, and helped create a context within which the harm was possible. For this reason, courts have held that employers, in some limited cases, are at least partially responsible for the unauthorized wrongdoing of their staff. The legal doctrine that imposes this responsibility on employers is vicarious liability.

In the following sections, you will learn about the conditions for the imposition of responsibility on a recreation provider under the doctrine of employer's liability. You will also learn about the special circumstances that can give rise to vicarious liability of the employer for the unauthorized acts of staff.

Employer's Liability

As you learned above, the doctrine of **employer's liability** means that an employer must share legal responsibility for any harm caused by a staff person in the ordinary course of business and while the staff person is carrying out a job duty. For example, if a recreation provider runs a gymnastics program that includes the use of a trampoline, the recreation provider will generally provide "spotters" who stand around the trampoline to physically redirect participants who jump too near to the edge. If a participant is relying on these spotters but one of them walks away in the middle of a session (permitting the participant to fall off the trampoline and break his neck), the recreation provider is directly liable for the participant's injuries. Liability flows from the fact that the recreation provider failed to follow its own safety procedures with respect to spotters.

The basis for employer's liability seems simple; however, many cases have turned on two factual questions: (1) what is the ordinary course of business and (2) what are job duties. Consider, for example, a company that provides local walking tours for senior citizens. If the staff, in carrying out their ordinary job duties, lead the senior citizens through a construction site, and someone trips and is hurt, the company is directly liable. But let's assume that while waiting in the parking lot for the participants to assemble, a staff member mentions that his muffler is falling off his car. He is overheard by a participant, who offers help re-attaching the muffler and hits her head when climbing out from under the car. The accident has occurred in the employer's usual place of business (the parking lot in front of the seniors' residence) and during usual working hours. However, supervising a client while the client works on the staff person's muffler is not a standard job duty.

In this example, the employer is likely to be held responsible because of the staff member's general duty to supervise; however, the facts of the case do not precisely fit the definition of employer's liability. If the facts deviate even more—for example, if, instead of helping the staff person fix his muffler, the elderly client accompanies the staff person on an unauthorized "coffee run" and is hurt in a car crash—the case becomes more complicated. Here the employer may *not* be liable for what is clearly no longer an accident that occurred in the ordinary course of business.

When training staff, recreation providers should explain that their risk management policies, procedures, and equipment are designed to manage the risks that arise *when all staff are doing their job as directed*. As soon as staff deviate from the work that they have been trained to do, move out of the usual work location, or interact with clients outside standard working hours, the employer is unlikely to be fully responsible for accidents that may happen. Instead, employees may find themselves personally liable for a lawsuit, or they may cause their employer to bear some unusual liability that may not be covered by insurance (a bad career move).

employer's liability
legal doctrine under which liability is imposed on an employer for harm caused by an employee in the ordinary course of business while carrying out a usual job duty

If staff work with vulnerable participants, the employer should make it particularly clear that staff are not permitted to seek clients as new friends outside the context of the recreation program. For the purpose of this instruction, a vulnerable participant is anyone who:

- is under the age of 18;

- has a cognitive deficit, a mental illness, or emotional problems;

- is physically vulnerable (as a result of disability, injury, or advanced age); or

- views the staff person as a person in authority (even if this view is unreasonable).

In some situations, and especially in small communities, a total ban on outside-program interaction between staff and clients is impractical; however, recreation providers who operate in these settings should be aware that they are potentially vulnerable to employer liability, and should screen their staff with great care.

Thorough training and clear communication of staff job duties are also essential, and are an employer's best insurance against liability for the mistakes and missteps of their staff.

Vicarious Liability

A number of unfortunate cases, notably within boarding schools, have brought the issue of organizational liability for staff actions to the attention of the Canadian public in recent years. Recreation providers are beginning to learn that situations that place vulnerable participants—the very young, the very old, and the disabled—in one-on-one private contact with staff create a potential for physical and sexual abuse. Teachers and staff in boarding schools have been found guilty of abusing children, and staff in nursing homes and group homes have been found guilty of abusing adults. An overnight setting, however, is not essential to create the potential for abuse: any time that vulnerable participants and staff are not properly supervised, the potential for problems arises.

Under earlier versions of the law of vicarious liability, an organization could not be liable for acts of violence perpetrated by staff, with one exception: if the staff person's job *required* the use of force (including self-defensive force), the employer could be liable for instances in which the staff person used *excessive* force. Jobs that require the use of force include, for example, police officers, prison guards, and security guards. This rule was consistent with the general principle of employer's liability. The reasonable use of force was authorized by the employer and therefore occurred in the ordinary course of business; the excessive use of force happened while the staff person was doing the job (though not doing it properly). A distinction was made between this kind of violence on the one hand, and unexpected violent acts by staff that were totally unrelated to the job on the other. Surely, the courts reasoned, an employer could not be held liable for an individual's intentional criminal act.

This reasoning no longer describes the law.

In light of our society's new awareness of the prevalence of abuse between recreation participants and staff, courts have begun to look differently on employee violence, sexual violence, and abuse. In 1999, the Supreme Court of Canada considered the case of *Bazley v. Curry*. In this case, Curry, an employee of a residential facility for emotionally troubled children, sexually abused a child in the facility's care.

Curry's opportunity to commit the sexual abuse arose because the facility provided complete parenting-style care for residents: staff were charged with bathing children, dressing them, and tucking them into bed at night. After someone complained of abusive behaviour, Curry was immediately fired. An investigation and criminal trial led to Curry's conviction on 19 counts of sexual abuse, two of which related to Patrick Bazley. Curry was sentenced, served a prison term, and by 1999 had died.

After Curry was convicted, Bazley (then grown into a young man) brought a civil lawsuit against the non-profit foundation that operated the residential home. Bazley claimed that even if the foundation was not negligent in hiring or supervising Curry (the foundation had checked Curry's background before hiring him), it should be held vicariously liable for the sexual abuse.

At the time, the courts did not recognize vicarious liability for intentional criminal acts of employees unless these acts were either (1) *authorized* by the employer (as police services authorize the use of force by police officers) or (2) so closely connected with authorized acts that the criminal acts could be said to be a *mode of performing* authorized acts. What happened between Curry and Bazley did not fit either of these categories.

However, the Supreme Court changed the law of vicarious liability in this case by upholding the Court of Appeal's finding that the foundation was liable. In expanding the doctrine of vicarious liability, the Supreme Court came to the following conclusions:

- Instead of relying on technical rules (such as the authorized act rule and the "mode of performing" rule), courts should consider fairness. They should think about the interests that the law of vicarious liability is meant to serve— that is, to hold parties that create a risk responsible for the consequences of that risk. (This conclusion makes sense because the party that creates a risk is best able to manage the risk.)

- Imposing vicarious liability on employers in appropriate cases is important from the perspective of deterrence. An employer that recognizes that it may be held legally responsible for the criminal acts of its employees is motivated to screen employees thoroughly and to supervise them closely.

- When deciding whether an employer organization should be held vicariously responsible for the acts of its employees, courts should consider the following matters:

  - Do fairness and good public policy support finding an employer liable in the specific circumstances of the case?

  - Is the harm done by the employee sufficiently related to the work authorized by the employer to justify vicarious liability? In the words of the Supreme Court (at paragraph 41), "Vicarious liability is generally appropriate where there is a significant connection between the creation or enhancement of a risk and the wrong that accrues therefrom, even if unrelated to the employer's desires."

> – In determining whether the harm is sufficiently connected to the conduct authorized by the employer, the court should review the facts of the case on the basis of the following factors (see paragraph 41):
>
>> (a) the opportunity that the enterprise afforded the employee to abuse his or her power;
>> (b) the extent to which the wrongful act may have furthered the employer's aims (and hence be more likely to have been committed by the employee);
>> (c) the extent to which the wrongful act was related to friction, confrontation or intimacy inherent in the employer's enterprise;
>> (d) the extent of power conferred on the employee in relation to the victim;
>> (e) the vulnerability of potential victims to wrongful exercise of the employee's power.

- Having considered all of these factors, a court must find that the employer *significantly increased the risk of harm to the victim* before it can decide that the employer is vicariously liable for the harm.

This test for the imposition of vicarious liability may seem very complicated. However, as a recreation provider, you have a duty to review and understand it. It is worth noting that many aspects of vicarious liability boil down to simple fairness and common sense, and that the great majority of acts that may attract vicarious liability for an employer can be avoided by properly screening, training, and supervising all employees.

At the same time that the Supreme Court changed the law in *Bazley v. Curry*, it heard another vicarious liability case: *Jacobi v. Griffiths*. The *Jacobi* case considered sexual abuse perpetrated by an employee of a boys' and girls' club—an organization that provided daytime recreation activities to young people, many of whom came from disadvantaged or troubled backgrounds. The employee, Harry Griffiths, was a very popular program leader, and all but one of the assaults that formed the basis of the lawsuit occurred off club property; in some cases, the assaults occurred at Griffiths's own home.

In considering whether the club should be held vicariously liable for the actions of Griffiths, the Court applied the *Bazley* analysis described above. However, unlike the unanimous decision in *Bazley*, the decision of the seven-member Court in *Jacobi* was divided 4–3. The three judges in the minority found that the sexual assaults were sufficiently connected to the employee's work to attract vicarious liability for the employer. The children were more vulnerable than average, Griffiths had been encouraged by his employer to form friendships with them, and his "god-like status" in the eyes of the children made it easier for him to abuse them. But the four judges in the majority disagreed.

In deciding that there was no basis for vicarious liability in *Jacobi*, the majority focused on the following factors:

- The legitimate activities of the club took place in a well-supervised environment, with volunteers present and little opportunity for privacy between staff and participants.

- In order to create opportunities to abuse the children, Griffiths had to "subvert the public nature of the club's activities"—for example, by luring children into the privacy of his own home.

- Finally, the off-premises sexual assaults were not a natural outgrowth of the club's activities. Rather, they were part of a chain with many links and only a weak connection to the enterprise of the employer organization.

While this case needs to be viewed with caution because the Court was so divided, it should be encouraging for recreation providers to see that providing proper supervision of staff–participant relationships can help to avoid the risk of vicarious liability.

The new law of vicarious liability introduced by the *Bazley* and *Jacobi* cases has created a whole new context for looking at interpersonal risks in recreation settings. Some aspects of this new context are touched on later in this chapter under the heading "Avoiding Sexual and Physical Abuse of Participants."

Contractors

Contractors—third parties hired by others to do specific jobs—have not traditionally been subject to vicarious liability. Historically, this has meant that participants who were harmed by a contractor could sue the contractor, but could not sue the party that hired the contractor.

contractors
third parties hired to do specific jobs

An example, in the recreation sector, is a case in which a self-employed yoga teacher rents a school gymnasium in the evening to run a yoga class. Under the traditional law of vicarious liability, the school would not be liable for harm to a participant that flowed from the yoga teacher's negligence (or the teacher's intentional wrongdoing).

There are, however, some exceptions to the traditional rule. The notion of fairness is very influential in this area of the law, and the courts are often willing to look beyond the *form* of an arrangement (for example, whether it involves an employee or a contractor) to analyze its *substance*. In many cases, the lines between a contract and an employment relationship can be blurred. If the person who employs the contractor is enjoying considerable economic *benefit*, it seems unfair that the contractor, who shares her profit with that person, should bear 100 percent of the risk of lawsuits.

In Ontario, it is not uncommon for public schools to offer their facilities to community groups and programs free of charge, or for a nominal charge. The programs, in turn, do not confer many benefits on the schools. They don't serve to attract new students or to market the school in any way. An evening yoga teacher, for example, may retain nearly 100 percent of his profit from the course. It's unlikely that the school will be required to share in liability for an injury to a participant, especially if the injury is unrelated to the condition of the school premises.

But consider, instead, the case of a self-employed ski instructor whose services are sought out by a large ski resort. The ski resort may be eager to attract new business. By offering ski lessons through the independent contractor, the resort may be able to make the sport of skiing accessible and attractive to beginners who would otherwise be too afraid to tackle the slopes on their own. For this reason, the activities of the contractor confer a clear benefit on the recreation provider. The recreation provider also provides considerable support for the contractor's activities because it provides the ski hill and ski rentals. Without a ski hill and rental shop, the contractor could not run her business. The ski resort will also advertise the availability of lessons in its brochures and on its website, and may even dress the ski instructor in a jacket that bears the resort's logo. In a case like this, the businesses of the recreation provider and the ski instructor are very closely intertwined, both from a business perspective and in the eyes of the clients. Forcing the ski instructor to bear the full burden of liability for injuries to a participant would seem unfair.

In these circumstances, a court may well impose a share of liability on the ski resort by finding that the conditions of the ski hill contributed to an injury, and that the injury was not exclusively the fault of the ski instructor. If this is not the case, however, the court may, after analyzing the relationship between the ski resort and the instructor, make a determination that the relationship is actually one of employment, not contract; and that the ski resort is therefore vicariously liable.

There is a third option for transferring liability to the ski resort in this case. One exception to the traditional rule that contractors are solely responsible for the harm they cause is another rule: the non-delegable duty rule. The **non-delegable duty rule** states that a party cannot evade liability for dangerous activities by hiring a contractor to perform these activities. One case (*Const. Scarmar Ltée v. Geddes Contr. Co.*) that helped establish this rule involved BC Rail, a railway company, and Scarmar Ltée, a company that owned power lines. BC Rail hired a contractor, Geddes Contracting Company Ltd., to use explosives to regrade railway land. The blasting damaged power lines owned by Scarmar. The court found that BC Rail could not avoid liability for harm caused to its neighbours by delegating dangerous work—in this case, blasting—to a contractor.

It can be a stretch to define teaching, supervising, or other recreational duties as "dangerous duties." However, the non-delegable duty rule has been applied successfully in some interpersonal risk situations. For example, in *B. (M.) v. British Columbia*, the Court of Appeal of British Columbia upheld the lower court's imposition of vicarious liability on the government of British Columbia for sexual assaults on a child by her foster parents. The foster parents were not employees of the government; as in most foster-parenting programs, they were independent contractors whose services were secured by the province. Without making any reference to foster parenting as a dangerous duty, the court held that providing care for children removed from their homes by court order was a non-delegable duty of the government. Therefore, the government was required to assume the risks related to this duty.

In light of this case and others in the area of vicarious liability and non-delegable duty, recreation providers should be aware that hiring an independent contractor to supervise, train, or otherwise interact with clients is not an effective way of insulating the organization against liability. Proper screening, training, and supervision of contractors who work with clients are essential in any recreation setting.

Volunteers

Many recreation providers have the good fortune of being able to recruit volunteers, who are not paid and generally do not receive benefits, to assist with program administration and delivery. Recreation providers' duties to volunteers differ from those owed to employees, clients, and the general public. However, there is little real difference between an employee and a volunteer. Recreation providers are usually

non-delegable duty rule rule that states that a party cannot evade liability for dangerous activities by hiring a contractor to perform these activities

fully responsible for the acts of volunteers because recreation providers receive considerable benefits from voluntary work, and therefore should bear the risks associated with it.

In order to protect the organization as much as possible from liability for the actions or wrongdoings of volunteers, employers should screen, train, and supervise volunteers as rigorously as they would employees.

AVOIDING SEXUAL AND PHYSICAL ABUSE OF PARTICIPANTS

Avoiding Sexual Abuse

The issue of sexual abuse of participants by recreation program providers was introduced above in the context of the *Jacobi* case. An important factor in the recreation provider's success in avoiding liability in *Jacobi* was the finding by the majority of the Court that the recreation organization's programs did not *enhance the risk* of abuse.

This finding was fairly contentious in light of the facts of the case. While the abuser was well supervised in his on-premises interactions with participants, the organization encouraged staff to develop personal friendships with participants—a dangerous practice in any organized recreation context.

In order to steer very clear of vicarious liability for physical or sexual abuse, recreation providers should take every possible precaution to avoid creating situations that enhance the risk of abuse. Some essential precautions include the following:

- *No private one-to-one interactions.* Unless *all* of the staff–participant interaction is public (for example, private ski lessons on a hill surrounded by other skiers and instructors), recreation providers should not allow staff to interact one-to-one with participants. When private conversations are appropriate (for example, when a coach must take a player aside to explain why he is being suspended from play), these conversations should take place out of earshot but in full view of other staff members. Under no circumstances should a staff person and a participant be alone in a private setting, such as a dressing room, washroom, bedroom, equipment room, closet, or private residence. Personal care attendants who help disabled participants with showering and dressing are the *only* exception to this rule.

- *No friendships between adults and youth or children.* If staff are adults and participants are youth or children, friendships that extend beyond the recreation setting should be prohibited.

- *No friendships between adults and vulnerable adults.* The "no friendships" rule should also cover any situation in which, *in the eyes of the participant*, the staff person is in a position of authority. Examples of situations covered by this rule include counselling services where the staff person interacts with adults who are struggling with addiction, mental illness, or emotional, health, or financial problems, or where the participant has a cognitive deficit or is elderly.

- *Strict limits on off-premises interactions.* Interactions between staff and participants should be restricted to the recreation premises, or to related premises (for example, trails used by a hiking club). Staff should not offer participants rides home, invite participants to their homes, or visit participants' homes unless supervision is assured. For example, supervision would be adequate in the case of a book club that meets at homes, because there are many witnesses to interactions.

- *No alcohol or drugs.* Staff should not be permitted to consume intoxicants in the presence of participants, or to interact with intoxicated participants. Because even a trace blood–alcohol level can affect the validity of liability insurance coverage, some recreation providers prohibit staff from consuming alcohol within a particular interval *before* undertaking supervisory duties.

- *No staff nudity.* Many recreation programs include dressing-room interactions between same-sex adult staff and participants. It is recommended that in these contexts, adult staff not be permitted to be nude, or even in their underwear, within the view of participants. This rule is more important when participants are children and youth.

- *No unnecessary intimacy in interactions.* In some settings, such as summer camps or camping expeditions, staff and participants are together while getting ready for bed, and at other times in which there is a heightened expectation of privacy. Staff should not be permitted to have any private interactions with participants in these settings, and should be discouraged from getting involved in intimate interactions, such as tucking participants into bed.

- *Strict limits on physical contact.* While recreation, by necessity, often involves physical contact between participants, all physical contact between staff and participants should be strictly monitored. Staff should be trained not to employ physical means of consoling injured players, such as hugging them or lifting them onto their laps.

Avoiding Physical Abuse

Lawsuits based on non-sexual physical abuse are somewhat less common than those based on sexual abuse. In general, recreation staff are fairly aware that striking, pushing, or otherwise assaulting participants is inappropriate. The issue of violence in sport is addressed in detail in Chapter 12. There is, however, one aspect of physical abuse that bears mention here: overtraining.

Many recreation pursuits can be highly competitive. Consider, for example, the sports that have a revered status in particular locations (high school football in many parts of the United States and minor hockey in many parts of Canada). Some studies have shown that coaches and parents are frequently more competitive, in their attitudes and expectations, than the players themselves. This is a worrisome finding, and is discussed below under the heading "Emotional Abuse, Harassment, and Discrimination." Harassment is not the only risk associated with excessively competitive attitudes, however; there is also the risk that coaches will make excessive physical demands on participants. This is of particular concern when participants are children, whose muscles, coordination, and stamina are still developing.

The myth that children have boundless energy is dangerous when believed by a sports coach. All athletes have physical limits, and young or vulnerable athletes may be more likely to conceal their discomfort when pushed beyond these limits by an intimidating coach. Children are also more sensitive to certain training factors, such as temperature extremes and weight of equipment.

According to Donald Pennington, an American orthopedic surgeon, overtraining injuries in children and youth are on the rise, and now account for 30 to 50 percent of child and youth sports injuries. Pennington attributes this phenomenon in part to a trend toward "specialization"—year-round participation, by young people, in a single sport. Historically, children were more likely to change sports with the seasons (for example, baseball or soccer in summer, football in fall, hockey or basketball in winter).

The Montreal *Gazette* reported, in September 2008, that the trend toward year-round hockey for young players is now being associated with burnout and overtraining injuries. Eager to retain their children's competitive status, parents are now enrolling children in summer hockey leagues and hockey camp, a practice that may in fact lead to injuries that were once uncommon in children and youth.

Overtraining is often unintentional. The onset of overtraining symptoms is unpredictable, and the signs can be subtle. However, some coaches combine heavy training with emotional abuse, and the result can be very dangerous. Staff should be trained to be conscious of the need to foster internal motivation in players, rather than to intimidate athletes into working harder. A player who is internally motivated to compete is much less likely to exceed his personal limits than one who is harassed. Even common expressions, such as the request that an athlete "give 110 percent" should be treated with caution.

Recreation providers should also be alert to the possibility of physical abuse when dealing with very elderly clients. There have been many reports of physical abuse of seniors by staff. These incidents generally happen in residential facilities, and not in the recreation context; however, the factors that increase the potential for senior abuse can also exist in recreational settings.

Elderly adults most at risk of abuse are those who have physical limitations (especially if they require physical help when rolling over in bed, or getting into a wheelchair), or who have problems communicating or being understood. In some cases, seniors who can communicate well do not have their concerns taken seriously, especially when they have a history of dementia.

Elder abuse is preventable in the same way as sexual abuse is preventable: interactions between participants and staff must be supervised, and private or intimate interactions must be strictly limited. Finally, complaints by older adults should always be taken seriously.

EMOTIONAL ABUSE, HARASSMENT, AND DISCRIMINATION

Whenever people with different strengths, weaknesses, opinions, and values are brought together, there is a potential for harassment, discrimination, and emotional abuse.

The Ontario *Human Rights Code* defines harassment as "engaging in a course of vexatious comment or conduct that is known or ought reasonably to be known to be unwelcome." Recreation staff can cause harm by harassing clients or each other, and recreation organizations can cause harm by permitting clients to harass each other without sanction.

Like physical and sexual abuse, harassment often occurs when there is inadequate supervision. In general, people recognize that harassment and emotional abuse are wrong, and avoid engaging in these behaviours in situations in which they will be overheard. However, it is also possible for the culture of an organization to become so corrupted that harassment occurs openly, with many staff people or clients participating. Hazing in sports, summer camps, private clubs, and educational settings is an example of institutionalized harassment.

Harassment and emotional abuse are most common in settings where people have a chance to get to know each other, and where power imbalances have an opportunity to develop. When clients participate in one-time recreational activities (for example, playing a round of minigolf or going on a trail ride), targeted emotional abuse is unlikely, though there is the potential for isolated discriminatory comments. Consider, for example, an overweight person being asked, pointedly, "Do you really want to squeeze yourself into that rollercoaster seat?" Requiring that staff deal with all clients with courtesy and without discrimination is an essential facet of staff training, and compliance can be monitored through adequate supervision.

Ongoing harassment, however, is less tractable. Institutionalized hazing also poses some difficulties, because it's common for the people conducting the hazing to have endured it themselves, and to declare it (in hindsight) to be "good clean fun."

There has been surprisingly little comprehensive research into the extent of harassment in recreation in Canada. An older, but oft-cited, study by S. Kirby and L. Greaves estimated that between 40 and 50 percent of Canadian sports participants reported having been made uncomfortable by abuse that ranged from mild harassment to rape.

Participants who suffer harassment in the course of recreation activities are often loath to report it. This reluctance results sometimes out of fear of an escalation in the harassment, sometimes out of fear that they will not be believed, and sometimes out of fear that they will lose their status within the organization (by, for example, being benched by a harassing coach).

According to the British Columbia Ministry of Healthy Living and Sport, signs of harassment in children may include:

- a change in behaviour, particularly if a child becomes withdrawn, loses interest in favourite activities, or appears unhappy or angry;

- unexplained injuries;

- sexual actions, talk, or knowledge beyond the norm for the child's age; and

- new friendships with older persons.

Adults who are harassed in the course of recreation may simply drop out of the activities that they once enjoyed, providing reasons that seem inconsistent with their original level of interest.

The British Columbia Recreation and Parks Association has published a useful and concise guide to resources for preventing discrimination in recreation settings.

Entitled "Anti-Discrimination in Sport and Recreation," the guide includes definitions of discrimination-related terms and a listing of (mostly Canadian) resources. The guide also provides practical suggestions for how "receivers" can respond to discrimination and harassment, and how observers can move from "dis-witnessing" or "passive witnessing" of discriminatory comments to the more productive "ethical witnessing and social action." For example, an ethical witness to a discriminatory comment is encouraged to:

- interrupt,

- identify the comment as discrimination,

- express disagreement,

- put the offender on the spot,

- support the receiver in seeking help, and

- approach other witnesses and request their backup.

Practical strategies like these can be taught to staff, and can help a great deal in creating a recreation environment in which harassment is not tolerated. There have been few lawsuits based purely on harassment in Canada. However, harassment that is permitted to continue unchecked has the potential to escalate into physical or sexual abuse, and participants are more likely to report these kinds of incidents. Such reports can lead not only to damages claims but also to criminal charges.

PARTICIPANT INTERACTIONS

Accidents and physical and emotional abuse can arise not only through interactions between staff and participants but also through interactions among participants themselves. In fact, in the context of competitive team sports, participants are more likely to be injured by other participants than by staff.

Recreation staff cannot completely prevent the harm that flows from participant interactions. However, good recreation providers understand that their policies and procedures, the training they provide to staff, and the messages that they send to participants have a very important role to play in setting the tone for participant interactions.

Because recreation providers benefit from repeat business and from ongoing relationships with participants, it is in their interests to create an environment that minimizes the potential for interpersonal harm. As explained above, practical anti-discrimination training can help create an atmosphere in which discriminatory comments are not tolerated. There are many other strategies that recreation providers can employ to minimize interpersonal harm. The following are a few examples:

- *General code of conduct.* Many recreation organizations have a code of conduct for staff and participants. Common issues covered in these codes are respect for others, the prohibition of discrimination, peaceful resolution of disputes, fair play, and rules prohibiting the use of profanity. Most codes of conduct make it clear that participants who violate the rules will be excluded from participation and will be required to leave the facility.

One of the most important features of an effective code of conduct is simplicity. The code should be brief enough that it is likely to be read, and can be posted on a reasonably sized sign. Fairly general statements—for example, "harassment of others will not be tolerated"—are preferable to very specific statements, such as "use of racial epithets will not be tolerated." General statements allow the organization to define inappropriate behaviour as widely as possible.

For a code of conduct to be effective, it must be communicated to all participants. Ideally, participants should be required to sign an agreement to comply with the code. The code must also be taken seriously by management. If participants regularly get away with violating the code without sanction, the code will be ignored by everyone.

- *Specialized codes of conduct.* Some organizations have specialized codes of conduct to regulate particular groups of patrons or activities. For example, a minor baseball association may have both a regular code of conduct and an additional code of conduct that applies specifically to the travelling team. The specialized code may have provisions related to the conduct of the team while on the road, to reinforce the need for travelling players to act as ambassadors for their town and to represent the organization with dignity. Other recreation facilities may have codes of conduct for spectators. For example, a golf club may have etiquette rules designed to limit distracting behaviour by spectators.

- *Fair play agreements.* There is currently a trend in minor sports to require parents and players to sign fair play agreements. These agreements are simply specialized codes of conduct. They are employed to reinforce the value of playing fairly, rather than winning at any cost, as a central feature of the organization's culture. Fair play agreements generally advise players that unethical play and poor sportsmanship will not be tolerated on the part of players, parents, or spectators.

- *Fair play as a determinant of standing.* A few sporting organizations have adopted the innovative approach of including fair play as a factor in the assessment of player standing. Players are ranked not only on the basis of skill and performance but also on the basis of fair play. Under this kind of system, a skilled player may justifiably be denied a place on a particular team when she has not demonstrated a commitment to fair play.

- *Effective, confidential complaint-handling mechanisms.* Harassment and discrimination often go unreported. Where the harassment occurs between participants, the recipient of the harassment may feel disinclined to report it if he is of the view that the organization can do nothing about it. Developing and publicizing a confidential mechanism for reporting complaints encourages reporting. In some cases, it may even be appropriate to permit complaints to be made anonymously. If more than one or two anonymous complaints are made about a particular individual, the organization can be fairly certain that the individual is indeed intimidating other participants, and that his behaviour must be investigated.

- *A drug and alcohol policy*. Because alcohol or drug abuse is sometimes associated with interpersonal violence, an organization should have a policy permitting the exclusion of participants who appear to be intoxicated. Enforcing this policy will not only help to prevent interpersonal harm but will also help to protect the safety of the intoxicated participants.

Finally, no matter how eager an organization is to retain customers, it is important to remember that a participant who threatens the quality of other participants' recreation experience always does the organization more harm than good. By acting quickly to sanction people who break the rules, and by terminating the participation privileges of repeat offenders, the organization will send the message to other participants that it is eager to create a safe, fun, and respectful environment—a move that is always good for business.

ABUSE BY SPECTATORS AND PARENTS

Spectators

Chapter 11 of this book is entirely devoted to spectator and visitor management in recreation; however, a discussion of interpersonal risk would not be complete without a mention of the potential for wrongdoing on the part of spectators.

New reports of spectator violence emerge each year. "Football hooligans" in England are commonly cited culprits, but all competitive sports events can be the focus of conflict between fans. Other events, such as music concerts, come with their own types of risks, which are explored in Chapter 11. When identifying and reducing the risks associated with their business, recreation providers should always include an assessment of spectator-related risks.

Parents

Because parents are viewed as the protectors of children, the prospect of a parent actually posing a risk to children in the context of recreation can sometimes be ignored. However, research indicates that many parents, caught up in the spirit of competition, knowingly or unintentionally cause emotional harm to their children.

Joyce Brennfleck Shannon, editor of the *Sports Injuries Sourcebook*, has identified emotional abuse as the most common form of abuse in youth sport, but the most difficult to identify. She cites the following examples: "rejecting; ignoring; isolating, terrorizing; name-calling; making fun of someone; putting someone down; saying things that hurt feelings; and/or yelling" (2002, pp. 169-170). Shannon also describes the following types of parental behaviour that may constitute emotional abuse:

- forcing a child to participate in sports;

- not speaking to a child after a poor sports performance;

- asking a child why he played poorly even though his performance meant so much [to the adult] and

- hitting, yelling at, punishing, or ridiculing a child for disappointing play.

A 1993 Minnesota study of youth sports participants found that 45.3 percent reported having been the victims of name-calling and insults, 17.5 percent reported physical assaults for poor performance; and 21 percent reported pressure to play while injured (Shannon, 2002, p. 171).

Preventing abuse of children by their own parents is a singularly difficult task for recreation providers. Parents are generally highly resistant to receiving advice about parenting from outside sources. There are, however, two things that recreation providers can do to help reduce the risk of this kind of abuse.

The first approach is to attempt to educate parents about the consequences of emotional abuse. Any educational campaign of this nature should be addressed to *all* of the parents, an approach that avoids singling out individuals, which can cause a defensive reaction. Coaches may address the issue informally, for example, in a post-game dressing-room chat with both parents and players. Using anecdotes to illustrate key points can be especially useful because it allows parents who may not be aware of their behaviour to recognize their mistakes. For example, after a practice, a gymnastics coach might say something like this:

> Well done, everyone, I can really see improvement. Another thing I noticed today is that we're beginning to work together as a team. We're lucky to have so many talented girls on our team here in Littleville. I think that demonstrates that we're having fun. Some teams struggle with many girls dropping out around this age, 12 or 13. I'm not sure why, but in some cases I think that girls who are growing quickly can go through a clumsy stage, and parents who don't realize that this is natural tend to get frustrated. Sometimes a girl faces a lot of criticism at home, and then gymnastics suddenly isn't fun anymore, and she drops out. I'd like to reassure all you parents that the best way to get through plateaus and awkward stages is to stick with it, keep things light, help your daughters to laugh off little stumbles and mistakes, and remind them that sport is supposed to be fun. Can I get your support in doing that?

A more formal approach might involve handing out brochures about emotional abuse in sport, and then following up the handout a few days later with a quick discussion. What did the parents think of the handout? Do they have any questions? Do they think parental pressure is a problem in this sport, or on this team?

Discussing emotional abuse and parents' potential role is best done *in front of the children*. This arms children with the knowledge that the recreation provider does not support the actions of an abusive parent, and does not believe that emotional abuse has a legitimate place in sport. This knowledge may make children more likely to reject or challenge parental abuse, or even to report serious abuse to a coach.

The second strategy for dealing with parental abuse involves creating an anti-abuse team culture. Good coaches know that they are responsible not only for helping players acquire skills but also for setting the tone for the team, developing a vision of what success means for the team, and creating an environment that supports that success. Studies of youth sport have demonstrated that developing physical and social skills within an abuse-free, cooperative environment is an achievement that may actually be more satisfying to participants than simply winning games and contests. Coaches need to spend time identifying the best interests of their clients—children—and developing a team culture that best supports these interests. For many youth sports teams, this means adopting a zero-tolerance attitude toward emotional abuse. Ways in which this message can be communicated to parents include:

- requiring parents to sign a fair play agreement;

- requiring that only encouragement, never instruction or correction, be provided from the sidelines;

- curbing verbal abuse by requiring parents to watch youth sports from out of earshot of the players;

- praising participants in front of their parents and other witnesses (this may make it more difficult for parents to criticize their children later);

- openly discussing, and rejecting, emotional abuse in sport;

- challenging emotional abuse when it's overheard; and

- providing a mechanism whereby children can report emotional abuse and get help.

Authors Jordan D. Metzl and Carol Shookhoff recommend that when mild abuse becomes evident to a coach, parents be encouraged to consider whether their own personal objectives for a child's sport participation are in line with, or in conflict with, their children's objectives. Some studies suggest that parents place a much higher value on competitiveness and winning than their children do. Parents often fall into the trap of living vicariously through their children, expecting "the child to redeem the failures of the parent, to avenge the parent for any remembered insult or slight, whether in high school, the workplace, or elsewhere" (Metzl & Shookhoff, 2002, p. 23 and Chapter 2).

If abuse persists or is serious, a sports coach is legally required, under the *Child and Family Services Act*, to report the abuse to a children's aid society and, where appropriate, to the police.

DUTY TO SCREEN

Recreation providers, especially those who deal with vulnerable clients, have a duty to inquire into the suitability of all staff who work with clients. Where clients are vulnerable, or where staff work closely or intimately with clients, this duty is heightened. Careful attention to screening is beneficial to the employer as well because it helps to avoid the hiring (and subsequent firing) of problem employees, sometimes at a significant financial loss.

Because privacy laws have been strengthened in recent years, obtaining useful information about a potential employee can be challenging. Former employers were once a good source of references, but now they often follow a policy of providing no information about a previous employee's tenure, other than to confirm the fact of employment and perhaps provide start and end dates. To obtain a fuller reference, a hiring manager now usually needs the candidate to supply the name and contact details of individuals who are willing to do more than confirm employment. When asking for references, the employer should request explicit, written consent to contact these references, which can be done by means of a form at the interview stage.

If you request that a candidate supply references, it is essential to follow up. Contacting references by telephone is usually most productive because the references are less likely to limit their comments. If possible, a candidate should provide references who can vouch for her performance in a position similar to the position being contemplated, or in a position that required a similar level of interaction with clients.

When a candidate has difficulty providing references, the potential employer should give some thought to why this might be the case. There are some legitimate reasons for not having references. Being young and new to the workforce (or the country) tops the list. However, where a candidate's resumé shows several former employers, and the references are not people who seem to be natural choices (recent employers or employers in the same industry) or where there are unexplained gaps in the candidate's employment history, the potential employer is entitled to be wary. Fairness should motivate the potential employer to ask further questions. For example, a potential employer might ask about what the candidate was doing during an employment gap, or whether the candidate can provide references from more recent employers.

If an employee or volunteer is being recruited for a position that requires particular expertise, the employer may also have the duty to take steps to confirm certain credentials. In most cases, employers simply accept what is written on an applicant's resumé, especially when the applicant seems like a good fit with the organization. However, where an applicant is alleging that he has a credential that is required *for client safety*, it is not only the employer, but also the client, who stands to suffer harm if the applicant is lying about the credential.

Examples of credentials that have safety implications include coaching credentials, first-aid credentials (for example, St. John Ambulance or CPR training), and credentials that relate to completion of anti-abuse programs (for example, the "Speak Out" program used in Canadian minor hockey). When a credential is an occupational requirement, or when an employer is selecting one qualified candidate over another on the basis of the credential, the employer should ask to see (and photocopy for the files) the diplomas and certificates that relate to these credentials.

Many recreation providers take the additional step of requiring candidates to undergo a police records check (in the case of volunteers, a police check may be required instead of references). A police check involves a search of police records in a particular place or places (never everywhere) for current public information about the candidate. If police records checks are conducted, they should be conducted according to an explicit policy that doesn't single out individuals. Applicants should be advised in advance that a police records check is required, a step that can have the added benefit of allowing applicants to self-screen: potential applicants who know they will not pass the police check are unlikely to proceed with a job application.

A police records check has important limitations:

- It is valid only up to the date of the search (a police check conducted two years ago will not show an offence committed last month);

- Many places allow the retrieval of information relating only to certain "designated offences" (usually crimes that would make a person unsuitable for a position of trust and authority over children).

- Many police record-keeping systems allow for the removal of records relating to the period before a person turned 18 years old.

- Most standard police checks reveal only information about criminal convictions, and do not reveal other details about engagement with the criminal system. For instance, if a person is investigated but not charged with a crime, there is no record; if a person is charged but acquitted of a crime, there is no record; and if a person is convicted but later pardoned, there is no record.

- A police check applies only to the jurisdiction in which it is requested. In other words, if a potential employee committed a designated offence in a different place than the one in which she applies for a job, the police check will reveal nothing.

It's also important for potential employers to remember that most human rights codes prohibit discrimination against employees on the basis of their record of offences, except when such discrimination is necessary to fulfill a true occupational requirement. Consider, for example, the charge of simple possession of marijuana (non-trafficking possession). Where a conviction on this fairly common charge appears on the criminal record of a young man applying for a filing job at a community recreation centre, it would be difficult to exclude the applicant on the basis that a perfectly clear criminal record is a true occupational requirement for a filing job. If, however, the young man were applying instead to coach in an after-school basketball program for inner-city youth, the employer might be justified in preferring applicants with no evidence of any connection to local drug trafficking networks. Very often, a person may not have an absolutely clean record, but may nevertheless be suitable for many kinds of employment.

Before conducting any police checks, employers should decide which kinds of criminal offences are incompatible with the actual requirements of a particular position. This step, which can be documented in writing, signed, dated, and kept on file, may minimize allegations of discrimination based on criminal records.

Like all other information about potential employees, the results of a police records check must be held in strict confidence, filed securely, and destroyed when they are no longer needed.

Employers must screen not only employees but also volunteers and, in some cases, contractors. Some recreation providers feel hesitant to subject volunteers to screening because they are unpaid. This is a mistake. If screening is conducted fairly, with courtesy, and with respect for privacy, reasonable volunteers who care about the populations they serve will not object. A useful guide for screening volunteers has been prepared by Sport Safe, a multi-partner safety initiative. Sport Safe's volunteer-screening model is published by the government of British Columbia.

Finally, it is important for all recreation providers to remember that even thorough screening cannot prevent all incidents. Every abuser has a first time, and it's possible that the recreation provider will be the first to provide a potential abuser with the opportunity to harm someone. Good screening must always be supplemented with good training and supervision.

DUTY TO TRAIN AND SUPERVISE

Duty to Train

Employers often view paid training as economically unproductive, and therefore devote insufficient time to it. This approach, however, is short sighted and can lead to lost productivity—and lawsuits—in the long run. As explained in Chapter 4, Risk Management I: Identifying and Reducing Risk, program staff often have the greatest responsibility for communicating risks, a task that lies at the heart of risk management. Unless staff know and understand the risks associated with the recreation they provide, and know and understand how to communicate these risks, they will not be in a position to protect participants and the future of the organization.

Well-trained staff benefit any organization by:

- helping to build a polished image for the organization;

- attracting discerning clients;

- retaining satisfied customers;

- permitting the organization to offer advanced-level recreation, which is often more profitable than basic services;

- being easy to supervise;

- taking pride in their work and identifying with the organization's goals and values; and

- protecting the safety of participants.

Providing current and comprehensive training for all staff and volunteers (including seasonal staff) is never a wasted investment for any organization, and can contribute in a very measurable way to limiting liability. Good training should include the following general features:

- Training should be specific to the job, the activity, the premises, and the organization.

- It should be documented.

- Efforts to assess trainee comprehension should be made and documented.

- Content should be current.

- Refresher training and training to support new activities, initiatives, or equipment should be provided.

The organization should welcome trainees' comments about the training. In particular, it should be open to comments that suggest that the training is inadequate, confusing, or not sufficiently relevant to job duties.

Finally, training needn't flow only from the top down. Organizations that are safety leaders often provide opportunities for staff to share experiences and best practices in team meetings. (Staff should always be reminded to adequately protect the confidentiality of clients during these meetings.) Discussing problems that have arisen and the strengths and weaknesses of the organization's responses is a useful way of making up for new employees' lack of personal experience with the challenges of their work.

Duty to Supervise

Recreation staff require supervision in addition to screening and training. Good supervision can help reduce the risk of accidents and wrongdoing in several ways:

- by eliminating opportunities for private interactions between staff and clients;

- by providing support to staff dealing with problems such as belligerent participants;

- by providing backup in an emergency—for example, by supervising the rest of the participants while the program staff person deals with an injured or disruptive individual, or by calling 911;

- by providing an opportunity to observe problematic staff behaviour—for example, by noticing that a staff person hugs or touches participants;

■ by providing a witness to interactions between staff and participants, which can minimize participant fabrication or exaggeration of events; and

■ by providing a second opinion, backed up by experience—for example, a supervisor may wish to challenge a staff person's decision to allow a harassing client to continue to participate.

All employers have a statutory duty to supervise their *employees*. In Ontario, for example, section 25(2) of the *Occupational Health and Safety Act* states that an employer must "provide ... supervision to a worker to protect the health or safety of the worker." What constitutes adequate supervision varies from workplace to workplace. If an employee is doing work that creates little risk to herself and affords no opportunity to harm vulnerable participants, having a supervisor who looks in several times a day and is available by telephone or by walking down the hall may be fine. However, if staff perform risky work, closer supervision or, in some cases, constant supervision may be warranted.

Similar factors influence the duty of staff to supervise *participants*. Child participants (anyone under the age of 18), participants with cognitive deficits, and participants who have physical limitations that make it difficult to avoid risks must be continually supervised. Adult participants doing dangerous activities also require constant supervision. Adult participants performing very low-risk activities may not require continual supervision, but they should always know where and how to contact staff in the event of an emergency.

Failure to supervise participants has formed the basis of, or been a factor in, successful claims against organizations. For example, in the case of *Lam v. University of Windsor*, the university and two judo instructors associated with a judo club based there were found liable for a serious injury (quadriplegia) suffered by an unsupervised judo participant. In *Lam*, the court found the instructors liable even though the injured athlete—who was an adult and experienced—knew that the class was over and that he was sparring unsupervised, as was common practice at the club.

In finding the defendants liable, the court held that it was reasonable to expect that the risk of injury to the plaintiff was enhanced by the lack of supervision. Had the activity been supervised by an expert instructor, the plaintiff would likely have been prevented from sparring in the way he did with an inexperienced opponent who outweighed him by 40 to 50 pounds. The court found that the defendant instructors had a duty to provide constant supervision when students were in the class, even after the instructor had formally "bowed out" to end the class. It also found that the university, as occupier, had a duty to be aware of the activities taking place on its grounds, and to ensure that activities such as judo were conducted under competent supervision.

In developing policies to govern their facilities and programs, recreation providers must devote focused attention to the issue of supervision, and make determinations about the appropriate level of supervision for each recreational activity and/or group. They must also develop policies with respect to the minimum qualifications for supervisors.

KEY TERMS

contractors

employer's liability

interpersonal harm

non-delegable duty rule

ordinary course of business

respondeat superior

REVIEW EXERCISES

Review Questions

1. Under what circumstances is an employer automatically liable for harm that flows from the actions of staff?

2. List at least three circumstances that can limit employer liability for staff actions.

3. How does an employer's vicarious liability for staff actions differ from a typical case of employer's liability?

4. List some of the factors that support a finding of vicarious liability against an employer.

5. Can a recreation provider be held directly or vicariously liable for the wrongful actions of volunteers?

6. Can a recreation provider be held directly or vicariously liable for the wrongful actions of independent contractors?

7. How can recreation providers limit their exposure to liability for emotional, physical, and sexual abuse of participants?

8. How can recreation providers limit the likelihood that participants will suffer harassment or abuse at the hands of other participants?

9. Can a mandatory police records check satisfy all a recreation provider's screening objectives?

10. How can providing appropriate supervision benefit a recreation provider?

Discussion Question

Reliable staff are essential in a recreation business. However, many tourism businesses tend to hire students, young people, and/or seasonal staff. How do you feel about this trend? Why?

CHAPTER 8

Equipment and Products Law

CHAPTER OBJECTIVES

After completing this chapter, you should be able to:

- understand the basic principles of consumer protection and product liability law;

- explain the function of product safety standards, and how they are developed and recognized;

- describe a recreation provider's duties to participants who are using inherently dangerous equipment;

- list the considerations that apply to recreation providers who make equipment available for use by participants;

- list the considerations that apply to recreation providers who do not make equipment available to participants, but who require its use; and

- understand how a recreation provider can compel a manufacturer or supplier of equipment to assume a fair share of liability in the event of an accident.

INTRODUCTION

The equipment used in much modern recreation has undergone an incredible evolution over the past century and a half. User demands for improved performance—and willingness to pay for upgrades—have stimulated innovation. Equipment that was once passed down from grandparents to parents to children (for example, a pair of snowshoes or ice skates) is now often deemed obsolete after a few seasons of use. In some cases, changes to equipment are slight, and affect performance very little. Consider, for example, a tent that is advertised as weighing 15 percent less than its predecessor. In other cases, an innovation can spark a great leap forward: for example, the curved or shaped skis introduced in the 1990s made it markedly easier for beginners to learn how to ski.

Constant upgrading of equipment is not always necessary and can place a financial burden on recreation participants; however, improvements in *safety* make the regular replacement of equipment a worthwhile investment for recreation providers who make equipment available for their clients. Changes in safety standards should be monitored from a policy standpoint. When a safety innovation represents a marked improvement, recreation providers who *don't* furnish equipment may want to consider adopting a policy that requires participants to invest in equipment that meets modern standards. Common examples of participant-supplied equipment include: helmets for hockey, cycling, motor sports, skateboarding, horseback riding, or snowboarding; personal flotation devices for boating or watersports; and gear for scuba diving.

When an accident happens in the course of an activity for which safety gear exists, the adequacy of the gear is almost always scrutinized in any determination of liability. Providing gear that meets modern standards, or enforcing a policy that requires the use of such gear, can help to assure that liability is shared by everyone responsible for the accident, including negligent manufacturers or suppliers.

CONSUMER PROTECTION AND PRODUCT LIABILITY

Introduction

Whenever one party buys anything from another party, a contractual relationship is formed. Historically, the law applied the principle of "buyer beware" to these contracts, requiring purchasers of goods to investigate the goods and their suitability before buying them.

However, this approach sometimes operated unfairly, because the purchaser is in a poorer position than the supplier to determine the quality and fitness of the goods. Also, purchasers—especially individual purchasers—often had less negotiating power than suppliers, who were often large manufacturers or retailers.

For these and other reasons, the law began to build in protections (mostly codified in statutes) for consumers. Protective legislation includes the following: provincial legislation such as the Ontario *Sale of Goods Act*, which inserts certain basic conditions into goods-for-cash transactions, the *Consumer Protection Act, 2002*, and the *Electronic Commerce Act, 2000*; and the federal *Competition Act*, which prevents certain anti-competitive practices. Consumer protection legislation is much broader than sale of goods legislation because it applies not only to contracts for goods, but also to contracts for services.

Finally, because consumers don't always have a contractual relationship with the manufacturers or suppliers of the goods that they use, a branch of tort law called product liability has developed. Product liability law allows consumers harmed by defective products to sue the parties responsible.

Because the *Competition Act* does not apply to transactions between suppliers (including manufacturers) and customers, it is not discussed in detail here; however, recreation providers should know that the government makes some attempt to ensure that consumers have access to a range of goods from a variety of suppliers.

Sale of goods legislation, consumer protection legislation, and product liability law are all introduced below.

Sale of Goods Legislation

As a recreation provider, unless you are in the business of selling anything, you need not study sale of goods statutes in detail; however, it's important to understand that the law offers protection against sellers who:

- sell things they are not authorized to sell,

- sell things that do not conform to the description provided in the selling process,

- sell things that do not match samples provided in the selling process,

- sell goods that are not of "merchantable quality" (this can include fairly low-quality goods), or

- sell goods that are not reasonably fit for the purpose for which the buyer intends them *if the seller is aware of the buyer's purpose.*

In the context of recreation, fitness for purpose, the last of the **implied sales conditions** listed above, is likely the most important. An example of a case involving fitness for purpose is one in which an organizer of an outdoor event (for example, a "rib fest" cook-off in a city park) orders banners and signage from a printing company. The event organizer makes it clear that the banners and signs are needed for outdoor use, but the supplier provides signs painted in non-waterproof paint. If the paint runs at the first sign of rain, rendering the banners illegible, the purchaser will likely be able to successfully argue that the goods were not fit for their intended purpose.

implied sales conditions
terms inserted into contracts for the sale of goods by statutes such as the *Sale of Goods Act*

If a buyer claims successfully that a seller has violated a condition implied by sale of goods legislation, the buyer can generally **repudiate** the contract. When repudiating a contract, a buyer has two options: (1) she may refuse to accept the goods (and refuse to pay for them) or (2) if the defect was not apparent on inspection and becomes apparent after the goods have been accepted, she may sue for the return of her payment.

repudiate
reject

Sale of goods legislation has some limitations:

- it doesn't apply to the sale of services or to the sale of land;

- it doesn't apply to barter transactions (transactions in which money does not change hands); and

- it depends on the existence of a contract between the parties (therefore, if a buyer buys from a retailer, the buyer has no recourse against the *manufacturer* if something is wrong with the goods).

Consumer Protection Legislation

APPLICATION

Consumer protection legislation overcomes some of the limitations of sale of goods legislation. It applies not only to transactions for goods but also to transactions for services (except for certain kinds of professional services, such as legal or accounting services).

However, consumer protection law has a significant limitation for recreation providers: it defines a "consumer" as "an individual acting for personal, family, or household purposes and does not include a person who is acting for business purposes." This means that the protections afforded by this kind of legislation do not benefit a recreation provider directly; instead, they protect the recreation provider's clients.

The fact that consumer protection is for consumers, not for recreation providers, often forms part of a provider's rationale for deciding not to furnish clients with personal protective equipment. Instead, many recreation providers require that participants supply their own gear. However, there are some instances in which this requirement is impractical. For example, consider a go-kart operator, who provides recreation that is usually enjoyed on a one-time or occasional basis. The go-kart operator would likely lose business if it had to turn away riders who had not thought to bring a helmet, or who brought helmets that the provider feared were not acceptable for the purpose of go-karting. For this kind of recreation provider, purchasing and furnishing equipment is unavoidable. Fortunately, product liability law, which is discussed later in this chapter, allows consumers to sue suppliers and manufacturers of substandard equipment.

NO CONTRACTING OUT

In recognition of the fact that individual consumers have less bargaining power than corporations, the Ontario *Consumer Protection Act, 2002* makes it illegal to contract out of the implied conditions imposed by the *Sale of Goods Act*. Businesses are considered to be able to negotiate contracts that serve their interests, which, in some cases, means contracts that waive the application of sale of goods conditions. However, any attempt by a seller to contract out of these conditions when dealing with a consumer is not recognized by the courts.

NO FALSE ADVERTISING OR REPRESENTATIONS

The *Consumer Protection Act, 2002* further protects consumers by making it illegal for sellers of goods or services to make false, misleading, or deceptive representations about their products or about the fitness of their products for their purposes. Section 14 of the legislation lists several specific kinds of representations that are forbidden. It is illegal, for example, for a seller to allege that goods have performance characteristics that they do not, in fact, have. This means that a seller cannot advertise that its basketball shoes allow wearers to jump 50 percent higher, unless this advantage has been proven in formal, widely accepted scientific studies. The prohibition against making misleading representations about performance characteristics can provide comfort to purchasers, especially when it comes to safety equipment. If a reputable manufacturer claims that its equipment decreases the risk of injury, the consumer can be reasonably certain that the claim is supported by research.

The *Consumer Protection Act, 2002* also bans certain sales and contracting practices that are so unfair to the consumer that they are unconscionable. Examples of such practices are set out in section 15 of the legislation, but the list is not intended to be exclusive. Other practices that sellers may invent in the future will also violate the law if a court deems them to be unconscionable. One example of an unconscionable transaction mentioned in section 15 is a situation in which an uninformed consumer is sold goods or services at a price that grossly exceeds the standard price range for similar goods and services. Consider, for example, a tourist on a spa vacation who is so delighted with his thermal seaweed body wrap that he allows the esthetician to talk him into buying a small jar of the seaweed concoction for $250. If the product is simply a repackaged version of an almond oil and kelp mixture that is readily available at drugstores for $12.99 per jar, the consumer may be able to allege that the transaction was unconscionable.

REMEDIES

Consumers who have been treated unfairly have a year from the date of the transaction to give notice to the seller that they are repudiating the sales contract. Sometimes this notice prompts the seller to refund the consumer's money.

If the seller does not respond within 30 days, however, the consumer can bring a lawsuit for damages against the seller. The consumer can claim not only compensation but also **punitive damages**, an amount designed to penalize the seller for its outrageous behaviour.

In addition to lawsuits, consumers can bring complaints against unscrupulous sellers. These complaints can lead to fines—or even, in rare cases, imprisonment—for sellers.

punitive damages
sum that may be added to a damages award to compensate a plaintiff for a defendant's outrageous conduct

Product Liability Law

INTRODUCTION

Product liability law differs from consumer protection law on a very significant front: it is based not on contract law, but on tort law. If a consumer can prove that defects in a supplier's product caused harm, the consumer may sue the supplier *even though there is no contract between them.*

There are many instances in which a consumer may use a product that he did not purchase directly from the party (usually the manufacturer) responsible for the quality and safety of the product. For example, most consumers buy goods from retailers and other distributors, not directly from manufacturers. The *Consumer Protection Act, 2002*, already discussed, usually applies to these transactions and allows the consumer to rescind unfair transactions.

However, in many cases, an honest retailer sells a product to a consumer in the course of a reasonable and fair transaction in which neither party is aware that the product has a dangerous defect. Historically, when such a defect emerged and later harmed the consumer, the consumer was barred from suing the manufacturer because there was no contractual relationship between the two of them.

The obvious unfairness of this situation led to the development of product liability law. This branch of tort law imposes liability on the manufacturers of defective or dangerous products. These manufacturers are obliged to compensate anyone they can reasonably foresee using the product, whether or not the user bought the product from them.

Product liability law is significant for recreation providers because it distributes the responsibility for accidents equitably among all the parties who are at fault. Many recreation-related injuries are caused by equipment failure, or by a combination

product liability
subcategory of tort law based on a defendant's liability for harm caused to others as a result of its defective or dangerous products

of factors *including* equipment failure. Product liability law allows consumers to sue the manufacturers of problem equipment.

The liability relief offered to recreation providers by product liability law is indirect because product liability lawsuits must be brought by the injured party (the recreation participant). For example, consider the position of an operator of a go-kart facility who purchases a supply of helmets to be worn by go-kart riders. If a rider is injured because a helmet fails to offer the expected protection in a crash, the go-kart operator (who will likely be faced with a lawsuit for damages) cannot rely on consumer protection legislation in a lawsuit of his own against the helmet manufacturer or supplier. Instead, if the go-kart operator hopes to require the helmet manufacturer to share in liability for the customer's injuries, he must hope that the customer names the helmet manufacturer as a **co-defendant**. (In practice, these hopes are almost always fulfilled because the plaintiff's lawyer will strongly encourage the plaintiff to add the helmet manufacturer as a defendant. The manufacturer, which is likely to be found liable, will probably be in a better financial position to satisfy a judgment than the small go-kart operator would be.)

co-defendant
two or more defendants in the same case

Faulty helmet cases enjoy a fairly prominent place in product liability law. A well-known example is the second-hand helmet case of *Thomas v. Bell Helmets Inc.* In *Thomas*, a motorcyclist suffered irreversible and severe brain damage when he was involved in a crash while wearing a second-hand helmet. Even though the motorcyclist did not purchase the helmet from the defendant manufacturer, the manufacturer was found 25 percent liable for the motorcyclist's injuries. The main reason that the manufacturer was liable was that it either knew or should have known that there was a risk of injury to wearers from the helmet being knocked off on impact. The court found that the helmet should have displayed a warning (on the helmet itself and not on the original box), and/or instructions about how to conduct a "roll-off" test to evaluate a proper fit.

INHERENTLY DANGEROUS GOODS

Some otherwise harmless or helpful goods are dangerous as a result of a design flaw or a manufacturing defect. There is a duty on the manufacturer of any such goods to recall them or to warn users as soon as the problem becomes apparent.

However, certain other goods, even when well designed and properly manufactured, pose significant risks to consumers. Examples include: tools (from power tools to pocket knives), chemicals, inflammable goods, goods that can explode, and vehicles. Because of the "thrill value" in certain recreational pursuits, many kinds of sporting goods are also considered to be dangerous goods: consider, for example, hunting rifles, windsurfing equipment, pommel horses, and even the lowly skateboard.

If a consumer product is inherently dangerous, unless the danger is absolutely obvious, the manufacturer has a duty to warn consumers—including second-hand consumers—of the risks associated with the product.

Warning users can be challenging because in many cases the user and the manufacturer never meet. For this reason, most manufacturers of dangerous goods rely on labels to convey warnings. Effective warning labels appear on the goods themselves, not on the packaging, because the packaging may be long gone before a user ever gets her hands on the product.

To protect consumers, recreation providers who furnish equipment should ensure that warning labels are intact. If possible, they should also draw users' attention to these labels. In practice, warnings about equipment are often delivered as part of general warnings about dangerous activities. For example, a ski instructor usually advises students that pointing their ski tips directly downhill will result in rapid downward progress. The instructor does not generally add that the reason for this is that the undersides of skis are designed to minimize the friction that usually holds human feet in one place on snow.

Recognizing these realities, courts have held that where a risk is already known to a user, or is widely known in the community, failing to spell out this risk on every possible occasion does not lead to liability. For example, all adults with normal cognitive abilities know that knives cut. A cooking class instructor will not likely be held liable for failing to warn students of this risk every time they pick up a knife (though a general warning about knives may be advisable at the first class). Likewise, knife manufacturers are not faulted for failing to label the blades of all of their knives with the warning: Beware, this can cut.

The same principles apply to dangerous sports. Most individuals are aware that "extreme sports" are so labelled because they come with a potential for injury. Visual inspection of such things as skis, surfboards, in-line skates, skateboards, unicycles, and hang gliders leads most observers to understand that, especially in the absence of skill and experience, these things cause falls, and falls cause hurt. While most recreation providers do warn participants even when the risks of an activity are obvious, the law acknowledges that competent adult participants approach these sports, to some extent, at their own risk.

The less obvious the risk of an activity, the greater the duty to warn. For example, there have been cases in which horseback riders have successfully sued riding establishments over accidents that occurred when an apparently calm horse suddenly bolted when it was startled by a loud sound. Also, some equipment—all-terrain vehicles are a good example—lead to injury at a most unexpected rate. Other equipment leads to injuries that are unpredictable in nature or attracts a different category of participants than you might expect. Consider, for example, the sobering statistic that 44 percent of non-traffic fatalities involving children and cars occur when a car backs over a child who is outside the car and not visible to the driver.

The reasoning behind a supplier's duty to warn a consumer about a product's risks was summarized in *Lambert v. Lastoplex Chemicals Co.*:

> [T]he duty to warn is imposed due to the recognition that an imbalance of knowledge between the parties fundamentally affects the relationship between them. Where a danger is known or ought to be known to the supplier, but would not be known to the consumer, the duty to warn arises.

This principle was applied in *Rozenhart v. Skier's Sport Shop (Edmonton) Ltd.*, which was discussed in Chapter 1 under the heading "Striving for Balance Between Risks and Benefits." *Rozenhart* dealt with an injury to a person who had rented in-line skates, put them on while awaiting his instructor, and injured himself while attempting to brake. The court considered a supplier's duty to warn a user (in this case, the supplier was the sports store that had provided the rental skates). It found that the rental clerk did not have a duty to explain the braking system for the skates because the system was about to be explained in the lesson the client had booked. The client knew enough about in-line skating to understand that there were differences between in-line skating and ice-skating (which he knew how to do), and that there were risks involved.

Recreation providers need to be aware that, in many cases, they will fall within the definition of "suppliers" of dangerous goods. As suppliers, they are required to warn users about risks, especially when the dangers posed by equipment are not widely known or readily discernible.

SAFETY STANDARDS

Bringing a safe product to market benefits everyone: consumers are protected from injury, and manufacturers are protected from lawsuits. For this reason, manufacturers, safety associations, and governments devote time and money to the tasks of reviewing and testing products from the perspective of safety. Out of this process flow safety standards—minimum specifications and guidelines—designed to protect the consumer.

compulsory standards
standards for products that are mandated by legislation

Some products, such as the following, have **compulsory standards** backed by legislation:

- elevating devices;

- amusement park rides;

- drugs and some medical equipment;

- many foods;

- baby cribs, cradles, car seats, and other baby gear;

- buses, cars, motorcycles, snowmobiles, and all-terrain vehicles;

- boilers; and

- helmets for use on motorcycles or snowmobiles.

voluntary standards
standards developed and accepted by industry leaders that are not enforceable in law

Other products have voluntary standards. **Voluntary standards** are developed and accepted by industry leaders, and are designed to assist manufacturers in producing safe goods. They are not enforceable under the law; however, knowledge of these standards by consumers can help to guide purchasing choices.

Standard-setting organizations play an important role in communicating standards to the public and helping consumers choose safe goods. Examples of standard-setting organizations include:

- the Canadian Standards Association,

- the National Research Council Canada,

- the Standards Council of Canada,

- the Ontario Electrical Safety Authority,

- the Canadian Centre for Occupational Health and Safety,

- the Technical Standards and Safety Authority, and

- the American National Standards Institute.

Recreation providers should educate themselves about the safety standards, both compulsory and voluntary, that apply to the equipment that they provide to clients. In addition, they should make a commitment to purchase and offer for use only equipment that meets the most recent safety standards. Member associations involved in the particular kind of recreation that the provider offers can be helpful in supplying information about equipment standards and safety.

Using equipment that meets industry standards helps to minimize liability for recreation providers in case of equipment-related accidents.

PROVIDED EQUIPMENT

Introduction

Although there are some liability pitfalls, many recreation providers, especially those who offer one-time or occasional thrills, cannot avoid the need to make equipment available for use by clients. When deciding whether or not to provide equipment, recreation providers should consider whether potential clients would be deterred from participating by the need to supply their own equipment. In making this determination, a recreation provider will likely consider the cost of the equipment and industry standards. There is a clear business disadvantage, for example, to being the only roller-skating rink in the province that does not rent roller skates!

If the equipment is fairly inexpensive, and some participants make many repeat visits, recreation providers can attempt to shift some of the equipment liability risks to participants by charging a rental fee. This practice also helps to offset some of the recreation provider's costs, and can make it possible to upgrade equipment. Examples of recreation providers that often charge rental fees include:

- ice- and roller-skating rinks,

- ski resorts,

- surfing schools,

- bowling alleys, and

- scuba-diving schools.

A rental arrangement allows the occasional or beginner participant to have access to an activity without an initial outlay of money for equipment. Renting basic (but safe and serviceable) equipment makes it likely that beginners who become enthusiasts will eventually buy their own higher-performance gear and adopt the risks related to its use.

Recreation providers who are less likely to attract repeat customers are also less likely to charge rental fees, and more likely to roll the equipment costs into a higher overall participation fee. Examples of these kinds of providers include:

- whitewater-rafting companies,

- bungee-jumping facilities,

- sailing schools, and

- parachute schools.

CASE STUDY

No Safe Equipment Without Safe Operators: Enslev v. Challenges Unlimited

Enslev was a case tried in the fall of 2007 in Ontario. It involved a claim by a young woman who suffered very serious injuries in a fall from a swing on a "challenge course." The woman fell when the loop that secured her safety harness to the pendulum swing failed. The loop failed because the webbing from which it was made was weakened and cut because of friction from a "lazy line," a device used to return the harness to its starting position after the rider dismounted. The contact between the lazy line and the loop occurred because of operator error in routing the lazy line.

The victim brought a lawsuit against the resort that offered the swing ride, and against the company that installed the challenge course at the resort. The contract between the two defendants, the resort and the supplier, contained a waiver: the resort management agreed that:

> the risk of use of the Equipment shall be the sole responsibility of the Client [the resort]. For greater certainty, the Contractor [the supplier] assumes no liability for injury, loss or damage to any person or property, however caused, resulting from the equipment and materials and any authorized or unauthorized use of the Equipment.

The contract also provided that the resort was responsible for training operators of the equipment, and the resort did so with the help of a consultant and a trainer knowledgeable in the field.

After reviewing the evidence, the court held that the resort was 100 percent liable for the plaintiff's injuries, and that the supplier was not liable. In finding only the resort liable, the court held that "[a] manufacturer cannot escape liability simply because the defect only causes injury when coupled with the negligence or other wrongdoing of the user or third party." However, there was nothing wrong with the equipment. The cutting of the loop by the lazy line was not reasonably foreseeable to the supplier (there had been no other accidents in 450,000 use cycles of similar equipment across Canada). Therefore, there was no duty on the supplier to build in a feature that would have prevented this accident. The court quoted the following statement of the limitations of product liability law from *Canadian Tort Law*, a well-respected legal textbook (Linden & Feldhusen, 2006, p. 642):

> The law does not impose strict liability on manufacturers so they are liable for all injuries caused by their goods no matter what the circumstances nor does it require a manufacturer to produce articles which are accident proof or incapable of doing harm.
>
> The manufacturer is not an insurer of anyone who suffers injury while using or misusing a product.

In permitting its staff to set up and use the equipment improperly, the resort became entirely responsible for the plaintiff's injuries. For recreation providers, this decision is a sobering reminder that product liability law will not save a recreation provider from liability where an accident occurs because of its staff's improper use of otherwise safe equipment. ◇

Once a decision is made to provide equipment (whether for a fee or not), several new responsibilities arise. First, the recreation provider must choose a supplier and decide on the quality of equipment to buy. Next, the recreation provider must develop policies with respect to the maintenance, cleaning, and replacement of equipment.

Finally, the recreation provider must decide whether and how it will need to communicate with its clients about equipment risks.

Sometimes the equipment risks and the activity risks are more or less indistinguishable, as in the case of a bungee-jumping facility. If a recreation provider's general risk communication policies are adequate, they will usually satisfy the provider's duty to warn.

But consider a ski resort that rents skis, snowboards, and mini-skis. Because the risks vary depending on the user's choice of equipment, it will be necessary to provide separate equipment-related warnings. The rental transaction, if there is one, provides a good opportunity to communicate these warnings. The user can be asked to sign a rental agreement that contains a warning (or even a waiver), and the attendant can direct the renter's attention to the warning and ask whether the renter understands the risks.

If there is no rental transaction, program staff will need to orient users to the equipment and this orientation must include a summary of risks.

In a situation with no interaction between equipment users and program staff, such as an unattended, coin-operated batting cage, signage can be used to communicate risk. This option, however, is inferior from a liability standpoint. Unless an activity is risk-free or very low-risk, such as using coin-operated telescopes for bird-watching, there should always be an attendant available to answer participants' questions. In all cases, program staff should be well trained and knowledgeable about the features of the equipment, and should be able to communicate all risks and safety procedures accurately.

How Good Must It Be?

When choosing equipment, recreation providers should offer only limited opportunity for the user to tamper with sizing or settings. As well, it should consider safety, quality, durability, and performance. Equipment appropriate for public use should be:

- durable,
- easy to put on and remove,
- simple to operate,
- easy to clean, and
- compliant with the latest safety standards.

High performance is often *not* a priority when it comes to selecting rental equipment, partly because the operator may wish to encourage enthusiasts to invest in their own gear.

Remember that as soon as equipment is purchased, it begins to go out of date. Some kinds of equipment become dated faster than others, especially if a sport is undergoing a great deal of change. Where equipment does *not* become obsolete quickly, durability is a key concern for providers. Spending extra money on durable equipment may mean that the equipment will remain in good working order for several seasons.

It is generally not necessary to replace equipment every time there is an innovation. However, there is one exception: where the innovation significantly improves *safety*, a recreation provider must invest in the improved product if she wants to limit liability.

When Upgrades Are Not Affordable

In some cases, a recreation provider is faced with a situation in which equipment that is expensive and in good working order falls short of new safety standards, but there is no money in the budget to replace it. This problem has recently plagued many providers of children's playground equipment. Standards for playground equipment have evolved rapidly in recent years because new research has pinpointed many equipment-related causes of injuries. To make matters more complicated, safety research about playground equipment has shown that equipment that is safe and appropriate for older children may *not* be safe for younger children, and vice versa.

Faced with the knowledge that existing equipment falls short of cutting-edge standards and that funds are unavailable for new equipment, these providers are forced to make decisions about whether to tear down or fence off play structures that are still in good condition. It is often public schools or municipalities who face these choices, and inevitably the results of these decisions are criticized. Where equipment is torn down or placed off limits, parents cannot understand why their kids no longer have access to serviceable equipment that was enjoyed uneventfully for many years. However, if older equipment is allowed to remain in place, the fact that a recreation provider knew that it fell below modern standards is guaranteed to be raised by any litigant hurt on the equipment.

Analogous situations also arise in other recreational contexts. Deciding between obsolete equipment and no equipment at all is unpleasant. However, for the recreation provider who is serious about his moral duty to participants, the choice is simple: *if it isn't safe, it shouldn't be used*. In the wake of a serious injury or death, a recreation provider will get no sympathy for alleging that he could not afford to protect participants. A recreation business that cannot afford safe equipment is a business that cannot afford to operate. Where the removal of obsolete equipment provokes an angry response, the users who complain should be encouraged to donate to a fund dedicated to raising money for replacement equipment.

Maintenance

When budgeting for equipment and developing policies for its use, recreation providers sometimes overlook the essential issue of maintenance. All equipment, no matter how simple, requires regular maintenance. A good program of maintenance includes:

- regular inspection;
- regular testing of equipment to which performance standards apply (such as dive tanks);
- an assessment of any hazards and a plan for dealing with them in order of their severity;

- immediate elimination of serious hazards (if they can't be eliminated, the equipment must be taken out of service);

- a plan of action and a deadline for dealing with lesser hazards (for example, peeling paint on park benches, thinning gravel cover on trails);

- regular replacement of consumable aspects of the equipment (for example, wheels on roller skates, or padding on amusement park rides);

- regular cleaning;

- sanitizing equipment that comes into contact with bodily fluids (for example, snorkelling gear) after every use; and

- providing appropriate storage conditions.

Recreation providers should be aware that poor maintenance is a more common cause of equipment-related accidents than defects or design flaws inherent in the equipment.

PARTICIPANT-PROVIDED EQUIPMENT

Introduction

If a participant will be enjoying a recreation activity on an ongoing basis—for example, by taking lessons or by joining a team or a club—it is quite common for recreation providers to require that the participant supply her own equipment. This is especially true when sharing equipment creates a hygiene risk (in the case of helmets, socks, athletic protectors, shoes, mouthguards, and breathing apparatus, for example), or when equipment must be custom-fitted to the participant.

Requiring that participants supply their own equipment puts recreation providers in the position of determining what equipment should—and shouldn't—be compulsory. In a few cases, these decisions are already made by lawmakers (for example, motorcycle helmets are mandated by law). In many other cases, the research that supports the use of particular pieces of equipment (such as hockey helmets, football mouthguards, and heeled horseback-riding boots) is so compelling that recreation providers have no trouble enforcing their equipment policies with respect to these items.

However, in some cases, enforcement can be a challenge, particularly in the case of newly introduced equipment. Protective equipment for skateboarding is a good example. Since the flourishing of skateboarding in the 1970s, many skateboarders have been wearing no safety equipment at all. Skateboarding developed in urban settings, often serving as a means of transportation to school or work. Early skateboarders used existing features (curbs, park benches, railings) as their playground. They developed a distinctive style of dress (slouchy pants and jackets; ball caps; wide, flat-bottomed shoes, often with loose laces; shaggy hair) that is quite incompatible with the helmets, knee pads, elbow pads, and wrist guards that are now highly recommended as protection against falls. Providers of dedicated skateboard facilities have had a great deal of difficulty enforcing equipment requirements. Many skateboard parks still enforce only helmet rules (and only if there happens to be a staff person available to supervise the park).

Similar fashion obstacles to equipment requirements are seen in other sports: for example, helmets are new to many skiers who have skied for decades. In hockey, young players often grumble about the face cages and neck guards that they are required to wear, but don't see on their pro hockey idols.

Faced with these complaints, recreation providers have the responsibility of investigating for themselves, using the best available data, exactly which pieces of equipment to require. If a piece of equipment provides an established measure of protection, it will be very difficult for a recreation provider to convince a court that there was a legitimate reason for not enforcing its use.

When to Require Upgrading

A policy that sets out required equipment, like any other policy, cannot simply be developed and then ignored. Advances in safety continue to be made, and there will eventually come a time when it will be necessary to require users to upgrade outdated equipment.

This task is easier if industry standards exist. When a new standard is developed, a sticker confirming that a piece of equipment complies with the new standard may be affixed to the equipment. A recreation provider can then enforce its policy by reference to the standard—for example, by requiring all hockey players to wear helmets bearing the "CSA mark XXXX."

Should You Inspect Participant Gear?

An interesting and thorny issue in recreation is whether recreation providers should inspect participant gear for safety. In support of inspection are the following arguments:

- Recreation providers want participants to be safe (from a moral and a liability standpoint).

- Recreation providers often have knowledge about the adequacy of equipment that is superior to the knowledge of participants.

- Recreation providers inspect their own premises and equipment anyway so it is logical that they should inspect participant-provided equipment.

There are, however, valid arguments against the inspection of participants' equipment:

- It's time-consuming.

- Many equipment defects, fit problems, and wear-and-tear damages are not readily visible on casual inspection.

- The recreation provider may not be qualified to determine the safety of equipment.

- By inspecting and approving participant gear, the recreation provider may actually be guaranteeing the safety of the equipment, and the participant may be entitled to rely on this guarantee when using the equipment. This situation can lead to liability for the provider later.

Despite these liability pitfalls, some recreation providers feel morally obligated to check equipment, especially when it has been chosen by beginners and when its correct use is complicated. Consider, for example, scuba diving equipment (a scuba diving case is discussed in Chapter 9, Adventure Tourism and Other High-Risk Activities). A recreation provider who does inspect equipment should require participants to sign a waiver at the beginning of the program. This waiver should contain a statement that the recreation provider's inspection of equipment is simply a good-faith effort to detect obvious problems, and does *not* constitute any kind of guarantee or warranty that the participant-supplied equipment is in fact safe. As in the case of all waivers, the wording should be brought to the attention of participants by a staff person who is available to answer questions and to confirm that the participants understand what the waiver means.

Enforcing Equipment Policies

Once a policy concerning required equipment is in place, recreation providers must take steps to enforce it. The most natural enforcement rule is to exclude anyone who lacks a required piece of equipment from participation. If this rule seems harsh (for example, where a participant has simply forgotten to bring something), the recreation provider may wish to offer the one-time use of a piece of good quality provider-owned equipment. Where an individual continues to "forget to bring" his own equipment, the provider may wish to make discreet inquiries about whether the cost of the equipment is prohibitive to the participant; if this is the case, the organization may be able to provide subsidies.

KEY TERMS

co-defendant

compulsory standards

implied sales conditions

product liability

punitive damages

repudiate

voluntary standards

REVIEW EXERCISES

Review Questions

1. Why must recreation providers monitor new developments in equipment?

2. List three statutes relevant to the protection of consumers.

3. When purchasing equipment from a seller, how can a recreation provider bolster its *Sale of Goods Act* rights?

4. If consumer protection legislation is designed to protect users, not providers, why is it relevant to recreation providers?

5. What must recreation providers do to avoid falling afoul of consumer protection laws when they sell services to consumers?

6. What is the key distinction between product liability law under the common law, and the protections available to consumers under the *Consumer Protection Act, 2002*?

7. As a supplier of inherently dangerous goods, does a roller-skating rink operator who rents roller skates have a duty to warn participants about the dangers of these skates?

8. How can a recreation provider determine the minimum industry safety standards that apply to the equipment used in its programs or required by its equipment policies?

9. From a liability perspective, why is it better for a recreation provider to require participants to supply their own equipment?

10. What additional responsibilities does a recreation provider assume when it makes the decision to provide equipment?

11. Why might a provider offer rental equipment that falls short of cutting-edge performance standards?

12. How can a practice of inspecting participants' own equipment increase the liability risk for recreation providers?

Discussion Question

How have consumer protection legislation, sale of goods legislation, and product liability law created a legal environment in which liability for accidents is equitably shared between recreation providers and the suppliers of equipment?

CHAPTER 9

Adventure Tourism and Other High-Risk Activities

CHAPTER OBJECTIVES

After completing this chapter, you should be able to:

- understand the special liability challenges facing providers of high-risk recreation;

- explain the role of warnings and consumer education in high-risk tourism;

- explain the role of waivers as a risk-sharing tool;

- understand the limitations of waivers, and the factors that support and detract from their validity;

- explain the heightened responsibilities assumed by high-risk tourism staff, and the need to provide comprehensive training for individuals employed in these settings; and

- understand the role of public relations management in protecting the image and reputation of high-risk activity providers.

INTRODUCTION

Adventure tourism, which Transport Canada describes as including "a very wide range of activities that extends from heli-skiing to ocean kayaking," contributes approximately $2 billion to the Canadian economy every year.

Recreational activities enthusiastically described by marketers as "adventurous" and "extreme" (and cautiously described by lawyers and actuaries as "dangerous" and "high risk") appear to be gaining in popularity. This trend reveals a fascinating inverse relationship to society's increasing general emphasis on personal safety. Apparently, an increasingly safety-conscious world provokes in many people a desire to test their personal performance limits in situations that introduce an element of risk.

Since adventure tourism and extreme sports often require travel to remote locations or the use of specialized equipment, they can be expensive. Therefore, they tend to be marketed to people who have disposable income and who are willing to pay well for once-in-a-lifetime thrills. The potential for profit motivates many providers to offer these activities despite high liability risks and obstacles to obtaining insurance.

This chapter introduces high-risk recreation activities. It discusses what makes the risks involved in these activities high, how to reduce these risks, and how to limit liability related to intractable risks through the use of warnings and waivers. It also explains why the providers of high-risk activities must strive for excellence in consumer risk education, service, employee training, equipment fitness, and public relations.

DEFINING HIGH RISK

high-risk activity
an activity that is associated with frequent injuries, serious injuries, or both

Deciding how to define a **high-risk activity** is not as easy or as objective as it seems. In everyday parlance, certain sports have traditionally been viewed as "extreme" or involving a high degree of risk (consider heli-skiing, skydiving, high-altitude climbing, and mountaineering). Others, such as cycling or golf, have traditionally been considered leisure activities. These distinctions, however, relate more closely to a sport's image than to actual statistics. Cycling, for example, leads to many more injuries per year than skydiving, largely because participation in cycling is more common.

The nature of the injuries that can arise from an activity tends to skew our perception of overall risk. For example, we can easily imagine fatal consequences from a parachute jump in which the chute fails to open, but it's difficult to imagine circumstances that might lead to death on a golf course. When we think of skydiving accidents, we think of people plummeting to their deaths, and when we think of golf accidents, we think of aches and pains from the repetitive action of swinging a club. However, people die on golf courses every year as a result of lightning strikes; and the most common injury associated with skydiving is an ankle sprain.

A 2004 analysis performed by Loyola University Health System's Pietro Tonino, a doctor who studied US consumer product safety data, revealed the following highest-to-lowest ranking of some recreational activities based on the rate of non-fatal injuries treated in US emergency rooms:

1. basketball,
2. bicycles,
3. football,
4. soccer,
5. baseball,
6. swimming/diving,
7. softball,
8. trampolines,
9. skateboards,
10. weightlifting,

11. horseback riding,

12. volleyball,

13. golf,

14. in-line skating, and

15. roller-skating.

This list shows that we are much more likely to be hurt while enjoying accessible, affordable, everyday sporting activities than while trying an exotic extreme sport. It is also apparent that the economic impact of everyday sports injuries, in terms of health-care costs and lost work time, is likely much greater than the toll exacted by high-risk tourism.

One facet of extreme activities that may support the high-risk definition is the potential for fatal or catastrophic non-fatal injuries. While a fatal injury is a remote possibility in almost any sport, certain activities carry a risk of death or disability that is higher than the rate seen in most sports. Some recreational activities that carry a well-known and low but significant risk of fatal or catastrophic injury include:

- whitewater rafting;

- mountaineering and mountain climbing;

- skydiving and, in particular, base jumping;

- flying small, private planes;

- scuba and cave diving;

- cliff diving;

- bull riding;

- speed skiing; and

- street luging.

Activities in which the risks of fatal injury are *not* widely known, but are still significant, include:

- recreational boating (where a high percentage of deaths are the result of intoxication);

- trampolining;

- rockfishing; and

- cycling.

Sometimes an activity is advertised or defined as "adventure" or "extreme" not because it is particularly dangerous, but because it is exotic, unusual, or occurs in a remote location. Examples of these kinds of activities include:

- participating in other cultures' hunting, harvesting, or other activities—for example, spear fishing in the South Pacific;

- dogsledding or winter camping; and

- trekking in rainforests.

MANAGING RISKS

The Alpine Club of Canada

Many sport or activity-focused member associations collect statistics about accidents in a particular field, and develop recommendations about best practices that can help prevent future accidents.

The Alpine Club of Canada maintains a database of alpine accidents (hiking, climbing, mountaineering, skiing, and snowboarding, for example) organized by year, with possible causes listed. The club also makes recommendations, sorted by cause, for avoiding these mishaps. ◊

According to some analysts, such as sociologist Lori Holyfield of the University of Arkansas, some activities that are not very risky from an actuarial (statistics) standpoint are marketed as adventure activities because experiencing them as such appeals to consumers. As explained above, we live in a safety-focused society. One of the side effects of that focus is a drive, on the part of certain individuals, to inject a measure of risk or challenge into what they perceive as a boring, stifling, or conventional life. Some recreation providers cater to this consumer preference, offering commercialized adventure activities that, in many cases, have been designed to offer costly thrills but very little real risk.

SPECIAL RESPONSIBILITIES OF HIGH-RISK ACTIVITY PROVIDERS

Surprise! The providers of high-risk activities don't have any responsibilities that are distinct from those of the providers of less exotic activities. The legal rules that lead to liability for a provider are the same, regardless of the nature of the services provided. *Any* occupier of property is at least partly responsible for the safety of visitors to that property. And *any* person who creates a risk that could foreseeably threaten another person's safety has a duty to make reasonable efforts to warn and protect that person. It makes no qualitative difference in law whether a visitor or customer has come to a recreation business to watch birds or to wrestle alligators.

In fact, from at least one perspective, the providers of high-risk activities have a liability management advantage: consumers often already know that the activity offered is dangerous.

Any time a consumer willingly participates in an activity that she knows is risky, there is an automatic sharing of risk between the provider and the participant. While it is still essential for the provider to warn the consumer of the risks, and to confirm and document the consumer's informed consent, the law takes account of the fact that it is unfair to saddle providers with 100 percent of the burden of liability for the intractable risks that accompany dangerous activities.

A high-risk context requires no additions to the list of risk management steps that a recreation provider must take: identify risks, reduce manageable risks, insure against intractable risks, and communicate risks to participants. However, a high-risk context *does* warrant a "full court press" approach to each of these steps. For example, if risks can be reduced through the use of protective equipment, top quality equipment must be purchased, and its use must be strictly enforced. Insurance coverage

CASE STUDY

Anatomy of an Accident: Isildar v. Rideau Diving Supply

On June 7, 2003, 28-year-old husband, father, and hardware designer Ali Isildar drowned while attempting his first scuba "deep dive," a requirement for completion of the advanced open water (AOW) scuba training program offered by Rideau Diving Supply (RDS). Isildar's widow and child brought a lawsuit against various parties after the accident. Before trial, all claims were either dropped or settled except for the claim against RDS.

On June 7, after performing a night dive and a wreck dive (other AOW requirements) the day before, RDS took a group of seven student divers, two instructors, and one assistant by boat to a site in the St. Lawrence River known as the Belly Dumper. The water at this location was 85 feet deep, considerably deeper than the 60-foot depth deep-dive requirement. The water was very cold, and the bottom was silty.

The divers descended in groups, and because of their inexperience, the first group "thundered" to the bottom, causing a silt cloud in the area. When Isildar descended with his buddy, visibility was very poor. While swimming, Isildar kicked off his buddy's facemask. By the time the buddy replaced his mask, he could no longer find Isildar, and so he followed instructions and surfaced. The instructor, Sarah Dow, then descended to find Isildar. Dow discovered Isildar in a state of panic. He had removed his regulator and was grabbing at her regulator and mask. Dow returned to the surface for help. By the time other divers found and retrieved Isildar, he was dead or unconscious, and did not respond to CPR after being pulled from the water.

While the cause of Isildar's death was drowning, the specific cause of drowning was never determined. Isildar had enough air remaining in his tank to permit him to surface safely, and Dow had found him by following a trail of bubbles. However, cold water, silty conditions, pressure on the body and ears, and nitrogen narcosis (which affects some divers at depths below 60 feet) have all been known to cause a perception of air starvation on the part of divers. This perception can lead to overexertion, overbreathing, panic, and irrational behaviour.

In considering all the facts of the case, the court found that Dow was negligent in attempting the deep dive with her students because she had insufficient experience as an instructor. The court also found that her decision to surface for help amounted to poor judgment, since it is often more appropriate to wait near a panicked diver until the diver loses consciousness, after which the instructor has four or five minutes to raise the diver to the surface.

The court also found that the instructors were negligent in their choice of site for the deep dive, in failing to investigate site conditions (especially the silty bottom), and in their decisions about which instructor would supervise which students and which students would be paired as buddies.

Finally, the court found that RDS was negligent in allowing an instructor with Dow's limited experience to supervise students in a dive with the risk level that this dive entailed.

A well-drafted and clearly communicated release of liability (waiver) protected the company and its staff from liability in this case, even though the court made a clear finding of negligence against the defendant. Nevertheless, this case is very useful from a learning point of view: it demonstrates that it is possible for an accident to have not just one cause but a long list of possible causes. The relevant causes in this case are set out below.

Environmental/natural factors:

- excessive water depth for a beginner deep dive,
- very cold water temperatures,
- strong currents at the bottom, and
- an (unexpectedly) silty bottom.

Equipment factors:

- an inappropriate amount of lead weight carried by the diver and/or his buddy;
- lack of familiarity with rented equipment; and
- lack of familiarity, on the part of the diver's buddy, with unusual/outdated equipment.

Diver factors:

- early signs of Hashimoto's disease in the diver, which is sometimes characterized by anxiety;
- susceptibility of the diver to nitrogen narcosis; and
- trouble clearing the diver's ears (and the decision to dive anyway).

Instructor/personnel factors:

- lack of instructor experience with dive site,
- lack of instructor experience with diving and rescuing,
- too many students per instructor,
- lack of instructor training about dealing with panicked divers,
- lack of instructor experience with low visibility, and
- absence of a "clean diver" (diver with a full tank) on the boat to cope with emergencies.

Faced with such a long list of possible contributors to the accident, the court determined that the accident was caused by a chain of misfortunes that would not have been set in motion but for RDS's decision to put Sarah Dow and Chris Miller—inexperienced instructors—in charge of the AOW course.

This case makes it clear that while accidents can have multiple causes, a single poor decision on the part of a recreation provider can act as a catalyst for the interaction of risk factors, with tragic consequences. ◈

must be arranged at a level sufficient to satisfy the worst possible situations: multiple fatal injury or complete disability claims by young claimants with dependants. (The subject of insurance is discussed in detail in Chapter 4.) Communication of risks must be thorough and detailed, and participants' understanding of all risk information must be documented in writing. A recreation business must be so frank in its disclosure of risks that risk-averse participants will choose not to participate. Finally, in appropriate cases, waiver documents should be created and used to force participants to acknowledge their responsibility in risk-taking.

Strategies for communicating with participants about risks have been reviewed throughout this book. As you have learned, there are many ways to approach this task. At one end of the spectrum are self-serve techniques, such as signs, website notices, and small-print mentions in flyers and handouts. In the middle of the spectrum are techniques that include a step in which the recreation provider, through a staff member, draws participants' attention to the risk information.

At the most formal end of the risk communication spectrum are strategies in which a staff person directly communicates warnings, provides an opportunity for participants to ask questions, and obtains the participants' signed confirmation that they received and understood the risk disclosure. Ideally, these communications take place during one-to-one conversations with individual participants in which written supporting material is given to participants, and there is plenty of time for questions and answers.

Providers of high-risk activities should always choose risk communication strategies at this most formal end of the communication spectrum. The recreation provider should also regularly review what is actually happening between staff and participants: having a good risk communication policy is useless if staff are not complying with it.

Two obstacles that staff sometimes face are insufficient time with participants and participant impatience. Cutting back on communications, orientation, and participant education is not the answer to these problems. A provider of high-risk recreation must refuse to be pressured into the rushed delivery of services. Instead, the necessary time commitment should be communicated to the participant from the outset. For example, a skydiving provider should structure its services according to a non-negotiable formal schedule such as the following: first-time jumpers must complete a morning orientation consisting of one hour of in-class learning and 90 minutes of ground-based training before signing up for an afternoon jump. The in-class portion of the training can then be devoted in part to risk communication, a question-and-answer session, and the completion of a waiver.

WAIVERS

Introduction

waiver
agreement to give up a right, privilege, or benefit to which a person would otherwise be entitled

A waiver is the legal document that non-lawyers are perhaps most familiar with today. It would be difficult to find anyone who has not had the experience of signing one. A **waiver** is an agreement, on the part of the person who signs it or makes it verbally, to suspend a right or privilege that would otherwise arise under the circumstances.

Because a waiver is a contract, and contract law requires that a benefit flow to each side of the agreement, the party who signs the waiver must get something in return for signing the waiver. The legal term for this benefit is consideration, which was discussed in Chapter 2, Legal Liability in Tort and Contract, under the heading "Offer, Acceptance, and Consideration." In most waiver situations, the consideration given in exchange for the person's signature is simply the provider's permission for the person to participate in the activity. This concept is well understood by most consumers, who recognize that if they don't sign the document, they won't be allowed to play (or rent something or enter the premises). By making a signed waiver a condition of participation, recreation providers can strongly motivate consumers to sign on the dotted line.

A person can waive (or attempt to waive) almost any kind of right or privilege. Consider, for example, the child who waives her right to dessert in exchange for not being made to eat her vegetables. Most formal waivers, however, relate to legal rights, and specifically to the legal right to sue another party for damages.

Waivers do not always operate as anticipated: the party who has prepared the waiver is not always permitted, by courts, to rely on the waiver to escape liability in the event of an accident. However, many waivers, when well prepared, properly explained, and signed by a well-informed, non-pressured consumer, hold up to legal scrutiny. (In both cases summarized in this chapter—*Isildar* and *Knowles*—the waivers allowed the recreation provider to avoid liability.)

Even if a waiver can be invalidated by a court, there are solid reasons for preparing one, and enforcing its use in a recreation business. Waivers are detailed risk communication documents, and most consumers recognize that they contain a description of the risks of an activity. A participant who has signed a waiver before participating is faced with a formidable challenge in arguing that he was unaware that the activity was risky. For recreation providers, proving consumer awareness of activity risks is the first step in proving that the consumer should share responsibility for the consequences of participation.

What Makes a Good Waiver?

It's not possible to be certain whether a waiver's full legal intent will be supported by a court that is called on to review it. In all waiver cases, the court considers not only the content of the waiver but also the specific circumstances surrounding its signature, the nature of the activity to which it is meant to apply, and factors personal to the individual who signed it. Some such factors include whether the signer had ever signed a similar waiver before and whether or not she was familiar with the activity's risks.

There have been many legal cases interpreting waivers. The decisions in these cases have helped to identify what kind of content, organization, and structure tends to support a waiver's effectiveness. Many of the specific contents of a waiver are quite technical. A recreation provider who proposes to use a waiver in his business should have it drafted by a lawyer who understands the business and its services well. However, it is useful to be able to recognize the general strengths and weaknesses of waivers, and to be able to identify gaps. The following sections explore some of the features of effective waivers.

Waivers That Work:
Knowles v. Whistler Mountain Ski Corp.

In April 1989, a honeymooning couple visited Whistler Mountain for a ski vacation. The bride, Pamela Knowles, was a novice who had skied only a few times. Knowles signed up for ski lessons, and rented ski equipment at the resort's ski shop. When she rented her skis,' she provided information about her height, weight, and ability level, three factors that dictate how the mechanism that attaches the ski bindings to the boots is to be adjusted. (Safety requires that skis be released from the boots in the event of a hard fall.) Knowles also signed a waiver, which released the ski shop from liability and contained the following terms:

3. I agree to hold harmless and indemnify the ski shop and its owners, agents and employees for any loss or damage, including any that results from claims for personal injury or property damage related to the use of this equipment, except reasonable wear and tear.

5. I understand that there are inherent and other risks involved in the sport for which this equipment is to be used, snow skiing, that injuries are a common and ordinary occurrence of the sport, and I freely assume those risks.

6. *I understand that the ski-boot-binding system will not release at all times or under all circumstances, nor is it possible to predict every situation in which it will release, and is therefore no guarantee for my safety* [emphasis added].

7. I hereby release the ski shop and its owners, agents and employees from any and all liability for damage and injury to myself or to any person or property resulting from negligence, installation, maintenance, the selection, adjustment and use of this equipment, accepting myself the full responsibility for any and all such damage or injury which may result.

After a lesson on a mixed novice–intermediate hill with her instructor, Knowles returned later to the same hill with her husband. While skiing the hill, she fell and injured her knee. The ski on her uninjured leg released from her boot, but the ski on her injured leg did not.

Knowles sued the ski shop for negligence, alleging incompetence in the adjustment of her equipment. Though she admitted that she had signed the waiver, she alleged that the waiver was unconscionable (unreasonably unfair).

The court reviewed the waiver, and found that it was not unconscionable and that the ski shop was entitled to rely on it, thereby avoiding liability for Knowles's injury.

The court cited the following factors in support of its decision to uphold the waiver:

- The waiver's wording anticipated and sought to exclude liability for precisely the event that happened: an injury that resulted from bindings failing to release during a fall. It also provided clear disclosure of this risk.

- The release was signed under circumstances free of time pressure, duress, or coercion. The injured party knew that she had a choice: she could choose not to sign (and not to ski) if she felt that the release was too onerous.

- The injured party knew that she was signing a release, read the release, understood the purpose of it, and knew that there were risks associated with skiing (and with bindings adjustment).

- Finally, the content and effect of the waiver, and the circumstances in which it was signed, did not deviate from "community standards of commercial morality." ◇

CONTENT

An effective waiver should contain the features outlined below.

- The waiver clarifies *who* is being released from liability. The release may cover a named corporation, its staff, or the corporation's directors, for example.

- The waiver specifies the kinds of claims that the signing party is waiving. These claims may include claims for property damage and dependants' claims under family law legislation, for example.

- The waiver specifies the bases of liability for which the party is waiving claims, such as liability based on equipment failure, employee negligence, or inherent activity risks.

- The waiver requires that the signer indemnify the recreation provider for legal and investigative fees and costs.

- The waiver excludes liability for a properly described amount of time (for example, for the duration of a course of ballroom dance lessons), and for activities taking place throughout the provider's premises, including locker rooms, warm-up areas, and lobbies.

- The waiver describes many of the foreseeable risks of the activity, including risks of minor injuries as well as catastrophic harm. For example, the ski equipment waiver in the *Knowles* case described the risk that bindings might not release during a fall.

- The waiver explains that the description of risks is not exhaustive, and that the activity may have unforeseeable risks.

- The waiver makes it clear that the activity has inherent risks that cannot be controlled by the provider and must be assumed by the participant. For example, a trail-riding facility may explain in its waiver that the full range of horses' behaviour cannot be predicted.

- The waiver explains that certain characteristics of participants may increase the activity risks. Examples of these characteristics may include heart conditions, pregnancy, epilepsy, and obesity.

- Finally, the waiver contains an affirmation, by the signer, that she knows and understands the risks and agrees to assume liability for them.

STRUCTURE AND LAYOUT

Features of the structure and layout of an effective waiver are set out below.

- The waiver is a separate document. It is not attached to or combined with a registration document, service contract, or any other kind of document.

- There is a heading at the top of the waiver, in print that exceeds 10 points in size, that indicates that the document is a waiver. Possible headings include Release of Liability, Waiver of Claims, Assumption of Risks, or Indemnity.

- The content of the waiver is printed in dark ink, in at least 10-point type, with key sections—for example, the release of claims based on negligence—printed in boldface type.

- The waiver has a place for a signature at the end, immediately following the affirmation statement or statements. An affirmation statement is the sentence, usually beginning with "I/we, the undersigned," that sets out what the reader has agreed or consented to as affirmed by his or her signature.

- The waiver is no longer than three pages and preferably no longer than two.

- The waiver contains subheadings to alert the reader to particular topics (statement of potential risks, waiver of claims, statement of inherent risks, indemnification, and promise to obey safety rules, for example).

Recreation providers who want a more detailed overview of the elements of a waiver may benefit from reading "Evaluating Your Liability Waiver" by Doyice J. Cotten. This article provides a quiz-style analysis that can be applied to any waiver. While the quiz is written for owners of fitness businesses in the United States, it provides an analysis that is useful for most recreation businesses in Canada, regardless of the activities offered.

The Appendix to this book contains sample waivers from three recreation providers: the Kamloops Women's Recreational Hockey League; Yamnuska, a Canadian provider of hut-to-hut ski mountaineering trips; and Owl Rafting, a provider of whitewater rafting expeditions on the Ottawa River.

Waiver Procedures

Nearly as important as the content of your waiver are the procedures you have in place for securing your participants' signatures. If a participant is made to sign a waiver under duress or time pressure, or without knowing the nature and purpose of the document, the waiver is unlikely to stand up in court.

In the recreation context, it is fairly difficult for a participant to suggest that he was made to sign a waiver under duress, because people have a choice about whether or not to engage in recreation. (Duress is more often an issue in cases involving essential services, such as medical or dental procedures, or contracts that relate to housing or other basic necessities.) However, it is possible that a recreation participant may not learn about the need to sign a waiver until he has committed considerable time, money, or energy toward preparing for the activity. For example, a person may arrange to host a 40th birthday party at a "challenge ropes course." The consumer may invite friends, arrange transportation, and plan for a catered picnic on the provider's grounds. He may not anticipate having to sign a waiver (or requiring all guests to sign one). In such a case, if the waiver proposes the surrender of significant rights, the host may later allege that he faced pressure to sign the waiver or risk disappointing his guests.

Time pressure is another situation that must be avoided when presenting a waiver. When a participant arrives just in time for a scheduled event (a sunset hot-air balloon ride, for example), she may be urged to get paperwork—including the signing of a waiver—done quickly. In this situation, the provider runs the risk that the participant will allege that she did not have the time to read and consider the terms of the waiver.

Finally, providers should avoid allegations that a participant did not understand either that a document was a waiver or that it was meant to have particular legal effects. Explaining waivers is not a pleasant part of the recreation experience. It goes against a provider's sales instincts to draw participants' attention to the fact that they are assuming responsibility for a long list of potential calamities, but this responsibility must be taken seriously. Waivers should be kept separate from other documents, such as registration forms, and participants' attention should be drawn to them. Sufficient time to read the documents must be allowed, and staff should be available to answer questions.

In an attempt to avoid arguments about duress, time pressures, or lack of participant understanding, some savvy recreation providers post their waivers on their websites. In their description of the registration process, they include a statement that participants are required to sign a waiver, and provide a sample of the waiver on the web page. Providers who do not have web pages can mail a package that contains a sample waiver to registrants before the program day.

It is very dangerous, from a legal standpoint, to introduce a waiver after participants have completed the registration process, paid for participation, and begun an

MANAGING RISKS

Risks to Rescuers

Some high-risk tourism activities may result in participants becoming stranded in remote areas because of mishaps, ill health, getting lost, or inclement weather. When this happens, a rescue mission becomes necessary.

Rescue efforts nearly always come with significant risks to rescuers. The conditions that led to the rescue subject's distress (for example, a storm or an avalanche) often pose hazards to rescuers. And many rescue techniques (for example, flying an aircraft low to the ground, travelling through dense bush, or venturing out into rough seas by boat) are inherently risky.

Whether a rescue is conducted by public agencies, such as the police or the coast guard, or by staff of a private recreation business, protecting the welfare of rescuers is always of paramount concern. Organizers of a rescue are placed in the unenviable position of balancing the benefits of a successful rescue mission with the risks of an unsuccessful one in making decisions about rescue tactics and timing.

There are, however, ways to make these decisions responsibly. One key strategy is to take low-risk steps to stabilize the condition of rescue subjects so that a rescue can be carried out under the safest possible conditions. In an article for Search and Rescue Info, author Martin Colwell makes the following suggestion:

> [P]lacing signage, directional stringlines, using sound or visual attractors, are all techniques that can be used to encourage the subject to move from a higher risk environment, to a lower risk area. If the subject has been found but cannot be immediately rescued due to extreme terrain, poor weather conditions or approaching darkness, then dropping a survival kit, including clothes, food and a radio, can significantly reduce the level of risk to the subject. Once the subject has been stabilized in this manner a rescue effort can then be undertaken when conditions improve, providing a much safer rescue environment for the searchers. In this manner the Total Mission Risk can be significantly reduced for both the searchers and the subject. ◇

activity. This danger stems from the rule of consideration: any agreement, in order to be valid, must offer a benefit to each side *at the time the agreement is made*. If the recreation provider has already extended its permission for the participant to engage in the activity and then later requires the signing of a waiver, it is open for the participant to argue that she was given no consideration for her signature on the waiver.

CONSUMER EDUCATION

While it is important to prepare and use them, waivers should not be the only source of risk information given to clients of high-risk or adventure providers. Waivers are often viewed in a negative light by consumers, who see them as an attempt, by providers, to avoid responsibility. Using waivers as an organization's primary consumer education tool sends the message that the organization is more concerned about protecting itself from lawsuits than protecting its customers from harm.

The more significant and probable the risks associated with an activity, the more time and resources the recreation provider should devote to a program of consumer education. Consumer education activities should have the following goals:

- to explain both the benefits and the risks of an activity;

- to support consumers in their decisions about whether or not to participate in the activity;

- to communicate to consumers that the decision whether to participate or not is their own responsibility;

- to help consumers who are not well suited to the activity (because of an underlying health condition, for example) to screen themselves out;

- to teach consumers how they can minimize the risks of the activity (for example, by avoiding intoxicants before participating and by wearing safety gear properly);

- to explain the recreation provider's safety rules and to review the participants' comprehension of and familiarity with these rules; and

- to assist participants in acquiring the skills that permit them to enjoy the activity safely.

While some high-risk activity providers use signage to communicate safety information, it is essential that in-person communication form a component of the consumer education program. When safety information is communicated in person, the recreation provider can:

- encourage the participants to ask questions, and answer these questions;

- review the participants' understanding;

- notice factors specific to a participant that may increase his risk susceptibility (such as an unusually small or large body size, a disability, evidence of intoxication, a language barrier, long hair hanging loose, or untied shoelaces); and

- testify later, should it ever be necessary, that a participant did in fact listen to an explanation of safety procedures.

Where an activity, such as riding a snow-tube, carries a medium risk and does not require sophisticated skills, a basic orientation conducted just before the activity takes place may provide sufficient education. Such an orientation can include instructions on how to steer the tube, the importance of an appropriate riding position, and waiting until the hill is clear before launch.

If an activity, such as skydiving or scuba diving, carries a high risk and requires special skills, a dedicated consumer education class (or series of classes) is in order. With each new level of participation—for example, solo skydives or deep scuba dives—an additional education session should be required.

For a medium-risk activity that will take place over an extended period (for example, a five-day horseback expedition through the wilderness), a dedicated education session may be warranted. The purpose of such a session is partly to explain risks and partly to allow staff to familiarize themselves with the participants and their level of experience and anxiety. This approach can assist in planning. For example, anxious riders may be assigned horses that prefer to follow, not lead, the pack.

Where a consumer education program is in place, it should be designed so that participants can withdraw from participation at any stage before an activity begins, without feeling pressure or embarrassment, or incurring a cost. Educating individuals who decide *not* to participate is a very reasonable cost of doing business in the adventure tourism sector.

In fact, providing consumer education without cost to a large group of people—consumers who have not yet committed themselves to participating in an activity, but are interested in learning more about it—is a public relations strategy that may serve an organization well.

The content of any consumer education program depends on the nature of an activity, but such a program should always contain the following:

- risk information;

- information about how to minimize risk (for example, how to wear a safety belt);

- information about proper technique and examples of improper technique to be avoided;

- information about what can be expected in the course of an activity, including unpleasant aspects (for example, whitewater rafters should be told that they will get wet, they may collide with each other in the boat, there will be sudden jerky motions, and visibility will be poor at times); and

- detailed information about what a participant should do if she gets into difficulty or wants assistance.

Finally, the recreation provider must remember that while its own policies and procedures are very familiar to staff, this information is likely new to participants. Participants' recall of safety instructions may be faulty in emergency circumstances, when they are in a state of panic. All staff should be trained to monitor the behaviour of participants, and to respond quickly when a participant is not following instructions: a participant may simply be frightened, and may not remember the instructions or how to signal for help.

PUBLIC RELATIONS FOR ADVENTURE TOURISM PROVIDERS

Occasionally, a tragic accident occurs and draws negative public attention to a particular high-risk activity or form of adventure tourism. This negative publicity poses a challenge for providers in the industry because it can dampen public demand for their services.

Managing the reputation of a high-risk or adventure tourism offering is a significant challenge, but there are several things that a provider can do not only to combat negative publicity but also to promote the benefits of the activity. First, if a high-profile accident occurs in a provider's own business, the provider should be able to follow the public relations policies that it has created long before the accident. These policies will likely include protecting the privacy of the victims and their families; leaving media communications to a designated spokesperson only; and providing timely and honest disclosure about the causes of the accident, steps taken to compensate the victims and their families, and steps taken to prevent similar accidents in the future.

If an accident occurs at a competitor's business, other recreation providers also have responsibilities. They should take steps to learn about the causes of the accident, and compare the competitor's policies, equipment, premises, and staff with their own to determine whether there is a risk that a similar accident could occur on their own premises. If safety gaps are identified (for example, if the provider is using the same kind of equipment that proved faulty elsewhere), these gaps must be immediately closed and best practices must be put in place. Allowing tragic accidents to serve as learning opportunities shows respect not only for the victims but also for future consumers.

If press coverage of an accident has come to dominate media coverage of an activity, particularly an activity in which accidents are rare, it is up to all providers in the field to take steps to provide information to balance the negative press. Perhaps, for example, the provider offers mountaineering courses, and must cope with the news of a fatal mountaineering accident. Under these circumstances, it may be useful to point out that *without* mountaineering programs, there would be no trained rescuers to assist in the event of accidents such as high-altitude plane crashes. Publishing articles about the renewal of safety standards in the industry and about advances in equipment is also useful at such times, as is offering free seminars or making other efforts to improve the public's understanding of the activity.

Finally, it is never a waste of time to promote little-known beneficial aspects of your programs to a general audience, not just to the direct consumers of the activities. If a recreation provider offers "voluntourism" programs—for example, a trip to South America that includes time spent building a community school—the public will be interested in hearing about this. If a recreation provider has rehabilitated land that was previously polluted or abandoned, this should also be promoted. If a provider takes care, in designing its programs, to protect vulnerable ecologies or cultures, or if its activities help to bring tourism dollars into a region that needs a commercial boost, these aspects of the business should be highlighted as well. Publicity of this nature benefits not only the individual provider but also the industry as a whole.

KEY TERMS

high-risk activity

waiver

REVIEW EXERCISES

Review Questions

1. What is the current state of the market for adventure tourism and high-risk recreation?

2. Which high-risk sports account for the greatest number of injuries to Canadians annually?

3. Do providers of high-risk sports owe an enhanced duty of care to participants?

4. What impact should the level of risk associated with an activity have on a provider's choice of risk communication strategies?

5. Why is it important not to allow risk communication to be rushed, and what strategies can a provider use to eliminate time pressure for these communications?

6. What key lesson can recreation providers learn from the *Isildar* case?

7. What is a waiver?

8. Are waivers effective at eliminating liability for recreation providers?

9. What can a recreation provider do to support the effectiveness of its waiver?

10. List three essential matters that must be covered in a waiver.

11. List three formatting considerations that can help consumers understand a waiver.

12. Why is consumer education essential in the context of adventure tourism or high-risk sport?

Discussion Question

Is it immoral or otherwise wrong to request that customers waive their right to make a claim for damages against a recreation provider? Why or why not? Does your answer change if the customer is waiving her right to make a claim that is based on the provider's negligence?

CHAPTER 10

Recreation on Public Lands

CHAPTER OBJECTIVES

After completing this chapter, you should be able to:

- explain the legal position of governments under tort and occupiers' liability law;

- understand the relationship between the use a government makes of its land and its exposure to legal liability;

- describe some of the recreational activities that take place on public property, and list some of the regulations that apply to them; and

- discuss the role of public education campaigns as a strategy for protecting the recreational users of public lands.

INTRODUCTION

Most of the material in this book has focused on recreation activities that are undertaken by people on private property owned by individuals or corporations. Many recreation activities enjoyed in Canada, however, are carried out on public lands or waters that are under the control of municipalities, provinces, or the federal government.

This chapter examines the legal implications, for governments, of permitting recreation on public lands and in public bodies of water, and the duties of governments as hosts of these activities. Relevant topics include a government's liability as occupier, its duty to warn the public of outdoor risks, vehicle restrictions, traffic management, boating laws, hunting and fishing laws, and rescue operations carried out by government agencies, such as the police and the coast guard. Because public recreation is a very broad subject, these issues are touched on only summarily. If you are a provider or host of recreation on public lands, you will need to do additional legal research into the activities that you facilitate.

GOVERNMENTS AS OCCUPIERS

Introduction

A considerable proportion of Canadian land and water is owned and controlled by governments. In urban areas, the predominant kinds of government-controlled lands are parks and streets (generally controlled by municipalities under authority delegated to them by provinces) and highways, which are typically the responsibility of provinces. In rural areas, both provincially and federally controlled parks can be found, and provincial (and occasionally federal) governments also control the shorelines and waters of most lakes and many rivers, streams, canals, and creeks.

When the sheer area of government-controlled lands is considered, it may come as little surprise that the common law once held that governments were not responsible in negligence for injuries that occurred on government land. This absolute immunity for governments no longer exists in Canada. It has been replaced by the idea, contained in both provincial and federal statutes, that the **Crown** does indeed owe a duty of care to visitors to public land and may be sued in negligence.

Crown
government, either federal or provincial

In Ontario, the statute on which government negligence is based is called the *Proceedings Against the Crown Act*; other provincial statutes are similarly named. At the federal level, the relevant statute is the *Crown Liability and Proceedings Act*. Municipal lands are under the general control of provincial governments, but sometimes are covered by an additional layer of municipal legislation known as **bylaws**. Municipal bylaws sometimes give municipalities greater **immunity** than is contemplated under the provincial law.

bylaws
municipal legislation

immunity
protection from lawsuits

The Ontario *Proceedings Against the Crown Act* explains that the province is liable in tort as though it were an ordinary individual or corporation. However, there is a very important caveat that people injured on government land must note: in order to bring a negligence lawsuit against the Ontario government "in respect of any breach of the duties attaching to the ownership, occupation, possession or control of property" (which includes claims flowing from recreation on government land), the injured person must give the government notice of her claim *within 10 days* of the incident. This limitation period is extremely short and much stricter than the limitation periods that apply to claims against individuals and corporations. Similarly short notice periods apply to claims made against the governments of other provinces, and to claims against municipalities.

The Ontario *Occupiers' Liability Act* makes it clear that the liability of an occupier (including a government occupier) varies according to the following factors: the kind of land being occupied, whether people who come onto the land are invitees or trespassers, and whether the occupier charges a fee for recreational use of the land. In some cases, a person who comes onto certain kinds of land for a recreational purpose is considered to have personally assumed the risks associated with his activities when

- he is trespassing,

- he has come onto the land for the purpose of recreation,

- the occupier does not charge a fee for the recreation, and

- the occupier has not offered the trespasser living accommodation on the land.

The kinds of land to which these rules about assumption of risk apply are described in section 4(4) of the Ontario *Occupiers' Liability Act*:

> (a) a rural premises that is,
>> (i) used for agricultural purposes, including land under cultivation, orchards, pastures, woodlots and farm ponds,
>> (ii) vacant or undeveloped premises,
>> (iii) forested or wilderness premises;
> (b) golf courses when not open for playing;
> (c) utility rights-of-way and corridors, excluding structures located thereon;
> (d) unopened road allowances;
> (e) private roads reasonably marked by notice as such; and
> (f) recreational trails reasonably marked by notice as such.

If an accident occurs on federal land (for example, in the far North), the federal government is liable for harm that flows from its ownership of property only if it has actually taken steps to occupy the property. What exactly this means, in law, has not been explored very closely; however, it is likely that the federal Crown, like the provinces, can be found liable for its negligent acts or omissions that take place on its *developed* lands (for example, roadways, trails, mines, and supervised beaches).

There is one more important wrinkle in the law of negligence as it affects government: most governments can be held responsible for the effects of their operational decisions, but not for the effects of their policy decisions. A **policy decision** is a high-level decision, made by senior government staff, about how the government will spend money, how it will make decisions, or how it will deploy its resources. An **operational decision** is an ordinary, day-to-day decision that is made by government employees about the details of a policy's operation. For example, a province may, as a matter of policy, create a program under which it buys radio airtime to alert the public about high water levels in local rivers and streams after storms or spring thaws. When applying this policy, the government will make operational decisions about matters such as the level of high water that merits a broadcast and the stations on which the announcements will be placed. A family that loses a child to drowning in a neighbouring province that has no such policy will be unable to sue the government for failure to warn about water-level changes because the decision of that family's government not to adopt such a program is a policy decision and not an operational one.

policy decision
decision made by senior government staff, often concerning the management of governmental resources

operational decision
routine decision made by civil servants about the specifics of a law's operation

Duties of Care to Users

Statutes concerning proceedings against the Crown show that governments, like individuals and corporations, can now be found by courts to owe a duty of care toward others. A duty of care arises whenever a party does something or omits to do something that could foreseeably cause harm to another.

Claims based on duties of care are most likely to arise when a government has developed land, for example, by constructing highways, installing playground equipment, building public structures such as recreation centres or nuclear power plants, and clearing and providing road access to beaches and parks. (Traffic management and maintenance of developed lands are discussed in the following section.)

If a government simply owns land and has not developed it, it's less likely that a person who is injured on this land (for example, by falling off a cliff or being mauled by a bear) will have a claim against the government: the government cannot be expected to know and guard against all of the hazards that exist in wilderness areas. Exceptions, however, arise if a government becomes aware that people are using undeveloped land and encountering risks. For example, if a government agency learns that snowmobile riders are routinely crossing a particular lake to get from one highway to another, and there has been a related drowning accident on the lake, the risk of a future accident becomes foreseeable to the government. The government is therefore obliged to take steps to prevent future accidents by, for example, fencing the area off, posting "no trespassing" or "no motorized vehicles" signs, or perhaps clearing an alternate route.

As in any other negligence-based personal injury case, a court faced with a claim against a government must consider the particular facts to answer standard personal injury liability questions such as the following:

- Was the plaintiff injured on government property?

- Did the government owe the plaintiff a duty of care?

- Did the government do, or omit to do, anything that made the injury more likely?

- If the government did something to limit the risks to the plaintiff, were the government's efforts reasonable? Were they adequate? Did they rise to the appropriate standard of care, or did they fall short?

- Was the accident reasonably foreseeable?

- Was the plaintiff an invitee or a trespasser?

- Did the government create an attractive nuisance (something that lured trespassers in)?

- Was there an adequate causal connection between the government's actions or inactions and the accident to make it reasonable to hold the government liable?

- To what extent was the plaintiff responsible for the accident?

Any time a government allows people onto its land or is aware that trespassers are on the property, it shoulders the responsibility for considering how the risks to the users can be minimized.

Traffic Management and Maintaining Developed Land

Highways and streets are an important example of developed government land, not only because of the infrastructure introduced by the government but also because the public is invited onto the highways and streets. Because governments assume a duty of care to users of developed land, each province has a long and detailed traffic management statute that helps the province enforce safe driving on its roads.

Court decisions have made it clear that the government bears the responsibility not only for enforcing safe driving but also for monitoring the physical condition of its roads and traffic signs, and for maintaining its roads in reasonably safe condition. The government has generally taken this responsibility seriously, and a large number of safety innovations (high-tech pavement, guardrails, medians, shoulders, and signage, for example) are in use across Canada to improve highway safety.

The government also seeks to protect users by regulating what kinds of vehicles are allowed to travel on highways, and what the features of these vehicles must be. In the recreation context, some restrictions that users should be aware of include the following:

- restrictions against pedestrian and bicycle access on some major highways;

- restrictions against the use of motorbikes, dirt bikes, all-terrain vehicles, and motorized snow vehicles on highways;

- the need for highway-legal recreational vehicles (such as motorcycles) to pass safety certification and to be equipped with safety equipment; and

- rules for the use of trailers (many recreation participants transport vehicles such as boats and snowmobiles, camping trailers, and horses in trailers; all trailers must meet provincial regulations with respect to licence plates, lights, load weight, and load restraints).

Roads are not the only government lands that must be maintained and managed. As you have learned in earlier chapters, any organization that maintains a park for public use must take all reasonable steps (by providing signage, rescue equipment, supervision, and fences) to protect the public from known risks in the park.

Governments also need to protect the public from risks that exist on land that is *not* open to the public. Examples of potentially dangerous government sites include:

- docks and wharves;

- railways;

- mines;

- nuclear power plants;

- electrical equipment and infrastructure;

- natural gas pipelines;

- dams, locks, and reservoirs; and

- waste management facilities.

Because unauthorized and undetected public entry onto these sites can be extremely dangerous, governments have to take significant measures to exclude trespassers. These measures include providing high fences, clear and regularly spaced signs, alarms, security lighting, closed-circuit television systems, and security guards. Where it's difficult to exclude the public from a particular kind of dangerous site (for example, railways and railway crossings), public education campaigns about the risks associated with unauthorized entry can be useful.

In some cases, recreational users actually seek out government-developed sites because they are tempting from a recreation perspective. For example, divers may be attracted to abandoned mines that have been flooded, and snowmobile operators may be attracted to the cleared land along railways. Any developed area that may be tempting to recreational users can be labelled an "attractive nuisance" by a court. The law holds that a party who creates a danger that attracts curious trespassers must either remove the danger or take extra precautions to prevent trespassers from gaining access to the area, and where those precautions prove to be inadequate, compensate those who are hurt while trespassing. The most successful of these cases have involved child trespassers.

Right to Restrict Activities

Like any other occupier, governments have a right to restrict the activities in which visitors engage on their lands, and many governments choose to do so. A government that deems an activity dangerous, or considers the cost of protecting participants too high or too labour-intensive often chooses to prohibit the activity.

For private landowners, the main methods available for controlling unauthorized activities are posting signs and conducting patrols. Government agencies can—and should—use these methods, but they have another tool at their disposal: legislation. Governments can pass laws or bylaws prohibiting dangerous activities, and can create offences that can be charged against those who disobey these laws. They can also enforce the law through the use of penalties. Fines are the most common penalty for committing provincial offences, but provinces can also suspend or withdraw driving or fishing licences, for example. In some cases, governments can also recommend prison sentences for offenders.

In some cases, prohibitions against dangerous activities exist under federal law. The most important examples, in the context of recreation, are firearms offences. Because the misuse of guns presents a threat to peace, order, and good government, firearms are regulated by the federal government. Another area of federal regulation in the recreation sector is maritime law (the law of the sea). Maritime law falls under the federal jurisdiction because of its international aspects.

Many of the rules that restrict land use and are of interest to recreation participants can be found in the statutes that create or regulate provincial or national parks. For example, in Ontario, the *Provincial Parks and Conservation Reserves Act, 2006* provides general rules that apply to these types of parks, including rules that prohibit the use of these parks for commercial purposes, such as timber harvesting. The regulations made under this statute impose additional restrictions. For example, the Provincial Parks: General Provisions regulation prohibits the following activities:

- entering a park from a place other than a designated entry point;

- setting fires except in designated fireplaces;

- engaging in inappropriate conduct, which is defined as including "discriminatory, harassing, abusive or insulting language or gestures or [making] excessive noise or [disturbing] other persons in a provincial park";

- selling or begging;

- having a domestic animal off leash, except as specifically permitted;

- possessing or igniting fireworks;

- climbing rock faces, except in designated areas;

- powerboating, except in parks mentioned in Schedule 1;

- landing aircraft, except in parks mentioned in Schedule 2;

- using firearms, except as permitted under the *Fish and Wildlife Conservation Act, 1997* or in other narrowly defined circumstances;

- using all-terrain vehicles, except in designated areas or with the permission of the park superintendent;

- waterskiing in Algonquin Provincial Park;

- using jet skis, motorized surfboards, parasailing, or watersledding in certain parks;

- possessing or using power saws or augers in certain parks; and

- camping near the shoreline in certain parks in winter.

Similar restrictions pertain to use of national parks. At the federal level, the governing legislation is the *Canada National Parks Act* and the regulations made under it.

Parks have a wide range of strategies to publicize and enforce usage rules, including posting signs and distributing written material at entry points; posting signs in the park interior; posting information on websites; and having parks conservation and enforcement staff conduct patrols.

OFF-ROAD VEHICLES

Introduction

Some vehicles are intended for off-road use. In general, they cannot be driven legally on major highways (though there are some exceptions for four-wheelers), and they are usually ridden for recreational purposes on private property or on dedicated trails. The popularity of off-road vehicles has increased in recent years in Ontario. According to a news release from the Ministry of Transportation, the number of registrations for these vehicles increased 128 percent between 1996 and 2005 (2008, p. 1).

Off-road vehicles, such as snowmobiles, dirt bikes, motorbikes, and all-terrain vehicles, are involved in a fairly high number of collisions annually. The Ontario Ministry of Transportation cites a Canadian Institute for Health Information report and notes that "off-road vehicles are among the top three causes of sports and recreation-related severe injuries during the summer months," and teenagers are the group most likely to be hospitalized following an off-road crash (2008, p. 1).

Off-road vehicles are regulated by the provinces. Ontario's *Off-Road Vehicles Act* provides that owners of an off-road vehicle must obtain a permit for the vehicle, affix a government-issued number plate to the vehicle, and obtain insurance. The permit must be carried any time the vehicle is ridden off the premises of the owner. If a police officer requests it, proof of insurance must be produced by the owner within 72 hours of the request being made. Riders must also wear a helmet that has a chin strap and otherwise conforms with the regulations whenever they ride off their own premises.

The *Off-Road Vehicles Act* makes it an offence to drive an off-road vehicle "without due care and attention or without reasonable consideration for other persons," or to fail to stop when requested to do so by a police officer.

A person who rides an off-road vehicle onto another occupier's land assumes responsibility for all risks to herself *unless* the occupier charges a fee for the use of his land, or offers living accommodation to the rider. This means that resort or campground owners who allow visitors to ride off-road vehicles or operators of off-road vehicle parks who charge for access may be at least partly liable, under occupiers' liability law, for injury to riders.

Enforcing off-road riding safety is a significant challenge for both private occupiers and governments because the vehicles are not restricted to specified routes. A prominent issue in off-road safety is impaired driving: in Ontario in 2007, there were 27 deaths following all-terrain vehicle crashes, and the Ministry of Transportation reported that alcohol was a factor in over 50 percent of them. Impaired driving of an off-road vehicle carries the same penalties as impaired driving of a regular vehicle (and has the same impact on the rider's insurance rates); however, enforcement is very difficult. Where off-road riding is common, government agencies should divert some of the time and money currently devoted to enforcement to developing public awareness campaigns concerning the dangers of irresponsible off-road riding, especially for young riders.

The Canadian Off-Highway Vehicle Distributors Council has proposed the following Safe Rider Code (2009):

- Know Your Operator's Manual
- Check the ATV Before You Ride
- Wear Your Helmet
- Protect Your Eyes and Body
- Get Qualified Training
- Ride Off-Road Only, Never on Public Roads
- Ride With Others—Never Alone
- Ride Within Your Skills
- Carry No Passengers
- Respect Riding Area Rules
- Keep Noise Levels Low
- Ride Straight—No Alcohol or Other Drugs
- Preserve the Environment
- Be Courteous to All You Meet
- Lend Your ATV to Skilled Riders Only
- Always Supervise Youngsters

While this code was written with all-terrain vehicles in mind, it is useful in the context of other off-road vehicles as well. Riders of motorized snow vehicles should bear in mind that winter conditions merit additional safety precautions:

- Wear clothing suitable to weather conditions to prevent hypothermia.

- Inform others of your destination and estimated arrival time.

- Carry a first-aid kit and a survival kit.

- Check avalanche conditions in susceptible areas.

- Check ice thickness and confirm ice safety with local authorities before travelling over ice.

- Wear flotation devices.

Motorized Vehicles in Provincial and National Parks

Mechanized Travel in Wilderness Parks, a regulation made under the *Provincial Parks and Conservation Reserves Act, 2006*, provides that no "mechanized travel" is permitted in wilderness parks except under certain specified conditions. Examples of such conditions include undertaking government-mandated research or gaining access to private property within the park boundaries. "Mechanized travel" is defined as "travel using a vehicle, as defined in the *Highway Traffic Act*, a motorized snow vehicle, a boat, an aircraft or any other apparatus propelled by machine or by means of machinery." Ontario's designated wilderness parks are listed below:

- Kesagami Provincial Park,

- Killarney Provincial Park,

- Lady Evelyn-Smoothwater Provincial Park,

- Opasquia Provincial Park,

- Polar Bear Provincial Park,

- Quetico Provincial Park,

- Wabakimi Provincial Park, and

- Woodland Caribou Provincial Park.

HUNTING AND FISHING

Introduction

Because Canada still enjoys large wilderness areas in which wild animals can thrive, hunting, trapping, and fishing flourish here. Aboriginal peoples continue to hunt, both for sustenance and to honour their heritage, and many non-aboriginal devotees also enjoy these activities.

The federal government and all the provincial governments have policies for the management of wildlife, and these policies incorporate a role for hunters and fishers. In Ontario, the key policy-maker is the Fish and Wildlife Heritage Commission. Every year, hunters help to manage imbalances in Canada's wildlife ecology by reducing populations of animals that would disrupt the existing balance of natural resources or otherwise inconvenience human beings. In return, policy-makers work to identify hunting, trapping, and fishing opportunities—that is, areas in which the wildlife population can tolerate hunting and fishing.

The key laws in place to manage hunting and fishing in Ontario are the following:

- the *Fish and Wildlife Conservation Act, 1997* and regulations;

- the *Provincial Parks and Conservation Reserves Act, 2006* and regulations; and

- the *Endangered Species Act* and regulations.

There are also three federal statutes that touch on the regulation of hunting and fishing:

- the *Canada National Parks Act* and regulations;

- the *Migratory Birds Convention Act, 1994* and regulations; and

- the *Species at Risk Act* and regulations.

In general, these statutes require that a person possess a valid licence before hunting or fishing anywhere in Ontario. They also impose limits on the kinds of animals and fish that can be hunted or caught, the areas in which hunting and fishing can take place, the seasons in which particular game can be hunted, and the kinds of weapons that can be used. As a general rule, hunting is permitted in conservation areas and prohibited in provincial parks; however, there are many exceptions. All hunters should consult the regulations under the statutes listed above to determine whether or not hunting is permitted in the area where they propose to hunt.

Hunting

Hunting licences in Ontario now come in four forms:

1. the class H1 outdoors card: for trained adult hunters (those over 18 years) who use guns;

2. the class H2 outdoors card: for trained adult non-gun hunters, such as falconers;

3. the class A1 hunter apprenticeship safety card for supervised gun-hunting learners who are aged 12 or over and have a parent's permission if they are under 16, and who have passed both the Ontario hunter education course examination and the Canadian firearms safety course examination; and

4. the class A2 hunter apprenticeship safety card for supervised non-gun-hunting learners who are aged 12 or over and have a parent's permission if they are under 16, and who have passed the Ontario hunter education course examination.

The Ontario hunter education course and examination are administered jointly by the Ministry of Natural Resources and the Ontario Federation of Anglers and Hunters. There is also a separate course for hunters of wild turkeys, which must be passed if these birds are to be hunted.

When an apprentice is hunting with a trained mentor, the two hunters must share a single firearm, and any game hunted by the apprentice is added to the mentor's bag limit.

In addition to carrying the outdoors card or hunter apprenticeship safety card, bird hunters must carry a federal migratory game bird hunting card. Dogs who assist with hunting must also be licensed for the purpose.

Hunters of deer and moose are required to wear clothing and headwear in a bright colour called "hunter orange," as are bear hunters in some situations. Waterfowl hunters, wild turkey hunters, and archers hunting in archery-only seasons are exempt from the hunter orange regulations.

Some modes of hunting are illegal, even when the hunter is properly licensed, has a legal gun, and is wearing hunter orange. Illegal hunting includes activities such as:

- hunting from an aircraft,

- hunting from a boat,

- hunting from a snowmobile or all-terrain vehicle,

- pursuing animals from any of these vehicles, and

- hunting animals (other than waterfowl) while they are swimming.

There are some exceptions to the vehicle rules for certain people with disabilities.

In addition to licensing laws, firearms laws apply to hunters. In Canada, it is illegal to use handguns or fully automatic guns for hunting. There are also detailed and exacting standards for the storage and transportation of firearms and ammunition, which must be transported and stored separately in locked compartments. Loaded firearms are not permitted within eight metres of roads or rights of way, and firearms cannot be fired across a road or right of way.

In most hunting areas, firearms cannot be discharged after dark (from one half-hour after sunset until one half-hour before sunrise).

Should anyone be injured by the discharge of a firearm and require medical treatment, the incident must be reported to a conservation officer at the earliest opportunity. Careless use of a firearm is a criminal offence, and penalties consist of fines up to $25,000 and/or prison terms of up to two years.

Finally, hunters are prohibited from harming any endangered species of *animal, insect, bird, reptile, or plant* while they hunt. There are 42 such species, and hunters should make themselves familiar with the list, which is compiled under the *Endangered Species Act* and includes timber rattlesnakes, bald eagles, golden eagles, and eastern cougars. While coyotes and wolves are not on the list, there is no hunting season for these animals; should a hunter kill such an animal to protect property, the kill must be reported to the Ministry of Natural Resources. There is no legal hunting season for elk or caribou in Canada.

The *Canada National Parks Act* makes it an offence to traffic in Canadian wildlife; penalties for this offence and related offences are severe.

Fishing

Fishing in Ontario, like hunting, is governed by the *Fish and Wildlife Conservation Act, 1997*. The primary source of federal regulation for fishing is the *Fisheries Act*.

The *Fish and Wildlife Conservation Act, 1997* prohibits fishing in Ontario without a valid fishing licence. A fishing licence for Ontario residents over the age of 18 now consists of an outdoors card with a fishing licence tag attached. There are two kinds of fishing licence tags: one for sportfishing and one for conservation fishing. It is also possible to obtain a temporary fishing licence when applying for an outdoors card, or if the fisher is a non-Ontario or non-Canadian resident. If a person is fishing in a body of water that contains a border with Quebec or Manitoba, it is generally legal to fish with an Ontario licence.

Fishers must carry their fishing licences with them at all times, and present them to a conservation officer when asked. Fishing without a licence is a provincial offence.

Many other aspects of fishing are regulated, including:

- the kinds of fish that can be caught and retained;

- the size of fish that can be retained;

- the areas in which fishers can fish (zone maps are available from the Ministry of Natural Resources);

- the seasons in which fishing is allowed;

- the rules related to ice-fishing;

- the rules related to fishing equipment and bait;

- the rules related to the export of fish; and

- the rules related to methods for hunting bullfrogs and snapping turtles.

As noted below, there are also restrictions on the use of powerboats in many Ontario parks; these rules are important for fishers' consideration. Illegal trafficking in fish is a federal offence with severe penalties. It is illegal to remove several species, including frogs and turtles, from provincial parks.

PLEASURE BOATING

Introduction

Of the approximately 400 Canadians who die in water-related accidents every year, more than one-third are boaters. Of that one-third, three-quarters are recreational boaters.

According to the Lifesaving Society of Canada, two contributing factors are prominent in predicting which boaters will die: in 85 percent of cases, drowned boaters were not wearing a personal flotation device; and in 38 percent of cases, alcohol was a factor in the accident.

Pleasure boating is regulated by Transport Canada, but the laws relating to boating are enforced by a number of different agencies, including the Canadian Coast Guard and police marine patrol units. When a boat is operated in a provincial park or conservation area, the Ministry of Natural Resources can regulate whether or not it can have access to particular waterways, or what size or type of boat can be operated.

Licensing

Small vessels—any powerboat under 15 tons and any pleasure boat under 15 tons with a motor of 7.5 kilowatts (10 horsepower) or more—must be licensed under the *Canada Shipping Act, 2001*. A vessel cannot be operated until it is licensed. Licensed vessels must have their registration numbers clearly marked on either side of the bow, and if the vessel is stopped by enforcement officers, the operator must produce the licence for review.

There are licensing requirements for vessel operators as well. As of September 15, 2009, all operators of pleasure craft in Canada must provide proof of competency before being able to operate a pleasure craft. The most common proof of competency is the pleasure craft operator card, which is available from the federal Office of Boating Safety or from licensed private companies.

A pleasure craft operator card can be obtained after successful completion of a boating safety examination. In some cases, individuals will be permitted to establish competency in a different way—for example, by taking a dockside competency test from a boat rental company. This allows occasional boaters and visitors from outside Canada to use boats in Canada.

Besides the competency requirement, there are also minimum boater age requirements:

- Operators under the age of 12 cannot operate a boat over 7.5 kilowatts (10 horsepower) unless supervised by a person aged 16 or over.

- Operators aged 12 to 16 cannot operate a boat over 30 kilowatts (40 horsepower) unless supervised by a person aged 16 or over.

- No person under the age of 16 is allowed to operate a personal watercraft, such as a jet ski.

Safety Equipment

The Small Vessel Regulations impose minimum safety requirements for boats. These requirements are very detailed and vary depending on the size of the boat. The following regulation from section 16.02 of the Small Vessel Regulations is reproduced in its entirety to demonstrate the specificity of these safety standards. (These requirements are for a pleasure craft that does not exceed six metres in length):

(2) Personal protection equipment shall consist of
    (a) subject to section 16.08, one personal flotation device or lifejacket of appropriate size for each person on board; and
    (b) one buoyant heaving line of not less than 15 m in length.

(3) Boat safety equipment shall consist of
    (a) either
        (i) one manual propelling device, or
        (ii) an anchor with not less than 15 m of cable, rope or chain in any combination;
    (b) subject to section 16.09, one bailer or one manual water pump fitted with or accompanied by sufficient hose to enable a person using the pump to pump water from the bilge of the vessel over the side of the vessel; and

(c) one Class 5BC fire extinguisher if the pleasure craft is equipped with an inboard engine, a fixed fuel tank of any size, or a fuel-burning cooking, heating or refrigerating appliance.

(4) Distress equipment shall consist of
(a) a watertight flashlight; or
(b) three pyrotechnic distress signals of Type A, B or C.

(5) Navigation equipment shall consist of
(a) a sound-signalling device or a sound-signalling appliance; and
(b) if the pleasure craft is operated after sunset and before sunrise or in periods of restricted visibility, navigation lights that meet the applicable standards set out in the *Collision Regulations.*

Studies by the Canadian Coast Guard have shown that if the operator of a boat asks passengers to wear a lifejacket, the majority will comply. In addition, compliance generally varies based on the passenger's perception of risk, and the operator's request that passengers wear a lifejacket generally elevates the level of risk in the passenger's mind (Andrews, 2003, p. 12). An operator's failure to carry the required number of lifejackets constitutes an offence punishable by a fine of $250.

Alcohol

Operating a boat while under the influence of alcohol is a criminal offence, with penalties ranging from a $600 fine and prohibition from operating a vessel, up to imprisonment for life in the case of serious repeat offences. The serious penalties for impaired boating deter some operators; however, passenger alcohol impairment remains a problem, and many boating fatalities occur when a drunken passenger falls overboard. Boat operators should not only comply with alcohol avoidance and storage regulations; they should also take responsibility for ensuring that passengers are not so impaired that their safety is in danger. When in doubt, an operator should not permit an intoxicated person to come aboard.

Powerboating in Provincial Parks

Powerboating is prohibited in many Ontario provincial parks. Regulation 347/07 under the *Provincial Parks and Conservation Reserves Act, 2006* provides a list of parks in which powerboating is *permitted*. In some cases, powerboats are permitted throughout the park; in other cases, their use is restricted to specific bodies of water or to a particular season. Finally, in many cases, powerboating is restricted to the use of boats within a certain horsepower range (for example, 10 horsepower or less).

People Downplay Familiar Risks

Participant experience and familiarity with risks poses a unique problem for recreation providers. David Ropeik and George Gray, authors of *Risk: A Practical Guide for Deciding What's Really Safe and What's Really Dangerous in the World Around You*, point out that familiarity with and enthusiasm for activities can distort risk perceptions. The authors make the following observations:

- People have less fear of risks associated with activities in which they voluntarily participate than of risks that are foisted on them against their will or to which they submit reluctantly. Consider, for example, the number of people afraid of dentistry and compare it with the number of people afraid of bicycling.

- People are less afraid of familiar than unfamiliar risks.

- People are less afraid of risks that are accompanied by benefits than of risks that bring no benefits.

- People are less afraid of the risks involved with products and activities that are offered by familiar than unfamiliar people.

The familiar people mentioned above need not be people actually *known* to the participant. Ropeik and Gray cite a situation in which two people each offer the participant a glass of clear liquid, and the participant is required to choose one glass and drink its contents. If one of the two people is someone the participant has never heard of or seen before, and the other person is Oprah Winfrey, the participant is much more likely to choose Winfrey's offering, even if he has never met her (Ropeik & Gray, 2002, p. 17).

In the recreation context, of course, this tendency translates into people attributing less risk to recreation activities that are promoted by their own parents or by celebrity athletes. It also may lead to inappropriate risk-taking by participants who have many years' experience with a particular activity. ◈

KEY TERMS

bylaws

Crown

immunity

operational decision

policy decision

REVIEW EXERCISES

Review Questions

1. Can individuals who are injured while participating in recreation on government-owned land sue the government for compensation?

2. Are governments liable for accidents that happen in wilderness areas?

3. What kinds of outdoor recreation activities are subject to government regulation?

4. What responsibilities does a government assume when it takes steps to develop land?

5. List some of the ways in which governments restrict the use of off-road vehicles.

6. List some of the ways in which governments restrict hunting and fishing.

7. List two factors that contribute to a significant percentage of boating fatalities.

Discussion Question

In February 2009, Canadian recreational skier Marie-Josée Fortin died while stranded in the British Columbia wilderness after intentionally skiing out-of-bounds with her husband at Kicking Horse Mountain Resort. The couple was stranded for nearly ten days in severe cold and were pursued by wolves. Despite her husband's having created at least five SOS signs—three of which were spotted by authorities—Ms. Fortin was never rescued, and her husband, Gilles Blackburn, was not rescued until after the third SOS was spotted.

The search effort was delayed in part because of confusion about searcher jurisdiction, and the lack of a missing-persons report. The RCMP has admitted that its failure to begin a search sooner contributed to Ms. Fortin's death. However, the skiers made multiple errors of judgment of their own: They carried no cellphone, no locator beacon, and no survival supplies; they skied deliberately out-of-bounds of the resort; they did not advise anyone of their plans for the day (and had checked out of their hotel); and they failed to remain near their first SOS sign.

Should a court order damages against the RCMP? (Don't worry that you don't know the legal answer to this question; answer from a public-policy perspective.)

CHAPTER 11

Recreation Spectators

CHAPTER OBJECTIVES

After completing this chapter, you should be able to:

- understand the risks associated with allowing recreation spectators to enter playing fields, tracks, stages, and other participant areas;

- list some of the strategies a recreation provider can use to contain spectators in safe viewing areas;

- explain the importance of appropriate emergency planning for crowd management;

- understand the basic regulatory framework that governs alcohol sales and service, and the challenges that spectator alcohol consumption presents for recreation providers;

- list other restricted or illegal spectator activities that must be monitored by recreation providers; and

- discuss the problem of spectator violence, and suggest violence prevention and management strategies.

INTRODUCTION

In conducting an initial risk assessment of a recreation business or organization, owners and staff may focus on the safety of participants. However, it is important not to forget that many recreation businesses host not only participants but also spectators and other visitors. Spectators may be formally invited—for example, students, teachers, parents, and friends may be invited to a high school football game, sometimes for a fee. But spectators may also watch recreation on a more casual basis. Consider, for example, a crowd that gathers on the ground below a bungee swing ride in an amusement park, or a parent who watches his child's end-of-session swimming test from a pool deck. In all cases, the safety implications of the presence of spectators must be considered.

Assessing risks to spectators is much the same as assessing risks to participants; however, there are a few unique issues that need to be addressed. First, spectators sometimes run the risk of being hurt through contact with participants or equipment. This problem can arise either when a spectator strays from the safe observation area, or when a participant, ball, vehicle, or other piece of equipment strays from the field of play. Second, spectators occasionally run the risk of being hurt in a sudden evacuation of a recreation area, especially when many people are contained in a confined space. Third, spectators may, if given the opportunity, consume alcohol irresponsibly and be injured as a result. Alternatively, they may engage or attempt to engage in other restricted or illegal activities on recreation property. Fourth and finally, spectators occasionally allow their competitive loyalties to escalate into violence, either against other spectators, or against recreation staff or participants. Each of these risks is discussed below, along with strategies that recreation providers can employ to prevent or limit harm to spectators and staff.

SPECTATOR INJURY THROUGH CONTACT WITH PARTICIPANTS OR GEAR

Introduction

Most readers of this book will be familiar with sports blooper reels that include footage of spectators being run over by raging rodeo steers, speedboats that fly out of the water, and slam-dunking basketball stars. Participant–spectator collisions are common (the author of this text once had her pinkie finger broken by an airborne Larry Bird). These collisions frequently cause minor, and occasionally cause serious, injury. Preventing or minimizing them is a wise move for recreation providers who are eager to minimize claims against their liability insurance.

Participant–spectator collisions fall into three main categories; each is discussed in a subsection below.

No Safe Observation Area

In some cases, participants and spectators collide because the recreation provider has not thought to designate and enforce a safe area from which activities can be viewed. This oversight is most likely to occur

1. where it is unusual to have spectators watch the activities, or

2. where the recreation display is a temporary installation, and has not been properly planned.

A situation in which spectator viewing is unusual might arise if a resort permits fishing from a dock, a fisher catches an unusual fish, and many observers crowd onto the dock to get a look at the catch. This situation could easily result in a spectator slipping and hitting his head on a piling. A mishap at a temporary installation might occur if there is a tricks competition at a local snowboarding park and a spectator climbs the steep sides of the park to get a better view, but then slips and falls into the path of the boarders.

In the fishing example, it would have been very difficult for the resort owner to predict, and guard against, the overcrowding on the dock. A forward-thinking resort owner might have posted a sign limiting the number of people on the dock at any time, but it is unlikely that guests would have heeded the sign in their eagerness to view the unusual catch. A more effective strategy for the resort owner would have been to ensure that the deck and surrounding area were as safe as possible: no tripping hazards, no exposed pilings, no submerged rocks, and proper drainage to manage slip risks.

In the second example, however, the recreation provider could definitely have foreseen the risk, and should have taken steps to manage it. Possibilities include:

- installing barriers on the sides of the snowboard park behind which spectators are required to stand, and installing viewing platforms that provide safe footing;

- requiring all spectators to remain at the bottom of the hill behind a barrier;

- hiring additional staff for the competition day to enforce the rules about safe viewing;

- arranging for the presence of first-aid providers (for example, St. John Ambulance) on the event day; and

- purchasing additional insurance coverage to cover the unusual risks related to having spectators at an event.

In summary, in the case of activities where spectator viewing is unusual, the best way to minimize harm is to keep the premises as safe as possible at all times. When spectators are anticipated, however, even for a one-time event, it is necessary to plan and enforce a safe viewing area.

Accidents Involving Equipment or Participant Entry into Observer Areas

Some participant–spectator collisions arise out of highly unusual accidents. Barrier-jumping steers and flying powerboat incidents fall into this category. An event at which such an accident happens may have enjoyed a long safety history before a participant moves outside the playing arena in a manner that had previously been thought to be physically impossible.

Where an event truly could not have been anticipated, the best a recreation provider can do is to fully insure itself. However, freak accidents reveal that things that you might dismiss as impossible do in fact occur. Therefore, sensible planning may involve making a few imaginative leaps.

By contrast, in baseball and hockey, it is fairly common for balls and pucks to sail out of the playing area, and sometimes these events lead to lawsuits. The plaintiff generally alleges that she had an expectation of complete safety from flying balls or pucks, and the recreation provider usually alleges that a warning about flying balls or pucks was clearly provided on signs in the building. Similar disputes arise in the context of basketball and football: it is not uncommon for a player who falls or is driven out of bounds to collide with a nearby spectator (who has often bought a premium ticket to get close to the action).

In all cases—whether the risk is exotic, as in the case of being trampled by a rodeo steer, or statistically significant, as in the case of being hit by a baseball—the risk management approach is the same: the recreation provider must take all reasonable steps to protect the spectators to whom it owes a duty of care. These steps follow the same pattern that has been described elsewhere in this book:

- eliminate controllable risks,

- educate spectators about intractable risks and require them to assume a share of responsibility for consequences, and

- insure against risks that cannot be eliminated.

Protecting spectators against risks can be costly. For example, installing safety nets above the glass in hockey arenas can cost thousands of dollars, and the nets require regular maintenance. However, lack of affordability, as a reason for failing to take safety precautions, does not stand up well in court when a spectator is seriously injured. As you have learned elsewhere in this book, if a recreation provider cannot afford to make recreation safe, it cannot afford to offer the recreation.

Some protective strategies are less expensive than others, but require a compliance commitment on behalf of staff. For example, the people most likely to be hit by a flying puck at a hockey game are the players sitting on the bench. Most minor hockey arenas now have rules that require players on the bench to wear helmets at all times. Coaching staff should be required to enforce this rule with their players.

Spectators Who Are Intentionally Out of Bounds

The third situation that leads to participant–spectator collisions occurs when a spectator intentionally strays outside her respective safety zone, whether that is the playing field, the track or stage, or the safe viewing area.

The key to controlling these incidents is maintaining appropriate staffing levels for all spectator events, and training staff to handle spectators' attempts to cross barriers. If there are significant risks associated with crossing a barrier, it is appropriate for staff to request that an offending spectator leave the premises immediately. If the spectator fails to do so, it may be acceptable to use reasonable force to remove the spectator in some circumstances.

A recreation provider who anticipates the occasional need to use force should either hire specially trained security officers, or provide staff with comprehensive use-of-force training.

assault
crime involving intentional physical contact without consent

battery
tort involving intentional physical contact without consent

wrongful detention
tort, sometimes called false imprisonment, which involves unjustified restraint of a person

Inappropriate uses of force—those that are not necessary for self-defence or to protect the public—constitute **assault** under the criminal law, and the intentional tort of **battery** under the common law. Any intentional touching of another person can potentially form the basis for a lawsuit based on battery. However, if the recreation provider can prove that the use of force was necessary and reasonable, it is unlikely that a spectator will succeed in his lawsuit.

Even if the use of some force is reasonable, the use of excessive force can form the basis for a criminal charge or a lawsuit. In all cases involving use of force, security personnel must use the minimum force necessary to protect themselves and the public from the spectator's actions.

Finally, there is another tort that can form the basis for a lawsuit following a poorly executed security effort: **wrongful detention** (sometimes called false imprisonment). Any time a spectator is restrained, by being held or placed in a secured

> ## CASE STUDY
>
> ### The Everclear Stage Dive Case
>
> A popular, but dangerous, stunt sometimes performed by musicians is the stage dive, a move in which a musician throws himself into the crowd, hoping to be caught by fans in a facedown, horizontal airplane pose. Injuries from stage dives are common, both for the diver and for the catchers. In 2007, for example, Klaxons frontman Jamie Reynolds broke a leg performing a stage dive that was a routine part of the band's show. This accident, which happened in France, followed a similar, but fatal, accident in England two years earlier.
>
> Usually, fans who stand near the stage on which a band known for its stage dives is performing understand that they assume the risks of catching one of their musical heroes. However, being on the receiving end of a stage dive has not always been considered as an honour. In 1997, a fan was injured at an Everclear concert when a stage dive was performed, not by one of the band members, but by New England Patriots players Drew Bledsoe (a 233-pound quarterback) and Max Lane (a 305-pound lineman). The fan, 23-year-old Tameeka Messier, suffered head and neck injuries and filed a lawsuit in Boston. Messier sued not only the venue operators and the football players but also the band, even though the band members allegedly did nothing to encourage the stage dives.
>
> The players, the venue owner, and the band all contributed to a settlement of over $1 million paid to the injured fan. ◇

area, there is a risk that she will claim to have been wrongfully detained. To minimize the risk of such a claim or a criminal charge, a spectator should never be restrained for longer than is necessary to get her out of harm's way and, if appropriate, to arrange for attendance by the police. Under no circumstances should a detained spectator ever be prevented from using the washroom, obtaining food or drink, or telephoning a loved one or a lawyer; and under no circumstances should a person be kept in uncomfortable conditions, such as extreme heat, cold, or tight quarters.

Occasionally a participant intentionally moves out of bounds and injures a spectator. The Everclear case provides an example of such a situation. To prevent these kinds of accidents, participants should be made aware that safety requires that they remain in their designated area, and that any attempt to accost a spectator or to move deliberately out of bounds will result in their being ejected from the game, event, or performance.

CROWD CONTROL, MASS EVACUATIONS, AND OTHER MEASURES FOR CROWDED VENUES

While a recreation venue may be safe under standard operating circumstances, things can change quickly when a crowd is mobilized by panic or other strong emotions. Football hooligan incidents around the world have shown that crowds can inflict considerable harm in a short time. The trampling death of a Wal-Mart employee in 2008 on Black Friday, the traditional peak shopping day between US Thanksgiving and the weekend, highlighted the need for facilities to anticipate risks associated with poor crowd control. Recreation providers who invite spectators into their facilities must pay special attention to this issue.

The owner of any facility that accommodates crowds must ensure that the facility meets the requirements of the relevant building code, especially regarding the number of exits, the exit locations, and the exit markings. In the event of an evacuation, it is important that spectators have many routes by which to leave the building to minimize pushing, shoving, and trampling.

The building must also be in compliance with the relevant fire code, and be equipped with appropriate alarm systems and fire-fighting equipment.

Many spectator facilities and other facilities that host large numbers of visitors now choose to have a defibrillator onsite. A defibrillator is a device that can be used to stimulate the cardiac function of someone who has suffered a heart attack. Research has shown that minimizing the delay in gaining access to a defibrillator can save lives.

Finally, any building that hosts crowds must be staffed with an adequate number of well-trained security personnel, ushers, and other hospitality staff. The calm demeanour and rational problem-solving provided by well-trained staff who are familiar with the facility can go a long way toward ensuring that emergencies are handled as safely as possible.

ALCOHOL SERVICE AND MANAGEMENT

Introduction

Alcohol consumption often accompanies adult recreation pursuits and, from a legal liability standpoint, presents some challenges that require careful management. Alcohol, in Ontario, is closely regulated by the provincial government. A permanent or temporary licence is required to sell or serve alcohol in a public place, and it is illegal to sell or serve alcohol to youth under the age of 19. It is also illegal to permit the consumption of alcohol in public spaces other than those that are licensed as alcohol-service spaces, or that offer overnight accommodation (for example, hotel rooms or campsites).

When recreation participants or spectators combine alcohol with recreation, violence or accidents sometimes result. The combination of competitive high spirits and intoxication can lead spectators to take risks or enter into conflicts that they

---

MANAGING RISKS

Safeconcerts Promotes Crowd and Event Safety

An entertainment website called Safeconcerts, whose motto is "music not mayhem," gathers and publishes information about how to promote safety at music concerts, festivals, and other events that draw crowds. The site lists several articles on safety-related topics, such as "Crowd Surfing and Moshing" and reports on concert incidents and initiatives. It also provides links to information about how to host an environmentally sound music event. By providing up-to-date concert listings, adopting a practical approach to drug control, and posting videotaped safety tips from performers such as Wayne Coyne of the Flaming Lips and Billy Bragg, the site seeks to be interesting and relevant to those who have the most at stake in concert accidents: young music fans. ◇

would avoid when sober. For this reason, recreation personnel must be especially vigilant in identifying, and if necessary excluding, intoxicated and rowdy spectators. They must also take steps to ensure that alcohol is not being illegally smuggled into a recreation venue.

Licences

Ontario has made some recent changes to its alcohol licensing system. These changes, effective since July 2008, are intended to reflect a new, risk-based approach to alcohol management. If an establishment's history demonstrates an elevated risk of non-compliance with alcohol management laws, the Liquor Control Board of Ontario (LCBO) can place special conditions (such as restrictions on hours of service) on its liquor licence. For this reason, maintaining consistent compliance with all applicable alcohol management rules is important for any venue that wants to maintain its low-risk licence.

There are a number of different types of liquor licences. In the recreation context, the most important are the special occasion permit, which allows the sale and service of alcohol on a single occasion in a single location, and the liquor sales licence, which allows the sale and service of alcohol on an ongoing basis in a particular facility.

SPECIAL OCCASION PERMITS

Special occasion permits can be issued for private functions, such as weddings and fundraisers, and certain kinds of public functions. The LCBO provides the following list of public functions for which a special occasion permit can be obtained:

- auctions,
- community festival events,
- consumer shows,
- diplomatic events,
- fundraising events,
- market research events,
- receptions,
- significant events, and
- trade shows.

Descriptions of these events are available on the website of the Alcohol and Gaming Commission of Ontario (AGCO).

Special occasion permits, especially for outdoor events, must be obtained well in advance. The AGCO advises that the application, which is to be delivered to an LCBO store, must be submitted 30 days in advance, although some indoor reception permits can be rushed. The application process is fairly onerous. A party wishing to serve alcohol at a community outdoor event must, for example, "at least 21 days prior to the event, write to the local municipality, police, and fire and health departments informing them of the event. The building department must be notified as well if a tent or marquee is used." There are also rules about the service setup, especially about how the alcohol service area is to be separated from other public areas where minors are permitted. Receipts for all of the alcohol purchased for the event must be available at the event for inspection by LCBO staff.

LIQUOR SALES LICENCES

Liquor sales licences are available for the ongoing sale of alcohol by a premises that must also offer, at a minimum, "light meals." Application for a liquor sales licence is made to the AGCO by mail with supporting documents. A PDF version of the application form is available on the AGCO website.

Liquor sales licences can come with endorsements—that is, additional permissions that must be applied for separately and that attach to the basic liquor service licence. The endorsements currently available are as follows:

- brew pub endorsement,

- catering endorsement,

- golf course endorsement,

- mini-bar endorsement,

- room service endorsement,

- stadium endorsement,

- wine pub endorsement, and

- bring your own wine (BYOW) endorsement.

Establishments licensed to serve liquor must comply with a wide range of rules. It is the responsibility of every liquor-serving recreation provider to be familiar with and comply with all of these rules. Failure to comply can lead to suspension or revocation of the liquor licence, and/or charges under the Ontario *Liquor Control Act*.

Finally, a law known as "Sandy's Law" now requires restaurants and bars that serve alcohol to post signs in a specific format warning women that the consumption of alcohol during pregnancy can cause birth defects and brain damage.

Searches

If there is a risk that spectators may bring alcohol into a venue in contravention of the law, it may be appropriate to arrange for entry-point searches by door staff. As you may know, it is illegal for police (or anyone else) to perform any kind of non-consensual search on a person in the absence of reasonable grounds to suspect that the person is breaking, or will break, the law. However, there is a difference between non-consensual and consensual searches. When a spectator arrives at a venue that is conducting entry-point searches, she has a choice: consent to a search, or choose not to enter.

Because the potential legal liability of recreation providers increases any time a staff person touches a visitor, spectator, or participant, most recreation venues mandate touch-free visual searches. In this kind of search, after being asked permission and agreeing to be searched, the spectator may be asked to open a coat, remove a hat, or open a bag or purse for visual inspection. Possibly with the aid of flashlights, the searchers may look into pockets or purses, but may not touch the spectators or their belongings.

In settings where the risk of smuggling illegal objects is high (for example, in a nightclub with a history of drug use or knife fights), the recreation provider may choose to mandate pat-down searches. During these searches, staff physically pat down the clothed body of a spectator. The entrant must always be asked to give permission to be searched. If permission is denied, the entrant should be directed to the box office, where a refund should be made available for any entry fee paid.

A pat-down search sometimes involves fairly intrusive touching (putting hands into the entrant's pants pockets), and should only be used if deemed absolutely necessary. Female staff must be available to search female guests, and male staff to search male guests.

Should a search turn up illegal alcohol, the entrant may be asked to return the item to his car, dispose of it outside the venue, or turn it over to the staff. If there is a duty police officer on hand, the recreation provider may choose to report the find to her. Whether or not the spectator is charged will be up to the police officer.

Intoxicated Spectators

A liquor sales licence provides that the **licensee** shall not sell liquor to a person who is already intoxicated. All staff who serve alcohol must be required to complete alcohol service training (a recognized provider of this training, in Ontario, is Smart Serve). Alcohol service training includes tips about how to recognize the signs of intoxication, which can sometimes be quite subtle.

licensee
licence holder

Should an intoxicated spectator pose a threat to herself, to others, or to property, the recreation staff should ask her to leave. If she does not leave voluntarily, trained security personnel (who should know how to use minimal force) should be called to assist in removing her. An intoxicated patron must never be thrown out of the building without a safe means of getting home. Security staff must offer to call a cab, pay for a cab if the patron has no money, or take sincere steps to ensure that she has a ride home with a sober friend. Providing a guest with the opportunity to become intoxicated and then allowing her to leave at the wheel of a car constitute grounds for a negligence claim in Ontario.

OTHER REGULATED ACTIVITIES

Introduction

Besides alcohol consumption, there are other restricted or illegal activities that patrons may engage in while on recreation property. The recreation provider has a duty to monitor the behaviour of its guests at all time, and to avoid knowingly allowing illegal or restricted activities to occur on its premises. Covering these activities in detail is beyond the scope of this book; what follows is a very basic overview. Where a recreation provider identifies a heightened risk for any of these activities on its premises, further investigation of the relevant regulatory framework will be necessary.

Smoking

The *Smoke-Free Ontario Act* now makes it illegal to smoke tobacco in any public place. What constitutes a "public place" is described in the legislation. While it was once permissible to provide a smoking room or other indoor smoking area, this is no longer the case; all smoking must now take place outdoors.

There are restrictions on smoking outdoors as well. Some buildings have passed bylaws prohibiting smoking within a defined distance from the front door (10 metres is fairly typical), and there are rules governing outdoor smoking shelters.

Because they cater to a health-conscious clientele, sports recreation facilities are generally very scrupulous in enforcing smoking laws, and many of these facilities have restrictions on smoking near the entrance. Should a patron persist in illegal smoking, staff should obtain the help of security personnel to remove the person from the building.

Drugs and Controlled Substances

No patron of a recreation business should be permitted to bring controlled drugs onto the premises, or to consume them there. A facility that encounters a problem with drug use may choose to conduct entry-point searches. Should drugs be found, the police should be contacted and a report made.

To protect the safety of patrons, recreation staff should conduct regular checks of washrooms, locker rooms, and other public areas to ensure that no drugs or drug paraphernalia have been left behind by others. These searches should be especially thorough in settings that offer children's programming; some curious children will readily consume found substances, and the provider must take steps to protect its guests.

Should a spectator fall ill or seem disoriented in circumstances where drug use is suspected, a first-aid provider should be immediately summoned and 911 should be called.

Weapons

No weapons of any kind should be permitted in a recreation facility that is not a gun club (gun clubs are subject to strict rules under the *Firearms Act*). Weapons offences, while still rare in Canada, are on the rise in recent years, and recreation staff should be alert to the issue. Special vigilance is warranted in any situation in which there is a spirit of competition, especially between teams with a historic rivalry. Providers of martial arts training and competitions should also be vigilant, because some traditional martial arts weapons (for example, throwing stars and nunchaku) cannot legally be carried in Canada.

Where a recreation provider has reason to suspect that spectators or visitors may bring weapons onto the premises, the provider has a responsibility to conduct voluntary pat-down searches at the point of entry. Should a weapon be found, the spectator should be detained until police can be summoned.

Gambling

Like alcohol sales and service, gambling is a restricted activity in Ontario. Gaming and gambling are not permitted except in premises specially licensed for the purpose, or unless the party offering the game, raffle, or lottery holds a licence.

Since many charitable organizations depend on raffles, lotteries, and other games to raise revenue, the provincial government offers licences for these activities to successful applicants. Small-scale raffles, games, and lotteries with prizes under listed amounts—for example, $5,500 for a media bingo event, $50,000 for total prizes in a raffle, and $2 for maximum bets on wheels of fortune—are licensed by municipalities. Larger-scale schemes are licensed by the province directly. A first-time applicant must apply for a provincial licence 45 days in advance, and a repeat applicant must apply 30 days in advance.

A recreation provider that wishes to offer a game, raffle, bingo, or similar event must make a proper application within the application period. If a provider allows other parties to offer gaming on its premises (for example, if a hockey arena allows travel team managers to sell raffle tickets during a home game), it must ask to view the licence held by the game offeror. If the offeror cannot produce a satisfactory licence, the recreation provider should prohibit the gaming activity on its premises.

Privacy and Public Sex

The protection of privacy is increasingly important in modern society. In some recreation settings, privacy can be abused through the use of small and easily concealed cameras (including cellphone-based cameras) in locker rooms. Most recreation facilities ban the use of cameras and cellphones in locker rooms and washrooms for this reason. Recreation providers should be sure to post clear signs near the entrance to locker rooms and washrooms where such a ban is in place.

In a few recreation settings, there is the potential for violations of the obscenity-related provisions of the *Criminal Code*. This problem arises where spectators engage in sexual acts in public places (for the purpose of the *Criminal Code*, a washroom is a public place). Although there is an expectation of privacy in a washroom stall, if sexual activity there is detectable to people outside the stall, the activity will likely be deemed to be obscene. Any recreation provider who is aware of public sexual activity on its premises should take steps to prevent it by conducting patrols and increasing the lighting in dark areas of the facility.

SPECTATOR VIOLENCE

Introduction

Unfortunately, some recreation events have been marred by incidents of violence among spectators. While Chapter 12 in this book is devoted to the subject of violence in sport and other recreation, it focuses on *participant* violence. Recreation providers must also be prepared for the possibility of violent confrontations between spectators, and between staff and spectators, and must have procedures in place for defusing these incidents safely.

Minor League Sports

Spectator violence is not restricted to crowd situations. Minor sports games, which may attract only a small group of spectating family and friends, are a fairly common trigger for violence. In July 2000, during a casual hockey scrimmage between children in Reading, Massachusetts, a 44-year-old father attacked another father, who was acting as referee in the game. In front of the young players, the attacker punched the referee until he was unconscious, and then left the scene. The referee died of his injuries, and the attacker was eventually convicted of manslaughter.

Hockey parent rage occurs in Canada as well, as the *Reddemann* case study demonstrates, and conflicts among spectators and between spectators and referees can occur at almost any sporting event. The following strategies can help to reduce the risk that these conflicts will occur:

- Develop a code of conduct for the facility that prohibits profanity and abusive language, and that incorporates stiff penalties for infringement. Such penalties can include suspension of a participant from play if his parents or spectators violate the policy.

- Communicate a zero-tolerance policy in relation to violence or verbal abuse.

- Ban alcohol from the facility.

- Ban parents from dressing room areas unless they are needed to dress young children.

- Ensure that spectators are restricted to a safe viewing area where their comments cannot be heard by coaches, players, and referees.

- Provide separate "Home" and "Away" seating areas.

- Ensure that the facility has enough staff available to monitor the behaviour of spectators, and to react quickly with a call to security or police if violence erupts.

Perhaps most importantly, coaches and other team staff should take the time to develop a rapport with parents. They should tell parents that the object of children's sports is to promote the benefits of health and fitness, and to encourage the development of co-operation, leadership, teamwork, fair play, and good sportsmanship in young players. Good coaches are often able to have a profound influence not only on players but also on their parents. If coaches demonstrate that they actually share the values that they are promoting—for example, by giving all players a fair portion of playing time and by treating referees with respect—they can create an environment in which spectators do not feel at liberty to engage in violent outbursts.

Professional Sporting and Other Recreational Events

Where a recreation provider offers events that cater to a large audience, violence prevention tactics must be more general. The key to preventing and stopping spectator violence in a crowd situation is providing sufficient staff. If spectators perceive that their actions are being observed by a staff person who is in a position to quickly

---

CASE STUDY

The Mascot and the Trainer: Reddemann v. McEachnie

In April 2002, the Chilliwack Chiefs and the Vernon Vipers, two Junior A hockey teams, were engaged in a playoff series that was tied 2–2. Reddemann, the mascot for the Chiefs, travelled to Vernon with friends to see the game. He was seated in the first row, directly behind the Vipers' bench and assistant trainer Trevor McEachnie.

Reddemann, as was his custom, brought a loud drum to the game. He beat the drum on and off, and every time the Chiefs scored, he leapt to his feet and beat it.

After the Chiefs scored two goals in quick succession, the Vipers called a time out. Reddemann stood up and beat his drum four or five feet behind McEachnie, who could not, as a result, hear what the coach was saying to the players. McEachnie turned around, leaned over the glass, and punched Reddemann in the face. Reddemann fell to his seat and then to the ground, with McEachnie continuing to punch him.

Reddemann suffered some moderate soft-tissue injuries and missed a week of work. His pain was not completely resolved by the time of trial three years later.

The court determined that because McEachnie's reaction was "totally disproportionate" to Reddemann's actions, it would be inappropriate to reduce the damages on the basis of provocation or self-defence. The court awarded Reddemann $25,000 in damages for pain and suffering, and $10,000 in punitive damages to reflect the need to denounce the behaviour of those "who are not in a position to control their temper and their enthusiasm for the team they support." In awarding these punitive damages, the court cited the fact that the league and team owner imposed little or no penalty of their own on McEachnie. ◇

---

summon backup, violent outbursts will be much less likely to occur than if spectators do not feel that they are being monitored.

Staff must be trained to intervene swiftly and effectively if a problem appears to be developing, and should have the authority to remove problematic patrons from the facility. By acting quickly to remove violent fans (with a refund, in appropriate cases), staff send a message that viewing the event is a privilege earned through appropriate behaviour.

Also important, should violence break out, are good policies about crowd management and proper building design.

When crowd control is necessary, facility rules should require that events have assigned seating, and that participants remain in their seats unless travelling to areas such as snack bars and washrooms. Requiring that participants remain seated leaves aisles clear, which allows security personnel to move quickly toward an altercation, should one arise. Such a requirement also allows a pathway for emergency personnel, stretchers, defibrillators, or other emergency equipment.

In a very large facility, requiring ticket holders to enter through one of several designated gates also helps to prevent dangerous congestion of aisles, stairways, and exits. As noted above, any facility that hosts large crowds must have a number of clearly marked exits appropriate to the size of the crowd.

KEY TERMS

assault

battery

licensee

wrongful detention

REVIEW EXERCISES

Review Questions

1. List at least three circumstances that can threaten the safety of spectators on recreation premises.

2. What three basic steps must a recreation provider take to protect the safety of spectators?

3. Why is it important for recreation providers to establish a safe viewing area for spectators?

4. What must a recreation provider do if she wishes to sell and serve alcohol on her premises?

5. How can recreation providers minimize liability related to the abuse of alcohol on their premises?

6. Is it legal for recreation providers to search spectator pockets and purses at entry points?

7. What must a recreation provider do before holding a charity casino event, or other gambling or gaming-based fundraiser?

8. What is the most important element of a spectator violence prevention program?

Discussion Question

Should recreation providers ever be held vicariously liable for harm caused by spectators?

CHAPTER 12

Violence in Sport

CHAPTER OBJECTIVES

After completing this chapter, you should be able to:

- describe some of the challenges for recreation providers in drawing the line between sport and violence;

- explain the role of intent as an element of assault;

- suggest strategies for establishing the limits of participants' consent;

- understand the roles played by team leaders and sports culture in determining the potential for violence;

- list at least three factors that can make participants prone to sports violence; and

- explain how appropriate rules and a culture of fair play can reduce sports violence.

INTRODUCTION

As this chapter was being written, 21-year-old Don Sanderson, a York University student and senior hockey player with the Whitby Dunlops, lay in Hamilton General Hospital. Sanderson had fallen into a coma after hitting his head on the ice in an on-ice fight. News reports about the accident featured the usual views from both the anti-fighting and the fight-tolerant sides of the debate. Perhaps most prominent in the media coverage of Sanderson's accident, however, were the comments of Bob McKenzie, a popular TSN hockey commentator, who wrote:

> What's truly frightening is that what happened to Don Sanderson doesn't happen more often. When you think of all the levels of hockey and how many fights there are, and how many times players in the fights lose their helmet(s), how many times those players end up falling to the ice and how hard that ice is, well, it's almost beyond comprehension that this isn't epidemic.

Indeed, Sanderson's was not the only serious head injury associated with hockey fighting in recent years: in a highly publicized 2004 incident, NHL player Todd Bertuzzi hit opposing player Steve Moore from behind, causing him severe injury. That incident led to both a civil lawsuit and a criminal investigation, and Bertuzzi served a long suspension from major league play.

Violent assaults and consensual fighting have occurred in nearly every team sport. Baseball, soccer, lacrosse, rugby, cricket, football, and basketball have all had their reputations marred, at one time or another, by a violent player-against-player incident. Violence has also tainted individual sports, most notably those that are fighting-based, such as boxing and wrestling.

While general sports violence statistics are lacking, individual studies suggest that there have been at least 100 sports violence investigations in Canada since the beginning of the 20th century. Despite increases in these cases in the last 40 years, prosecutions are rare, and where convictions are entered, sentences tend to be light. When violent incidents have come before Canadian courts for adjudication (whether under the criminal law or in lawsuits), judges have often struggled, particularly with issues related to consent. In the earlier cases, defendants have argued that participants in certain sports—notably hockey and boxing—assume the risk of a certain degree of violence because this violence is the norm for the sport. Judges have agreed with this argument in many, but not all, instances, which has resulted in considerable inconsistency in their decisions.

Deciding whether or not an act of violence is sport or assault is a very difficult task in practical terms. However, such a distinction must be made by courts and the recreation organizations that regulate sport, because violence affects individuals and society long after its victims have recovered from their immediate injuries. Recent research into the lifelong effects of repeated head trauma has revealed that athletes

CASE STUDY

Skate-Blade Kick to the Head: R. v. Tropea

On February 12, 2005, in the course of a women's Intermediate A hockey game, 20-year-old Julia Tropea of the Niagara Falls Rapids cross-checked opponent Carly Bernard (also aged 20) of the London Devillettes to the ice. Tropea then kicked her forcefully in the helmet with her skate. Bernard suffered a concussion and a dislocated jaw.

After a criminal trial, Tropea was convicted of assault causing bodily harm. The judge sentenced Tropea to two years' probation, and noted that, had the Crown asked for jail time, he would have considered custody or "perhaps house arrest for a few months." The Crown did not, however, ask for a custodial sentence. In refusing to enter the **discharge** requested by Tropea's defence lawyer, the judge described the offence as "so egregious to me, [that] it wipes out any chance of a discharge." This comment was especially notable in light of the fact that NHL players Todd Bertuzzi and Marty McSorley *were* granted discharges as a result of their own serious on-ice transgressions.

The criminal conviction entered against Tropea attracted some negative media attention, including suggestions that there is a "double standard" when it comes to criminal charges against NHL players. However, according to experts, the violence of Tropea's attack against Bernard is without precedent in women's hockey. Many people have viewed Tropea's skate-blade kick to Bernard's head as an attack more serious and more clearly intentional than either the Bertuzzi or the McSorley incidents.

Tropea has effectively been banned for life from playing organized women's hockey (and has never played since the incident). If her conviction stands on appeal, she will likely have difficulty securing permanent employment in her chosen field of study (early childhood education) and, at least in the short term, in crossing international borders. ◇

discharge
a judge's disposition (order) that does not impose a criminal conviction on a person found guilty of an offence

who sustain serious head injuries may suffer a 20-year reduction in life expectancy. A study by University of Montreal researchers, published in January 2009 in Oxford University's journal *Brain*, found that even a single concussion sustained in early adulthood can affect the cognitive and neuromotor function of athletes more than 30 years later. Research has also shown a disturbing number of premature deaths resulting from suicide. Many of the athletes studied exhibited depression, poor coping abilities, difficulty holding a job, and family violence. Although most of the research has focused on professional football, repeated concussions are also common in other sports, such as hockey, rugby, wrestling, and boxing.

In addition, some researchers argue that victimization through violence presents only half of the picture of social harm. In a 2003 communiqué written by senior analyst Paul Roberts, the Canadian Council on Social Development (CCSD) noted that parents frequently expressed concern about their children's exposure to violence on television, in video games, and in the media. However, the communiqué went on to note that these same parents rarely mentioned the impact of violence in the sports that their children play themselves:

> Our research shows that pressure "to win at all costs" is widespread in sports programs, pushing children to violence which causes low self-esteem, anxiety and aggressive behavior—yet most parents did not cite violence in sports as a cause for concern.

In each of the sections below, a facet of violence in sport is discussed with reference to an actual case.

INTENTION: DRAWING THE LINE BETWEEN ROUGH PLAY AND ASSAULT

Section 265(1)(a) of the *Criminal Code* of Canada defines an assault as any incident in which a person "without the consent of another person ... applies force intentionally to that other person, directly or indirectly." Three key elements of the offence are evident from this definition:

1. Criminal assault requires the application of force.

2. The force can be direct or indirect, but its application must be intentional.

3. The victim must not have consented to the application of force.

One player's application of force to another is a feature of all contact sports, and so there is rarely any controversy in sports violence cases about whether or not force was applied. This leaves two issues—intent and the absence of consent—for consideration in determining whether an injury is simply an unfortunate consequence of sports play, or the result of a violent criminal act. This section focuses on the issue of intent.

In daily life, it's usually easy to determine whether or not one person's application of force to another is intentional. In the context of contact sports, however, the issue becomes murkier. In an environment where contact is frequent and expected, differentiating between intentional and unintentional contact is difficult, and not very meaningful. Instead, any discussion of intent tends to focus on one of two issues:

1. In some cases, analysis is focused on whether the person accused of violence undertook the violent act *with the intent to achieve a legitimate sports objective* (for example, to score a point or defend against a play) or *with the intent to hurt another.*

2. In other cases, analysis is focused on whether or not the person accused of violence intended to inflict injurious *harm* or whether the *injury* was unintended although the *contact* was intentional.

A review of the *Criminal Code*, however, makes it clear that the definition of assault does not turn on either of these finer points. *Any* intentional, non-consensual contact is an assault, regardless of the motives for the contact or the assailant's expectations about the consequences. It seems that players of contact sports escape charges of assault solely through reliance on their opponents' consent to otherwise objectionable contact.

Not every kind of sports contact, however, is socially accepted. While the precise dividing line between fair play and violence is difficult to draw, some acts committed by sports participants are met with significant social disapproval, and sometimes with criminal charges. While observers do not always agree about their reasons for denouncing these acts, improper motives and a reckless disregard for the safety of others are key factors in defining an act not as sport, but as violence.

Many analysts have tried to develop a definition for sports violence, or to establish criteria for differentiating fair play from violence. The Canadian Centre for Ethics in Sport (CCES) offers the following definition:

> Violence in sport is a physical assault or other physically harmful actions by a player that takes place in a sports context and that is intended to cause physical pain or injury to another player (or fan, coach, game official, etc.), where such harmful actions bear no direct relationship to the rules and associated competitive goals of the sport.

Canadian sociologist Michael D. Smith, in his oft-cited book *Violence in Sport*, divides incidents of sports violence into four categories. Smith's categories are based on the degree to which an incident deviates from the recognized rules of a sport or game, and the likelihood of criminal law consequences. Smith's categories can be summarized as follows:

1. *Brutal body contact.* This violence is an intrinsic feature of many sports, such as football, rugby, hockey, boxing, and wrestling. It includes contact that lies within the rules of a particular sport but that could form the basis of a criminal charge or tort lawsuit if it occurred in a non-sports context. Examples include fair tackles and bodychecks in football and hockey, and fair punches and holds in boxing and wrestling.

2. *Borderline violence.* This violence constitutes a violation of the formal rules of play, but does not fall outside the general expectations of participants and spectators of a sport. It almost never forms the basis of a successful criminal investigation or a civil lawsuit, because the defendant can usually argue that the victim assumed the risk of this standard violence. Examples include illegal or penalty-attracting plays or moves, such as boarding or high-sticking in hockey, "facemask" or other illegal

tackles in football, and low blows in boxing and martial arts. In hockey, this category also includes most fighting, because while fighting has nothing to do with the game of hockey, it is so common that it has become the norm for the sport.

3. *Quasi-criminal violence.* This category includes unusual acts of violence that fall outside not only the official rules but also the usual limits for a particular sport. Because these acts deviate so markedly from the rules of play and participant expectations, they sometimes result in criminal convictions or civil lawsuits. Examples include fighting in any sport in which fighting is uncommon; unprovoked or excessively violent or unusual acts, especially when serious injury results; and attacks from behind or other attacks that are unanticipated. Boxer Mike Tyson's biting the ear of opponent Evander Holyfield in a 1997 match would likely fall into this category, as would Todd Bertuzzi's assaulting Steve Moore in a 2004 hockey game.

4. *Criminal violence.* Where an act of violence is completely unconnected to sports play and clearly constitutes a violation of the criminal law, it is criminal violence, and is prosecuted as such. Examples include sports hooliganism, attacks on referees by fans, and sabotage attacks such as the 1994 attack on figure skater Nancy Kerrigan by associates of skater Tonya Harding.

For a recreation provider, preventing sports violence and avoiding liability for sports violence means ensuring participant consent. It also means being able to determine quickly and decisively when the line between sport and violence has been crossed, and consistently imposing appropriate sanctions on offenders. The practical application of this duty will vary from context to context, but strategies may include the following:

- Have strictly applied rules about who may, and who may not, engage in body contact. These rules may be based on age (for example, bodychecks involving players under age 12 or over age 50 may be prohibited); health status (for example, medical clearance may be required before a boxer can enter a competition); ability (for example, players below a particular training level may be prohibited from undertaking certain moves); league type (for example, defensive slides in slo-pitch softball may be prohibited); or receipt of a signed waiver of liability or consent form.

- Have well-trained referees and officials who understand the rules of play and the limits of fair play, and who are willing to penalize all infractions with fairness and consistency.

- Have an internal investigations program that supports the timely review of all incidents of violence, the decision about whether to report an incident to the police, and the imposition of appropriate consequences.

- Have clear and consistently applied policies about game expulsions, suspensions from participation, revocation of registrations, and participation bans that allow the recreation provider to remove problem players and, if necessary, prevent their return.

- Have an effective system for the review of coaches, instructors, and trainers that allows the recreation provider to remove a coach, instructor, or trainer who encourages or ignores violent play.

- Have well-trained facility staff who are supported by security personnel and do not hesitate to call for police or ambulance backup in the event of an act of violence.

- Have first-aid equipment onsite and staff with first-aid training.

- Have an effective system in place to receive and respond to complaints by players, parents, referees, coaches, spectators, or anyone else who may have concerns about sports violence.

These steps would likely not have prevented the Julia Tropea assault described in the case study. However, they can create a climate in which violence is less likely to occur, and in which staff are prepared to provide immediate assistance, conduct a timely investigation, and take decisive corrective action.

CONTACT SPORTS AND THE LIMITS OF CONSENT

As explained earlier in this chapter, the criminal law of assault in Canada makes it clear that an act is an assault only when the victim does not consent to the application of force. Most successful defences to charges of assault that arise in the context of sport have turned on the issue of consent.

In agreeing to participate in a sport, a participant is generally considered to have assumed the risks related to the kinds of body contact that are widely accepted as part of the sport. A victim is unlikely to be successful in alleging that she did not assume these risks unless she can prove very little prior knowledge of the sport—for example, unless she is a complete beginner, and the sport is unfamiliar to the general public. Such a situation is rarely encountered.

In most cases, registering to play a sport includes a requirement that the prospective participant sign a waiver that describes the risks of the sport. But this step is not essential to prove consent: courts have almost always held that choosing to participate, even informally, constitutes consent to well-known risks.

The risk of criminal or civil liability, therefore, arises only where what happens on the playing field diverges so markedly from the expected playing experience that the participant cannot be said to have anticipated it—or to have consented to it. In its 1991 decision in *R. v. Jobidon*, the Supreme Court of Canada considered the facts of a "consensual bar fight" that led to the death of one of the fighters. In finding that the accused was guilty of manslaughter, the Court explained that the common law imposes limits on what a person can consent to. The common law relating to consent co-exists with the provisions of the *Criminal Code*, except where the *Criminal Code* specifically overrides the common law.

The victim in *Jobidon* consented to being in a fair fight. However, for public policy reasons, the Court held that the law does not recognize a person's consent to serious bodily harm. When the *Jobidon* case is considered, it becomes clear that certain sports—notably combat sports, such as boxing or mixed martial arts—operate

---

CASE STUDY

Shoot-Fighting Instructor Injures Student: Parker v. Ingalls

Robert Parker was an athlete with an interest in a wide range of sports and fitness activities. In 1997, when he was about 30 years old, he signed up for classes in Kenpo karate at a local martial arts club. Nearly six years later, Parker was still studying the martial art, and expressed an interest in learning shoot-fighting, a martial art that his instructor, club owner Jodey Ingalls, had introduced.

Ingalls was a martial arts expert, and had studied shoot-fighting with experts. There was never any question of his personal competence in the sport. Ingalls explained to Parker that shoot-fighting was more dangerous than Kenpo karate, but Parker agreed to try it anyway. On January 23, 2003, Parker agreed to allow Ingalls to demonstrate a new shoot-fighting countermove on him. In the course of the demonstration, Parker suffered a serious and painful knee injury, and sued Ingalls and the club in negligence.

The court found that Ingalls had made a negligent error in demonstrating the move, and that this error was the cause of Parker's injury. After a careful consideration of three different releases that Parker had signed or seen during his involvement with the club, the court concluded that Parker's consent to participate in martial arts training included the acceptance of many of the standard risks of the sport. However, it did not include the risk that Parker would be injured by his experienced and trusted instructor in the course of a demonstration. Ingalls and the club were found liable in negligence. ◇

---

more or less *outside* the limits of Canadian law. To date, there seems not to have been a criminal case, in Canada, based on lack of consent in combat sports. There have, however, been cases that test the limits of consent in sports, such as hockey, where interpersonal violence is not the essence of play.

When tragedy strikes in a sports context, courts are forced to examine the facts of the incident to determine whether the line between rough play and assault has been crossed to the point where the accused's actions have exceeded the limits of the victim's consent. This analysis is nearly impossible in the context of combat sports. Unless a clear rule exists prohibiting the kind of move that caused the harm (for example, eye-gouging is not permitted in wrestling), it is difficult for the victim to argue lack of consent. The fact that combat sports seem to operate in direct conflict with the Canadian law of assault places the providers and facilitators of these sports in a very awkward legal position. It has also led to regular campaigns for the abolition of combat sports.

The CCES has suggested that defining the limits of consent, in some sports, is not only a legal issue but also a question of morality:

> As a society, can we claim that all violence in sport is morally wrong and therefore should be penalized or banned outright? The obvious answer is "yes," but like many ethical issues, on closer examination this question is more complex. For example, some sports, as part of their rules, require intense physical contact which may cause pain, injury or other harm. In such cases, are the sports themselves morally unacceptable?

This book does not attempt to answer this question because morality is highly personal. Those who choose to engage in violent sports clearly consider these sports to be morally acceptable to them. Coming to this conclusion, however, requires an in-

---

CASE STUDY

The 99 Call: The British Lions and the Springboks

In 1974, the British Lions rugby team was set to face the Springboks from South Africa in the course of a highly successful, though violent, tour. The Springboks had a reputation for aggressive and sometimes violent play.

In preparing their strategy for facing the Springboks, the British Lions devised a play known as the 99 call. The play was to be used at the first instance of violence, on the part of a Springboks player, that went unpenalized by the referees.

On hearing the call of "99!," every British Lions player was required to immediately and violently attack the Springboks player closest to him. The reasoning behind the play was that the referees would be so overwhelmed by the sudden chaos that they would have to choose to throw either every Lions player out of the game, or no Lions player out of the game.

In practice, the play worked: no Lions player was ejected. Because of limited video coverage of the game, no charges or followup punishments were ever imposed, even though the violence was blatant. (For example, J.P.R. Williams ran 60 metres down the pitch to punch a Springboks player in the face.) The game, which became known as the Battle of Boet Erasmus Stadium, is remembered by rugby fans as one of the most violent of all time. ◇

---

formed consideration of all of the foreseeable consequences of participation. Providing the necessary information is the duty of the recreation provider. Providers must be aware, though, that even the best risk education and risk communication program cannot overcome the legal reality that a person *cannot* in law consent to serious bodily harm.

PART OF THE GAME: LEADER-SANCTIONED, CULTURAL, AND ENDEMIC VIOLENCE

The infamous rugby 99 call described in the case study was not only premeditated but also devised by the team's captain. It is a perfect example of leader-sanctioned violence, a particularly dangerous form of sports violence. Canadian sports history is marred by its own leader-sanctioned incidents: for example, Bobby Clarke's slash to the ankle of Russian hockey star Valeri Karlamov in the sixth game of the 1972 Summit series between Canada and Russia is rumoured to have been ordered by assistant coach John Ferguson Sr.

Malice, violence, and intentional harm run completely counter to the values and goals of recreational sport. Recreation leaders, including coaches, team captains, and instructors, set an example for participants. They play an essential role in shaping participants' sports experiences, in instilling values, and in setting the tone of play. There is no legitimate place in recreational sport for leaders who encourage, sanction, reward, or even turn a blind eye to violence. Recreation providers must be vigilant in identifying leaders, either staff or volunteers, who tolerate or encourage violent play. Providers must also take immediate and decisive steps to correct the behaviour of these leaders. If a sports leader has been warned about her attitude toward violence and has not changed it, she must be removed from her position of authority and, if necessary, from any form of participation. Allowing a leader who sanctions violence to remain in a position of authority amounts to an invitation to legal liability for the recreation provider should an injury result from the leader's actions.

Where support for violence can be traced to a particular individual, the recreation provider's remedy is fairly straightforward. However, in some cases, a team demonstrates violent play that is *not* ordered by team leaders, but that occurs spontaneously, and with the support of at least some of the other players. This problem can best be attributed to deficiencies in the general sports culture of the team. Sometimes, one or two incidents occur, earning a team a reputation for rough or violent play. If team members see an advantage to this reputation, they may embrace it, creating a team culture of violence that can endure through many playing seasons. An example of a sports organization with a culture of violence is the Philadelphia Flyers hockey team of the mid-1970s, who were known as the "Broad Street Bullies." While the Flyers are an NHL team, individual teams with violent reputations can be found in a wide range of sports, and at every level of play—including children's recreational leagues.

At the professional sports level, a team's violent reputation and culture can often be changed by trading the players most closely associated with the violence and by replacing the coach. At the recreational level, the problem is best handled through a program of education that helps participants to understand that violence is not an attribute for which a team should strive. In most cases, bully teams lose the respect of their peers, particularly when they play poorly.

When dealing with a team with a violent culture, recreation providers should realize that a successful cultural shift can be accomplished in the course of a single season. One of the best methods is to introduce a forceful new leader or co-leaders who openly dissociate themselves from the culture of their predecessors. Most players are eager for the mentorship of strong leaders, and will quickly adjust their performance to please them.

Finally, some sports violence flows not from leadership direction or team culture, but from the roots and reputation of a sport itself. Where violence has long been accepted as a feature of a sport, it becomes endemic. The best-known Canadian example of a sport in which violence is endemic is hockey; internationally, rugby is a good example.

Coping with endemic violence is a significant challenge for recreation providers. However, it's worth noting that not all Canadian hockey is violent. Fighting is almost unknown in young children's hockey, and is rare at all levels of girls' and women's hockey. This proves that it *is* possible to separate hockey from fighting by promoting non-violent competition at all levels of play.

Another way in which recreation providers can help to reduce violence in rough sports is by emphasizing the boundary between fair and foul play, and by characterizing all acts of violence as foul play. By equating violence with unsporting conduct, or even cheating, recreation providers can help to create an environment in which violence is deplored rather than admired. This strategy will succeed best if participants (and parents, in the case of children's activities) are regularly reminded of the true goals of sport: physical fitness, teamwork skills, and recreation. It also doesn't hurt to remind players that the likely result of violence is personal injury.

INDIVIDUAL FACTORS: HUMAN TIME BOMBS

While it's possible for violence to be endemic in a sport, or to be part of the culture of an individual team, most incidents of sports violence arise from the isolated actions of individual athletes who have momentarily lost their self-control. Well-known examples include boxer Mike Tyson's biting the ear of opponent Evander Holyfield in a 1997 boxing match, and soccer player Zinedine Zidane's head-butting opponent Marco Materazzi in a 2006 World Cup match.

Most often, these kinds of incidents occur when emotions erupt in the heat of competition, and the perpetrators are generally contrite and apologetic afterward. However, a few athletes show a tendency toward acts of violence, and their actions require close monitoring. A recreation provider who has identified a participant with a tendency toward violent outbursts has a duty to protect other participants from the actions of that person. Discharging this duty may include warning the participant to get his behaviour under control, providing anti-violence training or education, or banning the athlete from play in serious cases.

Recreation providers must be particularly vigilant about controlling participants whose outbursts appear to be motivated by racism or other forms of prejudice, or who use violence, verbal abuse, or anger to intimidate others. These participants can poison the recreation experience for their peers, and their actions must be closely controlled. If a participant's bad behaviour shows signs of escalating over time, it is generally appropriate to suspend him from participation pending a decision about whether his behaviour can be adequately controlled by staff.

CASE STUDY

Murder–Suicide Linked to Brain Injury: The Case of Chris Benoit

In June 2007, professional wrestler Chris Benoit killed his wife and seven-year-old son before committing suicide in his home in Fayetteville, Georgia.

The investigation of the incident revealed four factors that may have motivated Benoit's actions. First, it was revealed that Benoit's son Daniel probably suffered from fragile X syndrome, a genetic condition that has been linked to family discord. Second, medical records showed that Benoit was receiving testosterone therapy for testicular damage caused by a long history of steroid use. Testosterone supplementation has been linked, in some cases, to violence. Third, Benoit's history of steroid use was suggested as a factor.

Finally, an examination of Benoit's brain, conducted on the recommendation of Christopher Nowinski, a former wrestler and brain injury researcher, revealed damage to all four lobes and to the brain stem. This damage provided evidence of significant and repeated head trauma during the wrestler's career. According to the autopsy, Benoit's brain was comparable in appearance to that of an 85-year-old Alzheimer's patient. Traumatic brain injuries sustained through sports have been linked to shortened life expectancy, difficulty coping with life's challenges, domestic violence, and suicide.

Benoit was well known during his career as a wrestler who specialized in certain stunts that involved blows to the head. ◇

CASE STUDY

Takeout Slides: R. v. Anderson

In May 1997, a Vancouver slo-pitch recreational softball team called the Spartans found itself short a player for an upcoming game. The team recruited 22-year-old Edward Taylor, a player on another team in the same league, to fill in. Taylor was considered to be talented within the league.

At the bottom of the fourth inning, the Spartans were at bat, and the opposing team—the As—were in the field. John Anderson, the third baseman for the As, made a defensive error and allowed a Spartan runner (not Taylor) to reach base. In response to this error, some members of the Spartan team jeered at Anderson from the sidelines. Anderson became very angry, and remained so while the inning ended and the fifth inning began.

In the fifth inning, Anderson was first at bat, and made it to first base. The second batter's hit was caught just beyond second base by the Spartans' second baseman, and thrown to Taylor at shortstop. Taylor ran to second base, forcing Anderson out. However, in an attempt to prevent Taylor from throwing to first (for a double play), Anderson, who was still angry from the earlier incident, slid hard, feet first, into Taylor. This play—where the runner is out but attempts to interfere with a defensive play—is known as a takeout slide.

At 275 pounds, Anderson outweighed Taylor by 100 pounds. The collision between the two resulted in a severe injury to Taylor: a clean break of both the tibia and fibula that required surgery, insertion of a metal rod into a bone, five days in hospital, and six weeks on crutches.

Anderson was charged with assault causing bodily harm, and the case went to trial. The court found Anderson's actions to be foolish. However, by agreeing to participate in a softball game in which sliding was permitted (and there was no rule against take-out slides), Taylor had consented to the application of force by Anderson. ◇

In a few cases, violent behaviour has its roots not simply in personality, but in other causes that may involve

- drug use including the use of performance-enhancing drugs, such as anabolic steroids;

- alcohol abuse or the abuse of recreational drugs;

- the perpetrator's own history as a victim of domestic abuse or abuse at the hands of an authority figure;

- a recognized behavioural disorder, such as autism spectrum disorder or attention deficit hyperactivity disorder;

- a head injury or a history of concussions; or

- a mental illness, such as schizophrenia or depression.

When an athlete commits a violent act, a recreation provider's first responsibility is securing the safety of other participants. However, once their safety is assured, the provider has a duty to treat the violent participant fairly. Fair treatment includes taking into consideration the possibility that the athlete's actions may have been influenced by an addiction, an illness, or another problem that may be alleviated by referring the athlete to a physician or other specialist. Supporting the athlete in obtaining help is simply good customer service.

Finally, where violence occurs on a recurrent basis within a recreation organization, the recreation provider must consider whether its own policies, practices, and culture contribute to the problem. For example, in certain sports, such as body-building, baseball, and track and field, the use of performance-enhancing drugs is prevalent. The recreation provider has a duty to consider whether, by turning a blind eye to drug use—for example, by failing to require drug tests to verify the fairness of competition results—the provider may in fact be supporting these practices.

POLICING SAFETY: CAN RULES PREVENT VIOLENCE IN SPORT?

The incident in *Anderson* was not exactly accidental. Anderson, knowing that he greatly outweighed the opposing player and that an impact would likely cause injury, slid into second base despite the fact that he knew he was already out. His actions were reckless and motivated by anger and a desire for revenge.

Rough play fuelled by anger occurs every day in Canada, across a wide range of sports played at various levels. Reckless play that causes serious physical injury is highly problematic for recreation providers who are committed to providing safe and enjoyable recreation.

However, a careful reading of the *Anderson* case shows that there *is* something that can be done about it. Because the rules of the game permitted sliding *and did not ban takeout sliding*, Taylor's consent to the risks of the sport included consent to the risk of being hit by a takeout slide. Had the rules banned takeout slides—which were described, by one expert, as a "rare" play in recreational softball—the assault charge may well have succeeded.

In many cases, sports experts are well aware of the kinds of plays most likely to cause injury. In some cases, experts are also aware of the plays most likely to lead to retaliation. This knowledge has permitted many providers of recreational sport to ban certain kinds of plays for the safety of all players.

For example, most children's baseball and softball leagues have a rule prohibiting intentional body contact between a runner who is out and a defensive player who is standing on base. In hockey, many leagues enforce "no-touch icing," wherein the referee blows the whistle to declare icing as soon as the puck crosses the opposing team's red line (to prevent players from racing toward the boards). At all levels of football, players are prohibited from tackling each other after the ball is dead.

According to the authors of *Best Practices in Sport: A Vehicle for Positive Values and Ethical Conduct?*, 30 percent of hockey injuries are caused by illegal plays. Vigorous enforcement of the rules, especially in recreational play, has the potential to improve safety for players.

By adopting rules that prohibit the plays most likely to result in injury, and by making players aware of these rules, recreation providers can make the game safer and limit the risks to which participants consent. With appropriate rules in place, a participant who makes an aggressive illegal play cannot rely on the victim's consent to the illegal action in a subsequent criminal or civil trial.

By the time this section was written, hockey player Don Sanderson, mentioned at the beginning of the chapter, had succumbed to his injury. After Sanderson's death, many prominent hockey experts were recommending that hockey leagues adopt a penalty for players who remove their helmets voluntarily (a practice known as "buckets off," undertaken by players to prevent hand injuries to an opponent) in the course of a fight.

A CULTURE OF SAFETY: PROMOTING FAIR PLAY AS AN ANTIDOTE TO VIOLENCE

While rules designed with safety in mind can go a long way toward reducing the potential for violence, rules have their limitations. Most sports incorporate a penalty system for enforcing rules. Because this system introduces predictability into the enforcement process, it allows a player to weigh the pros and cons of making an illegal play; therefore, at least in some cases, players may *choose* to make illegal plays. In addition, referees do not detect all illegal plays, a reality that rewards players who are skilled at concealing their dirty deeds. And finally, rules are a negative, external motivator: they are imposed by someone else, which makes them a weaker motivator than a player's own goals and objectives, and there is no reward for compliance, only a penalty for non-compliance.

The most effective way to change behaviour is not to enforce rules; rather, it is to awaken in participants positive and internal motivations to avoid violence by creating a culture of fair play within a team, league, or sport. Accomplishing this is not an easy task, but the rewards, for recreation providers, are considerable. If participants are motivated to play fairly and avoid violence, sports become more enjoyable for everyone.

The spirit of fair play is alive and well among sportspeople across Canada. One need only watch a Mite Select game to see that six-year-olds can play a style of hockey that is not only seriously competitive but also safe and fair; the same goes for most old-timers' leagues. Adult recreational softball, lacrosse, and ultimate Frisbee leagues thrive across the country, and are generally characterized by a "let's try not to get hurt because we have to go to work tomorrow" spirit of play.

In fact, the strongest motivator for fair play in adult recreational sport is the understanding, shared by the majority of team members, that sport is intended as a source of stress relief and socialization, and that avoiding injury—or even unpleasantly aggressive competition—is an important condition of participation.

Because children are less likely than adults to worry about the impact of an injury on the other facets of their lives, promoting fair play in children's leagues may require more formal efforts on the part of organizers. A number of fair play codes and programs are available as resources to recreation providers. A good first stop for research on promoting fair play is the website of the CCES, an organization independent of the government that was created through the merger of the Commission for Fair Play and the Canadian Centre for Drug-Free Sport.

With the help of a multifaceted approach to violence prevention that includes screening of staff and volunteers, development of anti-violence policies, careful design and vigorous enforcement of the rules of play, prompt and consistent responses to incidents of violence, and building a culture of fair play and safety, recreation providers can reduce the potential for violence in their programs and facilities.

KEY TERM

discharge

REVIEW EXERCISES

Review Questions

1. Has a criminal investigation or trial ever occurred in Canada because of an incident of sports violence?

2. Do sports violence incidents lead to criminal charges or civil lawsuits?

3. How does sports violence hurt participants and/or society?

4. What challenges do prosecutors and plaintiffs face when trying to prove intent on the part of a sports assailant?

5. Does a participant's consent to play a sport eliminate her right to sue in tort for assault or to request a criminal charge?

6. How can a recreation provider help establish the limits of participants' consent?

7. How can a sports leader's attitude influence the potential for sports violence? What should a recreation provider do if faced with a leader who encourages violence?

8. What can a recreation provider do to overcome a culture of violence in a team or league?

9. How can rules of play influence player safety?

10. How can promoting a culture of fair play improve player safety?

Discussion Question

Recent studies have established a significant link between head injuries suffered during sports participation and problems in later life, including reduced life expectancy. Where a recreation provider offers access to sports or other activities that are accompanied by a risk of head injury, what are the recreation provider's moral responsibilities to its clients? Is it, in fact, immoral to offer access to the most dangerous activities, such as football, boxing, professional wrestling, and hockey?

Sample Waivers

Kamloops Women's Recreational Hockey League
2007/2008

RELEASE OF LIABILITY, WAIVER OF CLAIMS, ASSUMPTION OF RISKS
AND INDEMNITY AGREEMENT

NAME OF PARTICIPANT: _____

ADDRESS OF PARTICIPANT: _____

_____

_____

BIRTH DATE: _____   PHONE NO: _____

EMERGENCY CONTACT:_____

RELATIONSHIP: _____TELEPHONE:_____

DISCLAIMER CLAUSE
The Kamloops Women's Recreational Hockey League (KWRHL), their officers, directors, agents, contractors, employees, volunteers, members and representatives (all hereafter collectively referred to as "KWRHL") are not responsible for any injury, loss or damage of any kind sustained by any person while participating in the KWRHL, including injury, loss or damage which might be caused by the negligence of the KWRHL.

DESCRIPTION OF RISKS
In consideration of my participation in playing ice hockey with the KWRHL, I acknowledge that I am aware of the possible risks, dangers and hazards associated with my participation in the KWRHL including the possible **risk of severe or fatal injury** to myself or others.

INDEMNIFICATION
In consideration of the KWRHL allowing me to participate in league games and skills sessions I agree:
1. **TO ASSUME AND ACCEPT ALL RISKS** arising out of, associated with or related to my participating in league games and skills sessions even though such risks may have been caused by the negligence of the KWRHL;
2. **TO BE SOLELY RESPONSIBLE FOR ANY INJURY, LOSS OR DAMAGE** which I might sustain participating in league games and skills sessions even though such injury, loss or damage may have been caused by the negligence of the KWRHL;
3. **TO HOLD HARMLESS AND INDEMNIFY KWRHL** from any and all liability for any damage to the property of, or personal injury to, any third party, resulting from my participation in league games and skills sessions.
4. **TO INDEMNIFY AND HOLD HARMLESS** the Kamloops Women's Recreational Hockey League and each of their respective directors, officers, agents, contractors, employees, volunteers, members and representatives from any and all claims, demands, actions and costs which might arise out of my participating in the KWRHL even though such claims, demands, actions and costs may have been caused by the negligence of the Kamloops Women's Recreational Hockey League.

ACKNOWLEDGEMENT
I UNDERSTAND THAT THIS IS A LEGAL AGREEMENT. It is binding upon myself as well as upon my heirs, executors and representatives, in the event of my death or incapacity. **I HAVE READ AND UNDERSTOOD ALL THE TERMS OF THIS AGREEMENT**, and by signing this agreement voluntarily, I am agreeing to abide by these terms.

Signed this _____ day of _____, 20 _____, at Kamloops, British Columbia.

_____   _____
Signature of Member/Participant/Parent/Guardian   Signature of Witness

_____   _____
Print Name   Print Name

YAMNUSKA INC.
Operating as Yamnuska Mountain Adventures

RELEASE OF LIABILITY, WAIVER OF CLAIMS AND ASSUMPTION OF RISKS AND INDEMNITY AGREEMENT

BY SIGNING THIS DOCUMENT YOU WILL WAIVE OR GIVE UP CERTAIN RIGHTS TO SUE OR TO CLAIM COMPENSATION FOLLOWING AN ACCIDENT

PLEASE READ CAREFULLY!

_____
Signature of Guest

To: Yamnuska Inc. operating as YAMNUSKA MOUNTAIN ADVENTURES and To: HER MAJESTY THE QUEEN IN RIGHT OF THE PROVINCE OF BRITISH COLUMBIA and its directors, officers, employees, agents, guides, independent contractors, subcontractors, sponsors, assigns and representatives (all of whom are hereinafter referred to as "the RELEASEES")

DEFINITION

THE RELEASEES' programs include, but are not limited to, mountaineering, ski touring, telemarking, cross-country skiing, rock climbing, hiking, waterfall ice climbing, glacier travel and high altitude climbing and travel teambuilding initiatives and exercises, canoeing, kayaking and general physical exercise both outdoors and indoors.

In this Agreement, the term "wilderness activities" shall include but is not limited to: hiking, nature study, snow sports, touring, mountaineering, rock or ice climbing, expeditions, trekking, glacier travel, mountain biking, horseback riding, swimming, boating, fishing, watersports, and all activities, services and use of facilities either provided by or arranged by the Releasees including orientation and instructional sessions or classes, transportation, accommodation, food and beverage, water supply, rescue and first aid services, and all travel by or movement around vehicles, helicopters, other aircraft, horses and pack animals, all terrain vehicles, watercraft or other vehicles.

ASSUMPTION OF RISKS

I understand that the Releasees' programs involve intrinsic hazards, not all of which can be listed here. Among the more obvious and frequent are:

1. Steep terrain where a fall, whether roped or unroped, may cause injury or death.
2. Falling rock, ice or other objects, which may cause injury or death.
3. Violent and unpredictable weather, which may cause injury due to extremes of heat or cold, and which may prevent travel to, from or within an area.
4. Unfamiliar country, where the program participants may get lost, off route or be separated from the rest of the party.
5. Wild animals, which have been known to maul, sometimes fatally, mountain travelers.
6. Avalanches, which are highly dangerous and may be triggered by the activities of skiers or climbers or by natural forces.
7. Remoteness of location with poor communications and inability to get rescue or medical assistance quickly or easily.
8. Medical problems arising from climbing at high altitudes or in areas where adequate supplies of clean food or water may be unavailable.
9. Transport by public or private motor vehicle, helicopter and light fixed wing aircraft or through the use of animals.
10. Hazards involved in canoeing, kayaking and other water activities such as capsize, striking rocks in rivers, and drowning.
11. Scrapes, bruises, fractures and other injuries sustained in physical activity indoors and outdoors.
12. **NEGLIGENCE ON THE PART OF THE RELEASEES, INCLUDING THE FAILURE BY THE RELEASEES TO TAKE REASONABLE STEPS TO SAFE GUARD OR PROTECT ME FROM THE RISKS, DANGERS AND HAZARDS OF WILDERNESS ACTIVITIES.**

I AM AWARE OF THE RISKS, DANGERS AND HAZARDS ASSOCIATED WITH WILDERNESS ACTIVITIES AND I FREELY ACCEPT AND FULLY ASSUME ALL SUCH RISKS, DANGERS AND HAZARDS AND THE POSSIBILITY OF PERSONAL INJURY, DEATH, PROPERTY DAMAGE AND LOSS RESULTING THEREFROM.

NON-SCHEDULED OR EMERGENCY EVACUATION, RESCUE OR FIRST AID
I acknowledge and agree that all expenses associated with non-scheduled or emergency evacuation, rescue or first aid will be my responsibility and will not be covered by the Releasees.

NOTICE TO SNOWBOARDERS AND TELEMARK SKIERS – INCREASED RISK
Unlike alpine ski boot/binding systems, snowboard, and some telemark boot/binding systems are not designed or intended to release and will not release under normal circumstances, thus increasing the risk of not surviving an avalanche.

Initials

YAMNUSKA INC.
Operating as Yamnuska Mountain Adventures

RELEASE OF LIABILITY, WAIVER OF CLAIMS AND INDEMNITY AGREEMENT

In consideration of the Releasees accepting my application for any of the Releasees Mountain Adventures programs or activities I agree to this release of claims and waiver of liability as follows:

1. **TO WAIVE ANY AND ALL CLAIMS** that I have or may in the future have against **THE RELEASEES** from any and all liability for any loss, damage, expense or injury including death that I may suffer, or that my next of kin may suffer, as a result of my participation in wilderness activities DUE TO ANY CAUSE WHATSOEVER, INCLUDING NEGLIGENCE, BREACH OF CONTRACT, OR BREACH OF ANY STATUTORY OR OTHER DUTY OF CARE, INCLUDING ANY DUTY OF CARE OWED UNDER ANY APPLICABLE OCCUPIERS' LIABILITY LEGISLATION IN THE PART OF THE RELEASEES, AND ALSO INCLUDING THE FAILURE ON THE PART OF THE RELEASEES TO TAKE REASONABLE STEPS TO SAFEGUARD OR PROTECT ME FROM THE RISKS, DANGERS AND HAZARDS REFERRED TO ABOVE;

2. I am not relying on any oral or written statements made by the Releasees or their agents, whether in brochures, advertisements or in individual conversations to lead me to become involved in this program on any basis other than my assumption of the risks involved.
3. I accept all of the risks and the possibility of death, personal injury, property damage and loss resulting from my involvement with the program I am taking with the Releasees
4. I certify that I am physically capable and fit to participate in this activity and I have no medical conditions or needs other than those listed.
5. I confirm that I am eighteen years of age or older. (Younger participants must have a parent or guardian read and sign this document.)
6. I confirm that I have read over this agreement before signing, that I understand it, and that it will be binding not only on me but also on my heirs, my next of kin, my executors, administrators and assigns.
7. I hereby irrevocably submit to the exclusive jurisdiction of the courts of the Provinces of Alberta and I agree that no other courts can exercise jurisdiction over the agreements and claims referred to herein. Any litigation to enforce this agreement shall be instituted in Alberta and nowhere else.
8. **I HEREBY AGREE TO HOLD HARMLESS AND INDEMNIFY THE RELEASEES** from any and all liability for any property damage or personal injury to any third party resulting from my participation in wilderness activities.

I HAVE READ AND UNDERSTOOD THIS AGREEMENT PRIOR TO SIGNING IT AND I AM AWARE THAT BY SIGNING THIS AGREEMENT I AM WAIVING CERTAIN LEGAL RIGHTS WHICH I OR MY HEIRS, NEXT OF KIN, EXECUTORS, ADMINISTRATORS, ASSIGNS AND REPRESENTATIVES MAY HAVE AGAINST THE RELEASEES.

Witness's Signature	Guest's Signature
Witness's Printed Name	Guest's Printed Name
Date	Signature of Parent or Guardian if guest is under age 18

CLIENT INFORMATION

LAST NAME	FIRST NAME
ADDRESS	CITY
PROVINCE/STATE	POSTAL/ZIP CODE
COUNTRY	EMAIL

MEDICAL INFORMATION

EMERGENCY CONTACT	PHONE
ALLERGIES	
MEDICATIONS	
MEDICAL CONDITIONS	
OTHER HEALTH OR MEDICAL INFORMATION	

OWL Rafting Inc.

RELEASE OF LIABILITY, WAIVER OF CLAIMS, ASSUMPTION OF RISKS AND INDEMNITY AGREEMENTBY
SIGNING THIS DOCUMENT YOU WILL WAIVE CERTAIN LEGAL RIGHTS, INCLUDING THE RIGHT TO SUE.

Initial Here [   ]

FIRST NAME OF PARTICIPANT   LAST NAME OF PARTICIPANT

APT #   STREET ADDRESS

CITY   PROV/STATE   POSTAL/ZIP CODE

AREA CODE   HOME PHONE #   AREA CODE   WORK PHONE #   DATE OF BIRTH   D D M M Y Y

TO: OWL RAFTING INC. and its directors, officers, employees, instructors, agents, representatives, volunteers, independent contractors, subcontractors, sponsors, successors and assigns (hereinafter collectively referred to as the "Releasees").

DEFINITION
In this agreement the term "Whitewater Activities" shall include all activities in any way related to the river rafting trip, kayaking, or canoeing and all other recreational activities offered by the Releasees including, but not limited to, orientation and instruction sessions, transportation or travel to and from the river, loading and unloading of vehicles, rafts and boats, camping, backpacking, fishing, hiking, backcountry travel and all recreational activities offered (hereinafter referred to as "Whitewater Activities").

ACKNOWLEDGEMENT - WHITEWATER / RIVER RAFTING SAFETY
I acknowledge that I have been advised to wear a helmet and lifejacket while participating in the Whitewater Activities. Instruction in the proper use of the helmet and lifejacket is available from the guides. I am aware that the physical exertion required by Whitewater Activities and the forces exerted on the body can activate or aggravate pre-existing physical injuries, conditions, symptoms, or congenital defects. I have been advised to seek medical advice if I know or suspect that my physical condition may be incompatible with the Whitewater Activities. I acknowledge that I am not nor will I be under the influence of drugs or alcohol while participating in the Whitewater Activities.

ASSUMPTION OF RISKS
I am aware that Whitewater Activities involve many risks, dangers, and hazards including, but not limited to: accidents which occur during transportation or travel to and from the river; the overturning or upsetting of rafts or boats; sudden violent and unexpected movement of the boat or raft; entrapment by trees, logs, rocks or equipment; hypothermia due to exposure to very cold water; falling from the boat or raft into long sections of continuous rapids; impact or collision with rocks, trees, logs, deadfall, other vessels, and other boating equipment; encounters with domestic or wild animals; high winds; equipment failure; variation in the water conditions, surfaces and currents; and negligence of other boaters and rafters. I am also aware that fishing, hiking, backpacking, camping and back country travel involve many risks, dangers and hazards, including but not limited to: steep slopes in their natural state that may contain many obstacles and hazards; terrain that may not have been travelled on or climbed before and is not regularly patrolled or inspected; becoming lost or separated from the guide or party; rock slides; rapid and extreme change in weather conditions; negligence of other participants. Communication in the backcountry terrain is difficult, and in the event of an accident; rescue and medical treatment may not be available. I am also aware that there is a risk of **NEGLIGENCE ON THE PART OF THE RELEASEES, INCLUDING THE FAILURE BY THE RELEASEES TO TAKE REASONABLE STEPS TO SAFEGUARD OR PROTECT ME FROM THE RISKS, DANGERS AND HAZARDS OF THE WHITEWATER ACTIVITIES. I FREELY ACCEPT AND FULLY ASSUME ALL RISKS, DANGERS AND HAZARDS ASSOCIATED WITH THE WHITEWATER ACTIVITIES AND THE POSSIBLITY OF PERSONAL INJURY, DEATH, PROPERTY DAMAGE OR LOSS RESULTING THEREFROM.**

Initial Here [   ]

RELEASE OF LIABILITY, WAIVER OF CLAIMS AND INDEMNITY AGREEMENT
In consideration of THE RELEASEES agreeing to my participation in the Whitewater Activities and permitting my use of their equipment, vehicles, parking and other river rafting facilities (hereinafter referred to as the "rafting facilities"), and for other good and valuable consideration, the receipt and sufficiency of which is acknowledged, I hereby agree as follows:

1. **TO WAIVE ANY AND ALL CLAIMS** that I have or may in the future have against THE RELEASEES AND TO RELEASE THE RELEASEES from any and all liability for any loss, damage, expense or injury including death that I may suffer, or that my next of kin may suffer as a result of my participation in Whitewater Activities, DUE TO ANY CAUSE WHATSOEVER, INCLUDING NEGLIGENCE, BREACH OF CONTRACT, OR BREACH OF ANY STATUTORY OR OTHER DUTY OF CARE, INCLUDING ANY DUTY OF CARE OWED UNDER THE OCCUPIERS' LIABILITY ACT ON THE PART OF THE RELEASEES, AND FURTHER INCLUDING THE FAILURE ON THE PART OF THE RELEASEES TO SAFEGUARD OR PROTECT ME FROM THE RISKS, DANGERS, AND HAZARDS OF THE WHITEWATER ACTIVITIES REFERRED TO ABOVE;

Initial Here [   ]

2. **TO HOLD HARMLESS AND INDEMNIFY THE RELEASEES** from any and all liability for any property damage or personal injury to any third party resulting from my participation in Whitewater Activities;
3. That this Agreement shall be effective and binding upon my heirs, next of kin, executors, administrators, assigns and representatives, in the event of my death;
4. That this Agreement shall be governed by and interpreted in accordance with the laws of the Province of Ontario; and
5. That any litigation involving the parties to this Agreement shall be brought within the Province of Ontario, and shall be within the exclusive jurisdiction of the Courts of the Province of Ontario.
6. **PHOTO RELEASE** – I consent to photographs taken of me during my participation in the Whitewater Activities, and to publication of the photographs by the Operators for advertising, promotional and marketing purposes.
7. **MARINE LIABILITY ACT:** The Marine Liability Act, S.C.2001,c.6, may limit the liability of the Operators in the event of an accident resulting in injury or death.

In entering into this Agreement I am not relying on any oral or written representations or statements made by the Releasees with respect to the safety of Whitewater Activities, other than what is set forth in this Agreement.
I CONFIRM THAT I HAVE READ AND UNDERSTOOD THIS AGREEMENT PRIOR TO SIGNING IT, AND I AM AWARE THAT BY SIGNING THIS AGREEMENT I AM WAIVING CERTAIN LEGAL RIGHTS WHICH I OR MY HEIRS, EXECUTORS, ADMINISTRATORS, ASSIGNS AND REPRESENTATIVES MAY HAVE AGAINST THE RELEASEES.

Signature of Participant_____ Print Name Clearly _____

Signature of Parent or Guardian if participant under 18 years old_____

Signed this _____ day of_____ , 20 _____ Office Witness_____

Group Organizer name_____

Bibliography

Adams, M., Burton, J., Butcher, F., Graham, S., McLeod, A., Rajan, R., Whatman, R., Bridge, M., Hill, R., & Johri, R. (2002). *Aftermath: The social and economic consequences of workplace injury and illness.* Wellington, New Zealand: New Zealand Department of Labour and the Accident Compensation Corporation.

Alcohol and Gaming Commission of Ontario. www.agco.on.ca.

Alpine Club of Canada, Edmonton Section. (2005). Alpine accidents in Canada. http://alpineclub-edm.org/accidents/index.asp.

Anderson, R. v. 2000 CanLII 1590 (BC S.C.).

Andrews, S. (2003). Five year study shows "perceived risk" to be key factor in wearing PFDs. *SARSCENE 13*(2), 12-13.

B.(M.) v. British Columbia. 2001 CanLII 227 (BC C.A.).

Bazley v. Curry. 1999 CanLII 692 (S.C.C.).

British Columbia. (n.d.). Volunteer screening model [Model developed by Sport Safe]. www.hls.gov.bc.ca/sport/docs/sportsafe/screening_volunteers_guide.pdf.

British Columbia Ministry of Healthy Living and Sport. (n.d.). Dealing with harassment and abuse. www.hls.gov.bc.ca/sport/abuse_violence_prevention/index.htm.

British Columbia Recreation and Parks Association. (n.d.). Anti-discrimination in sport and recreation [Resource supplement]. Burnaby, BC: Author.

Canada National Parks Act. (2000). S.C. 2000, c. 32.

Canada Shipping Act, 2001. (2001). S.C. 2001, c. 26.

Canadian Centre for Ethics in Sport. (1999, February). *Building a new brand of sport©—What about violence?* [Discussion paper on violence in sport]. www.cces.ca/pdfs/cces-paper-violence-e.pdf.

Canadian Charter of Rights and Freedoms. (1982). Part I of the *Constitution Act, 1982*, R.S.C. 1985, app. II, no. 44.

Canadian Council on Social Development. (2003, September 15). *Children increasingly exposed to violence—Parents can help* [Communiqué]. Ottawa: Author.

Canadian Human Rights Act. (1985). R.S.C. 1985, c. H-6.

Canadian Off-Highway Vehicle Distributors Council. (2009). Safe rider code. www.cohv.ca/ridercode.html.

Canadian Paediatric Society. (2002; updated February 2007). Preventing playground injuries [Position statement by the Injury Prevention Committee]. *Paediatrics & Child Health, 7*(4), 255-256.

Child and Family Services Act. (1990). R.S.O. 1990, c. C.11.

Colwell, M. (2006). Walking the tightrope: Managing risk in SAR. www.sarinfo.bc.ca/ManagingRiskInSAR.htm.

Competition Act. (1985). R.S.C. 1985, c. C-34.

Const. Scarmar Ltée v. Geddes Contr. Co. 1989 CanLII 2777 (BC C.A.).

Constitution Act, 1867. (1867). (U.K.), 30 & 31 Victoria, c. 3.

Constitution Act, 1982. (1982). R.S.C. 1985, app. II, no. 44.

Consumer Protection Act, 2002. (2002). S.O. 2002, c. 30, Sch. A.

Corbett, R., Findlay, H.A., & Lech, D. (2008). *Legal issues in sport: Tools and techniques for the sport manager.* Toronto: Emond Montgomery Publications.

Cotten, D.J. (2008). Evaluating your liability waiver. *Fitness Management,* June, 40.

Courts of Justice Act. (1990). R.S.O. 1990, c. C.43.

Cowan, S. (2008, September 13). Hockey obsession leading to burnout among young players. *Montreal Gazette.*

Criminal Code. (1985). R.S.C. 1985, c. C-46.

Crown Liability and Proceedings Act. (1985). R.S.C. 1985, c. C-50.

De Beaumont, L. et al. (2009). Brain function decline in healthy retired athletes who sustained their last sports concussion in early adulthood. *Brain 132*(1).

D.N. and D.S.G. v. The Corp. of the Dist. of Oak Bay. 2005 CanLII 1412 (BC S.C.).

Electronic Commerce Act, 2000. (2000). S.O. 2000, c. 17.

Endangered Species Act, 2007. (2007). S.O. 2007, c. 6.

Enslev v. Challenges Unlimited Inc. 2007 CanLII 45408 (ON S.C.).

Evergreen. (2008). Toyota Evergreen Learning Grounds: Transforming the outdoor landscape of Canada's schools. www.evergreen.ca/en/lg/lg.html.

Firearms Act. (1995). S.C. 1995, c. 39.

Fish and Wildlife Conservation Act, 1997. (1997). S.O. 1997, c. 41.

Fisheries Act. (1985). R.S.C. 1985, c. F-14.

Fowler Kennedy Sport Medicine Clinic at the University of Western Ontario. (n.d.). Corporate sponsorship opportunity for the Primary Care Sport Medicine Fellowship Program. www.fowlerkennedy.com/sponsors/primarycare_fellowship.cfm.

Gegax, T., with Bolsta, P. (2007). *The big book of small business.* New York: HarperCollins.

Gray, D., & Gray, D. (2000). *The complete Canadian small business guide* (3rd ed.). Toronto: McGraw-Hill Ryerson.

Hall (Litigation guardian of) v. Powers. 2002 CanLII 49475 (ON S.C.).

Hamstra v. BC Rugby Union. (1989), 1 C.C.L.T. (2d) 78 (BC S.C.).

Highway Traffic Act. (1990). R.S.O. 1990, c. H.8.

Holyfield, L. (1999). Manufacturing adventure: The buying and selling of emotions. *Journal of Contemporary Ethnography, 28*(1), 3-32.

Horse Riding Safety Act, 2001. (2001). S.O. 2001, c. 4.

Human Rights Code. (1990). R.S.O. 1990, c. H.19.

Hutchison v. Daredevil Park Inc. 2003 CanLII 25623 (ON S.C.).

Isildar v. Rideau Diving Supply. 2008 CanLII 29598 (ON S.C.).

Jacobi v. Griffiths. 1999 CanLII 693 (S.C.C.).

Jobidon, R. v. 1991 CanLII 77 (S.C.C.).

King v. Redlich. (1986), 35 C.C.L.T. 201 (BC C.A.).

Kirby, S., & Greaves, L. (1996). *Foul play: Sexual harassment and abuse in sport.* Paper presented to the Pre-Olympic Scientific Congress, Dallas, Texas.

Knowles v. Whistler Mountain Ski Corp. 1991 CanLII 1037 (BC S.C.).

Lam v. University of Windsor. (2001, March 9). [Unreported decision]. (File No. 97-GD-39502) (ON S.C.).

Lambert v. Lastoplex Chemicals Co. 1971 CanLII 27 (S.C.C.).

LeBlanc, J., & Dickson, L. (1996). *Straight talk about children and sport.* Gloucester, ON: Coaching Association of Canada in partnership with the Royal Bank of Canada Charitable Foundation.

Lifesaving Society of Canada. (2003). *National boating fatalities report* (2003 ed.). Ottawa: Author.

Limitations Act, 2002. (2002). S.O. 2002, c. 24, Sch. B.

Linden, A.M., & Feldhusen, B. (2006). *Canadian tort law* (8th ed.). Markham, ON: LexisNexis Butterworths.

Liquor Control Act. (1990). R.S.O. 1990, c. L.18.

McKenzie, B. (n.d.). Parenting trumps journalism at a time like this [Blog]. www.tsn.ca.

Mechanized Travel in Wilderness Parks. O. Reg. 346/07.

Metzl, J.D., and Shookhoff, C. (2002). *The young athlete: A sports doctor's complete guide for parents.* Boston: Little, Brown and Company.

Migratory Birds Convention Act, 1994. (1994). S.C. 1994, c. 22.

Motorized Snow Vehicles Act. (1990). R.S.O. 1990, c. M.44.

Municipal Act, 2001. (2001). S.O. 2001, c. 25.

Negligence Act. (1990). R.S.O. 1990, c. N.1.

News-Medical.Net. (2004, August). Basketball and cycling rank highest in U.S. recreational injuries. www.news-medical.net.

Occupational Health and Safety Act. (1990). R.S.O. 1990, c. O.1.

Occupiers' Liability Act. (1990). R.S.O. 1990, c. O.2.

Off-Road Vehicles Act. (1990). R.S.O. 1990, c. O.4.

Ontarians with Disabilities Act, 2001. (2001). S.O. 2001, c. 32.

Ontario. A message from the Government of Ontario. *2007 Hunting regulations summary.* www.noto.ca/images/general/2007huntingregseng.pdf.

Ontario Ministry of Transportation. (2008, May 16). Ride safely both on and off the road [News release]. http://ogov.newswire.ca/search_e.html.

Ornish, D. (1999). *Love and survival: The scientific basis for the healing power of intimacy.* New York: Collins Living.

Orzeck, T. (2004, June 6). *Harassment & abuse in sport: Understanding and taking responsibility for safe sporting environments.* Paper presented to Canadian Centre for Ethics in Sport.

Parker v. Ingalls. 2006 CanLII 942 (BC S.C.).

Parks Act. (1986). S.S. 1986, c. P-1.1.

Proceedings Against the Crown Act. (1990). R.S.O. 1990, c. P.27.

Provincial Offences Act. (1990). R.S.O. 1990, c. P.33.

Provincial Parks and Conservation Reserves Act, 2006. (2006). S.O. 2006, c. 12.

Provincial Parks: General Provisions. O. Reg. 347/07.

Public Health Agency of Canada, Healthy Living Unit. (2003). The benefits of physical activity. www.phac-aspc.gc.ca/pau-uap/fitness/benefits.html.

Reddemann v. McEachnie et al. 2005 CanLII 915 (BC S.C.).

Ropeik, D., and Gray, G. (2002). *Risk: A practical guide for deciding what's really safe and what's really dangerous in the world around you.* New York: Houghton Mifflin.

Rozenhart v. Skier's Sport Shop (Edmonton) Ltd. 2002 CanLII 509 (AB Q.B.).

Rylands v. Fletcher. (1868), L.R. 3 H.L. 330.

Safeconcerts. www.safeconcerts.com.

Sale of Goods Act. (1990). R.S.O. 1990, c. S.1.

"Sandy's Law." Ontario Bill 43. *An Act to Amend the Liquor Licence Act.* (2005).

Sea Horse Ranch. (n.d.). [General information and "ride at your own risk" policy]. www.horserentals.com/seahorse.html.

Shannon, J.B. (Ed.). (2002). *Sports injuries sourcebook* (2nd ed.). Detroit: Omnigraphics.

Small Vessel Regulations. C.R.C., c. 1487.

Smith, M.D. (1989). *Violence in sport.* Toronto: Canadian Scholars' Press.

Smoke-Free Ontario Act. (1994). S.O. 1994, c. 10.

Soccer Quest Coaching Inc. v. The Ice Box Arena Co. 2008 CanLII 49 (BC P.C.).

Species at Risk Act. (2002). S.C. 2002, c. 29.

Stein v. Sandwich West (Township). 1995 CanLII 1239 (ON C.A.).

Sundown, R. v. 1999 CanLII 673 (S.C.C.).

Technical Standards and Safety Act, 2000. (2000). S.O. 2000, c. 16.

Thomas v. Bell Helmets Inc. 1999 CanLII 9312 (ON C.A.).

Tonino, P. (2004). Basketball and cycling rank highest in U.S. recreational injuries. www.news-medical.net/?id=3781.

Transport Canada. (2008). Marine policy. www.tc.gc.ca/policy/report/marine/rcpi2.htm.

Trevor Butterworth. (2008). How we calculate risk: Fear of flying after 9/11 led to increase in auto deaths. http://thestatsblog.wordpress.com.

Tropea, R. v. , 2007 ONCJ 241 (CanLII).

Turner, S., Brown, D., Buist, A., Fafard, M., & Goulet, C. (2003). Best practices in sport: A vehicle for positive values and ethical conduct? Canadian Centre for Ethics in Sport. www.cces.ca/pdfs/cces-paper-dps-e.pdf.

United States Consumer Product Safety Commission. (1999, May 4). New standard for soccer goals helps prevent tip-over deaths linked to unanchored goals (Release No. 99-106). Bethesda, MD: Author.

Western Australia Civil Liability Amendment Bill. 2003.

Wyseman, D.R. (2003). Risk and recreation [Unpublished sourcebook].

Glossary

alternative dispute resolution (ADR)
strategies, such as structured negotiation, mediation, and arbitration, that are designed to settle disputes without recourse to traditional courts

assault
crime involving intentional physical contact without consent

attractive risk
risk that tends to lure children into situations that endanger them

battery
tort involving intentional physical contact without consent

best practices
industry procedures that are most efficient in promoting and maintaining safety

but for test
test to establish causation in negligence action: but for the defendant's conduct, would the harm have resulted?

bylaws
municipal legislation

causation
the logical connection between harm and the negligent actions of the party accused of causing it

co-defendant
two or more defendants in the same case

compulsory standards
standards for products that are mandated by legislation

consideration
benefit that must flow to each party to make a contract binding

Constitution
document that establishes the framework under which all other laws are created and the basic principles to which all laws must conform

contract
agreement enforceable in law

contractors
third parties hired to do specific jobs

contributory negligence
role that a plaintiff may play in negligently contributing to the cause of or the aggravation of his own injury

controllable risk
a risk that can be eliminated or reduced

costs
a portion of the successful party's legal costs that is paid by the unsuccessful party

court of appeal
a court that reviews the actions and findings of trial courts

Crown
government, either federal or provincial

damages
monetary compensation awarded to a plaintiff for harm suffered

defendant
party who is required to defend a lawsuit

discharge
A judge's disposition (order) that does not impose a criminal conviction on a person found guilty of an offence

discretion
freedom to make decisions within limits set by legislation or common law

due diligence
defence requiring the defendant to prove that she did everything reasonable to prevent a tort from occurring

duress
pressure to enter into a contract by way of threat of physical or economic harm

duty of care
duty owed by one person to act reasonably that is the foundation of a negligence action

employer's liability
legal doctrine under which liability is imposed on an employer for harm caused by an employee in the ordinary course of business while carrying out a usual job duty

exclusion clause
contract term that limits the contractual or statutory liability of a party in the event of a breach of the contract

external policies
policies that govern the relationship between a recreation organization and its clients, including client participation, third-party relationships, and public relations

foreseeable
predictable by a reasonable person

high-risk activity
an activity that is associated with frequent injuries, serious injuries, or both

hold harmless agreements
agreements that make users of recreation facilities responsible for assuming risk of any claims arising from use

hybrid offence
offence that may be prosecuted using either summary conviction or indictable procedures at the discretion of the prosecution

immunity
protection from lawsuits

implied sales conditions
terms inserted into contracts for the sale of goods by statutes such as the *Sale of Goods Act*

indictable offence
serious offence that is prosecuted with full and formal criminal procedure

injunction
court order that is designed to prohibit an action or require an action

internal policies
policies that govern tasks and processes within a recreation organization

interpersonal harm
harm that results from interactions between participants and program staff or among the participants themselves

interpersonal risks
risks that arise through interaction between individuals

intractable risk
a risk that cannot be eliminated or reduced

invitees
people who are invited onto premises by an occupier

joint and several liability
a legal principle that makes the parties who contributed to harm jointly responsible for the full extent of damages, so that if one or more parties lack the means to pay, the remaining party or parties are liable for the full amount

jurisdiction
law-making authority

legal capacity
ability to contract that flows from being of sufficient age and mental ability

liability
legal responsibility

licensee
licence holder

limitation periods
time periods that limit when plaintiffs can launch lawsuits

misrepresentations
false statements of fact

negligence
failure of a person to act reasonably that results in harm to another

non est factum
claim that a party signed the wrong contract or signed a contract under a complete misunderstanding about its nature

non-delegable duty rule
rule that states that a party cannot evade liability for dangerous activities by hiring a contractor to perform these activities

occupiers' liability
duty that imposes liability on occupiers of land or buildings for any harm caused to visitors, invitees, or trespassers

operational decision
routine decision made by civil servants about the specifics of a law's operation

ordinary course of business
on an employer's premises, during usual working hours, and while an employee is performing her regular job duties

paramount legislation
legislation that takes precedence over all other laws

parol evidence rule
common-law rule stating that if the language of a written contract is clear and complete, courts do not look at evidence beyond the contract to interpret it

plaintiff
party who starts a lawsuit

pleadings
documents exchanged between the plaintiff and the defendant in a civil action that set out their respective cases

policy
governmental course or principle of action

policy decision
decision made by senior government staff, often concerning the management of governmental resources

precedent
court decision that affects future court decisions to ensure consistent application of the law

procedural law
law that describes the manner in which substantive law is enforced

product liability
subcategory of tort law based on a defendant's liability for harm caused to others as a result of its defective or dangerous products

provincial offences
offences created under provincial statutes

punitive damages
sum that may be added to a damages award to compensate a plaintiff for a defendant's outrageous conduct

remedy
judge's order to compensate a plaintiff

representations
statements or claims made by contracting parties in the course of negotiations

repudiate
reject

respondeat superior
legal doctrine under which liability is imposed on an employer for harm caused by an employee in the ordinary course of business while carrying out a usual job duty

specific performance
requirement that a breaching party complete his obligations under a contract

standard of care
degree of care that a person must take to prevent harm to others

standard of proof
amount, level, or persuasiveness of proof that is required at trial

strict liability
liability that requires no proof of intention or negligence

substantive law
law that creates rights and obligations by requiring or prohibiting certain activities

summary conviction offence
relatively minor offence that is prosecuted without a preliminary hearing or jury

Supreme Court of Canada
highest court of appeal in Canada

thin skull rule
rule in tort law that defendants take plaintiffs as they find them, even if hidden vulnerabilities make the plaintiffs more susceptible to injury than others

tort
harm done by people to others for which compensation can be sought

trespassers
people who come onto premises uninvited, or after business hours

trial courts
courts empowered to host full hearing of a case

tribunal
person or group of persons charged with making formal administrative decisions

unconscionability
serious unfairness

undue influence
pressure exerted on a weaker party that deprives him of the ability to exercise his judgment or free will

unilateral mistake
error made by one party with full knowledge of the other

vicarious liability
liability imposed on one party (often an employer) for the harmful actions or omissions of another (often an employee)

voluntary standards
standards developed and accepted by industry leaders that are not enforceable in law

waiver
agreement to give up a right, privilege, or benefit to which a person would otherwise be entitled

wrongful detention
tort, sometimes called false imprisonment, which involves unjustified restraint of a person

Index